WITHDRAWN

HARVARD LIBRARY

WITHDRAWN

THE ROMAN CATECHISM IN THE CATECHETICAL TRADITION OF THE CHURCH

The Structure of the Roman Catechism as Illustrative of the "Classic Catechesis"

Robert I. Bradley

UNIVERSITY
PRESS OF
AMERICA

Lanham • New York • London

Copyright © 1990 by
University Press of America®, Inc.
4720 Boston Way
Lanham, Maryland 20706

3 Henrietta Street
London WC2E 8LU England

All rights reserved
Printed in the United States of America
British Cataloging in Publication Information Available

Library of Congress Cataloging-in-Publication Data

Bradley, Robert I.
The Roman catechism in the catechetical tradition of the
church : the structure of the Roman catechism as
illustrative of the "classic catechesis" / Robert I. Bradley.
p.   cm.
Includes bibliographical references.
1. Catholic Church. Catechismus Romanus.   2. Catholic
Church—Catechisms—Latin.   3. Catholic Church—Education.
4. Catechetics—Catholic Church.   I. Title.
BX1959.B72   1990-   238'.2—dc20   89-27945 CIP

ISBN 0-8191-7646-X (alk. paper)

 The paper used in this publication meets the minimum requirements of American National Standard for Information Sciences—Permanence of Paper for Printed Library Materials, ANSI Z39.48–1984.

FOREWORD

"We have the Prophetic Word" (2 Peter 1:19). "You received the Word of God which you heard from us... not as the word of men, but as what it really is, the Word of God" (1 Thess. 2:13). Saints Peter and Paul specify what it is that the Church hands on in her catechetical teaching: it is the Prophetic Word of God out of the Prophetic Light, received as such by the member of the Church.

The Creed of the People of God speaks of "the immortal Tradition of the holy Church of God". The research accomplished by Father Robert I. Bradley, S.J., makes it clear that there is a catechetical component in this immortal Tradition, a component which is central to the Ordinary and Universal Magisterium of the Catholic Church. This Ordinary or daily form of the Magisterium of the Church is the handing on of this Prophetic Word by a formative teaching, accomplished by a definite pattern, structure or typos didachēs (see Rom. 6:17).

This catechetical content and structure illumines the catechumen from the higher order of the prophetical light. Its truths stand above progress in the natural order of the sciences and above cultural changes in philosophy. Hence it abides securely across the centuries, and in particular during these present times of Trent, Vatican I and Vatican II. "The teaching of faith which God has revealed," the Supreme Magisterium has stated in solemn definition, "has not been proposed as a philosophical discovery to be perfected by human ingenuity, but as a divine deposit... to be guarded faithfully." Far from suffering a dialectic of rupture between these manifestations of the Extraordinary form of the Magisterium, this catechetical tradition ministers in its own fundamental way to their continuity. Its official Catechisms, furthermore, are not in dialectical conflict or competition, for they express harmoniously and teach faithfully that same Word of God. They all teach the one-and-same Divine Deposit of Faith and Morals and apply its truths as the new Way of Life.

Father Bradley's work helps in a most timely fashion to make more visible this great catechetical fact which stands in the life of the Church from Jesus' teaching of His Apostles to the present. It is timely because of the well-known contemporary pressure upon the Church to give way to a Hegelian dialectic of opposition between Vatican I and Vatican II, especially in catechetical matters and this not least in the area of the Sacred Deposit of Morals. One need but read Father Bradley's introduction to see that his work is a fundamental vindication of the catechetical continuity between Vatican I and Vatican II, between both of them and the Council of Trent, and indeed between all of them and the Apostles who learned the content and structure of their teaching from the Lord Jesus Himself. In these times of deception, confusion and even threat of rupture within "the immortal Tradition of the Holy Church of God," Father Bradley's work has a special importance. It is recommended as a resource for catechetical teachers today.

Eugene Kevane

Notre Dame Apostolic Catechetical Institute
Feast of Sts. Peter and Paul
June 29, 1989

TABLE OF CONTENTS

FOREWORD	iii
TABLE OF CONTENTS	v
PREFACE	vii
INTRODUCTION	1
Notes to Introduction	4
CHAPTER I: THE "CLASSIC CATECHESIS": THE CATECHUMENATE OF THE FATHERS	6
Notes to Chapter I	19
CHAPTER II: THE COMPONENTS OF THE "CLASSIC CATECHESIS"	25
Notes to Chapter II	46
CHAPTER III: THE "CLASSIC CATECHESIS" AND SACRED SCRIPTURE	55
Notes to Chapter III	73
CHAPTER IV: CATECHESIS AND CATECHISMS	83
Notes to Chapter IV	101
CHAPTER V: THE ROMAN CATECHISM AND THE COUNCIL OF TRENT	110
Notes to Chapter V	127
CHAPTER VI: THE DIMENSIONS OF THE ROMAN CATECHISM	138
Notes to Chapter VI	156
CHAPTER VII: THE STRUCTURE OF THE ROMAN CATECHISM	166
Notes to Chapter VII	185
CONCLUSION	195
Notes to Conclusion	199
APPENDIX: A TOPICAL SYNOPSIS OF THE ROMAN CATECHISM	203
BIBLIOGRAPHY	220

PREFACE

As in the great world of ecclesial events since the Second Vatican Council, so in the small world of this writer's immediate experience through the same span of years, the Roman Catechism came late. I had heard of the "Catechism of the Council of Trent," but had scarcely studied it--much less made it the focal point of my studies--through my early years of formal education, my seminary years, and my more than score of subsequent years of teaching on the college and graduate levels in Catholic schools. It was only after John Paul II's <u>Catechesi Tradendae</u> and the invitation by the Rev. Msgr. Eugene Kevane to collaborate with him in putting out a new English translation of the Roman Catechism that I began to see the central contemporary importance of this four-hundred-year old work.

From the simplest pre-school catechesis in the family to the most advanced research and training such as was now available in the newly founded Pontifical catechetical institutes, what I saw as most needed at all its levels by Catholic education was a reacquaintance with the "classic catechesis": that instruction, at once elementary and comprehensive, which accompanied the faith from the beginning and which was therefore <u>timeless</u>. Although originating in a context of a specific historical period, the Roman Catechism contained this "classic catechesis" as no other single work, before or since, has ever managed to do. To a degree greater than I had ever expected, this timeless quality of the Roman Catechism was due to its <u>structure</u>: its four-fold content based exclusively on the Apostles' Creed, the sacraments, the Decalogue and the Lord's Prayer. As Msgr. Kevane summarized that four-fold content:

> Always and everywhere ... the substance of this teaching has been one and the same since its origin in the call of Jesus Christ: "The time has come, and the Kingdom of God is close at hand. Repent and believe the Good News" (Mk 1:14-15). It is first a teaching of what is to be believed, namely the Articles of Faith summarized in the Apostolic Profession; and then it is a teaching that helps them to repent and deepen their <u>metanoia</u> or conversion to God Incarnate. This repentance or metanoia is the new Christian way of life with its three principal activities: personal prayer, Gospel morality and

> Sacramental living. Thus the four areas of catechetical content, classical in the Catechumenate, come into view together with their roots in the life and work of the Divine Teacher.¹

The conjunction in the Roman Catechism of "belief and metanoia," with the latter composed of "personal prayer, Gospel morality and sacramental living," offered perspectives of structure which I was now convinced had immense value for our better understanding of what authentic catechesis is really all about. When, therefore, shortly after this first contact of mine with the topic of the structure of the Roman Catechism, I came upon the famous French lectures of Joseph Cardinal Ratzinger on "the sources and the transmission of the faith," and read the following passage as part of his conclusion, I knew that this topic was clearly momentous.

> The Apostles' Creed, the sacraments, the Decalogue, the Lord's Prayer. These four classic components and headings of catechesis have across the centuries served as matrix and resume of catechetical instruction. They have also served as introduction to the Bible and to the Church's life. We said that they correspond with the dimensions of Christian existence. This is what the Roman Catechism affirms when it says that in these components the Christian finds what he is to believe (the Creed), what he is to hope for (the Our Father), what he is to do (the Decalogue), and in what vital milieu he will find all three possible (the sacraments and the Church). At the same time this structure manifestly aligns with the four ways of reading Scripture which were worked out in the Middle Ages, and which can also be seen as a response to questions posed by the four stages of human existence. ²

As it happened, an opportunity for me to pursue a new doctorate at the Angelicum in Rome occurred at that same time (January 1983), and so began the project of this study. Interrupted by teaching and pastoral duties, the project was pursued along lines somewhat more modest than those outlined by Msgr. Kevane in his introduction to our edition of the Roman Catechism.³ Yet the exigencies of time and space were not the only reasons why I have limited the topic to the structure alone. The full implications of Cardinal Ratzinger's statement concerning the Roman Catechism and the meanings of Scripture eventually emerged as something more than justifying its being the exclusive object of this study.

Thanks to the genial and unstinting counsel of my mentor, Père Benoit Duroux, O.P., this study can at last be offered as a "footnote" to the magisterial work of Cardinal Ratzinger and Msgr. Kevane. May it contribute to a better understanding of the Roman Catechism as the greatest single instance of the "classic catechesis"--and therefore as an indispensable instrument for the renewal of authentic catechetics in our time. If in fact it has come late, may its very timelessness make of this circumstance a new beginning for us all.

This entire study would have been in vain, however, but for the dedicated, unremitting assistance of Dr. Betty Bosarge (both in Rome and in Virginia) and Mrs. Clara Picco in preparing the MS for publication. To them I owe a gratitude beyond words.

Robert I. Bradley, S.J.

Alexandria, Virginia

NOTES

1. Eugene Kevane (ed.), <u>Teaching the Catholic Faith Today: Twentieth Century Catechetical Documents of the Holy See</u> (Boston: St. Paul Editions, 1982), p. xxviii.

2. Joseph Cardinal Ratzinger, <u>Transmission de la foi et sources de la foi</u> (Paris: Tequi, 1983), pp. 34-35. See below, Conclusion, pp. 197-98.

3. Robert I. Bradley, S.J. and Eugene Kevane (eds.), <u>The Roman Catechism: Translated and Annotated in accord with Vatican II and Post-Conciliar Documents and the new Code of Canon Law</u> (Boston: St. Paul Editions, 1985), pp. xii-xiii.

INTRODUCTION

The "catechetical tradition" is a reality commensurate with Christianity itself. From its origins as recounted in the writings of the New Testament down to our own times, the Christian experience has been a continuum; and just as important as any other strand running through these two millennia[1] is that which has had for its task the handing on, precisely, of the knowledge of the Christian faith.[2] That essential teaching of the faith, called "catechesis,"[3] is essentially a "tradition": what is "handed on" can be said to be the "handing on" itself.[4]

For a starting point in this tradition we can cite the culminating passage in St. Matthew's Gospel: Christ's formal mandate to His Apostles to teach (Mt 28:18-20).[5] And for a statement to mark the contemporaneity of the tradition we have that most recent major magisterial document on catechesis: John Paul II's Apostolic Exhortation entitled--appropriately enough--<u>Catechesi Tradendae</u>.[6]

The Roman Catechism--or, to give its formal title, the <u>Cathechism for Parish Priests, as decreed by the Council of Trent and published by order of the Supreme Pontiff, Pius V</u>[7]--occupies a prominent, and in many ways unique, position in the catechetical tradition. Our present purpose is to study "the Roman Catechism in the Catechetical Tradition": how this one book, for all its uniqueness, indeed by virtue of its uniqueness, illustrates that tradition as no other one book does.

More specifically, we intend to demonstrate its fidelity to that most enduring and authoritative strand in that tradition, which we call the "classic catechesis." "Classic," for it has become <u>timeless</u>, dating from that first institutionalized instruction we call the "catechumenate," right down to the present auspicious renewal of that same institution following the Second Vatican Council.[8]

The fidelity of the Roman Catechism to the classic catechesis is most immediately illustrated by its very <u>structure</u>: the number and arrangement of its various components. However, as is true in so much of education, structure is more than mere framework. It is a living force, giving form, direction and proportion to the process of teaching and learning.9 If, then, the Roman Catechism is illustrative of the classic catechesis primarily by means of its structure, that is not merely because structure is the first thing we see in a given work; it is because it is also the last--the <u>innermost</u>--thing that is there. It is really not too much to say that, in this case at least, the structure is the <u>soul</u>.

The fidelity of correspondence between the classic catechesis as timeless tradition and the Roman Catechism as a privileged moment in that tradition lies, then, mainly in the structure which animates both. What is that structure? It is, both radically and adequately, nothing other than the <u>Sacred Scriptures</u> themselves. In the sense, that is, of the <u>senses</u> in which the Scriptures have been read in the Church.10 The correspondence which exists between the senses of Scripture and the components of the classic catechesis--and hence of the structural parts of the Roman Catechism--is the "thesis" of this present study. It is a thesis of such value, in my opinion, that we are quite justified in limiting this study to it alone.

Other theses are, of course, involved in this study, and they are in fact touched on to some extent. Because they, too, are important-- undoubtedly more important in the long run than the one we have pursued--it may be well to include in this introduction a brief description of what we can legitimately prescind from as "theses" proper to this study.

They are mainly two, and they can be said to lie at either end of the spectrum that is the continuum of the classic catechesis. At the far end lies the question of the precise linkage between the classic catechesis and the New Testament itself. That is to say, how precisely do the elements which made up the "curriculum" of the original catechumenate relate to the elements of the "curriculum" of Christ's and the Apostles' teaching?[11] For the purposes of our present study, that linkage is a postulate, and we leave it at that.

The second "thesis" outside the scope of this study lies at the near end of our chronological spectrum: the precise linkage between the Roman Catechism and the present time. As with the preceding instance, here too we can properly prescind from an investigation and verification that would obviously take us too far afield. What must suffice for now is simply to say that the <u>relative</u> "timelessness" of the Roman Catechism, as a faithful witness to the classic catechesis, grounds a postulate which amply sustains and guides our contemporary catechetical devices, as evidenced by <u>Catechesi Tradendae</u>--and by the <u>RCIA</u>.[12] But that is another topic, touched on in our <u>Conclusion</u>, and offering us an open-ended invitation hopefully to pursue it at some future date.

Having indicated what this study does <u>not</u> include, and why, let us now summarize what we intend to demonstrate. The Roman Catechism, primarily by virtue of its structure as consonant with the senses of Scripture as read in the Church, illustrates with unique clarity the classic catechesis, and so merits its position as a privileged moment in the catechetical tradition of the Church.

The thesis thus stated will be developed in two phases. We will first consider the classic catechesis itself (Chapters I - III): its Patristic heyday (Chapter I), its components (Chapter II), and its relationship to Scripture (Chapter III). We will then address the Roman Catechism (Chapter IV - VII): its catechismal antecedents (Chapter IV), its Tridentine origins (Chapter V), its literary "dimensions" (Chapter VI), and its Scripturally inspired structure (Chapter VII).

Then, serving as a kind of "epilogue" to this study, we will offer a few reflections on the Roman Catechism as it has affected the catechetical tradition from the time of its appearance until our own, and as it can affect the times to come.[13] By then, perhaps, we will better see why it can itself be called a "classic"--a timeless exposition of a timeless faith.

NOTES

1. Other such strands in the overall history of Christianity would be the "liturgical tradition," the "missionary tradition," the "tradition of works of charity," the "theological tradition," the "ascetical tradition," the "governmental tradition," etc.

2. "The faith" as an object or content, as distinct from an act or habit (i.e., "fides quae" as distinct from "fides qua"), has Scriptural warrant (e.g., 2 Tim 4:7). Although St. Thomas Aquinas did not use the terminology, he was deeply aware of the distinction itself (see S.T., II-II, 6, 1; in Rom., cap. 10, lect. 2).

   For two further fundamental insights presupposed by this study and hence notable in these introductory remarks, see St. Thomas' treatment of faith as related to proposition (S.T. II-II, 1, 2) and as related to grace (II-II, 4, 4).

3. For the etymology of "catechesis" and its Scriptural basis, see below, Chapter I, pp. 6-7.

4. The activity of "handing on" something from someone who has it to someone who previously has not had it is surely dominant in the thought of the Apostle who wrote about his "handling" the Word of life (1 Jn 1:1)! Yet, the balance between the activity and the object of the "handing on" is strongly suggested in the Pauline expression: "what was handed on to me I hand on to you" (1 Cor 15:3). In fact, "paradosis," the most traditional single term designating "tradition," refers primarily to "the thing received" and only secondarily to a "handing on." See Francis Zorell, S.J., Lexicon Grascum Novi Testamenti (3rd ed., Paris: Lethieulleux, 1961), cols. 987-89.

5. It is significant that the first agendum mandated by Christ is to "teach" ("matheteusate ... didaskontes," Mt 28:19-20). Although the distinction between proclamation ("kērygma," evangelization) and instruction ("katēchēsis," catechesis) is important--and can be said to underlie the distinction in this very mandate-text between "making disciples" and "teaching them to observe"--yet more important for the overall purpose of our present study is the fundamental unity of the "ministry of the word." This unity is substantiated by the overwhelming prevalence in the New Testament of the one term "didachē" to designate all teaching.

6   AAS 71:1277-1340.

7   Catechismus ex decreto SS. Concilii Tridentini ad parochos Pii V Pont. Max. iussu editus.

8   The renewed catechumenate, mandated by the Second Vatican Council (Sacrosanctum Concilium, 64; Ad Gentes, 14), is best identified in the United States with the Rite for the Christian Initiation of Adults (RCIA), originally issued by the Holy See in 1972.

9   An analogy with the human body comes to mind. The skeleton is every bit as alive as what is draped on it! But then, what gives form even to the skeleton--as to everything else in the body--is the forma corporis, the soul.

10 This is why our approach to Scripture in this study is exclusively hermeneutical--and "traditionally" hermeneutical at that!

11 Granting the obviously unsystematized character of New Testament teaching, we can nevertheless discern instances of the "typos didachēs" referred to by St. Paul (Rom 6:17), e.g., Heb 6:1-2. See below, Chapter I, pp. 6-7.

12 See below, Chapter I, notes 30 through 38, pp. 22-23.

13 See below, Conclusion, pp. 195-98.

CHAPTER ONE

THE "CLASSIC CATECHESIS"

THE CATECHUMENATE OF THE FATHERS

Our historical survey begins with the word "catechesis." It anchors our study in New Testament sources, and at the same time introduces us to the full sweep of the "successio apostolica" and the "sensus fidelium" thereafter. Although "katēchēsis" never occurs as an abstract noun in the New Testament, and even in its variant verbal and adjectival forms it occurs far less frequently than "didachē" and its variants,[1] it is nevertheless sufficiently present in the Pauline/Lucan corpus, sometimes as a mere synonym for "didachē," sometimes as having a more distinctive connotation.

The original etymological sense of "katēchein" (literally, "to sound down," hence, "to resound" or "to echo") connotes a kind of dialogue, an organized and elementary mode of instruction. To Theophilus thus "instructed" (katēchēthēs), St. Luke proposes to offer his Gospel as a more thorough narration of the history of the Word (Lk 1:4). It was Apollos thus "instructed" (katēchēmenos) in the way of the Lord who went on to teach about Jesus Christ (Acts 18:25). Five words spoken in such a manner that from them he can "instruct" (katēchēso), St. Paul tells his Corinthians, is worth more than ten thousand words spoken in tongues (1 Cor 14:19). Perhaps the best text of all is the phrase in Galatians where Paul mentions both the one "instructing" (katēchoun) and the one "instructed" (katēchoumenos) as having a mutual responsibility in sharing their goods (Gal 6:6). "Katēchēsis" therefore has in Scripture its essential connotation as a distinctive instructional term: it is brief but complete, elementary but systematic, following up the "kērygma" by introducing a more structured "didachē".

Clearly implied in the New Testament -- and its being implied and not expressly spelled out only enhances the fact of its antiquity and "lived-ness" -- is the "<u>didachē</u>" of the Apostles as <u>the rule of faith</u>. In the heart of his magisterial discourse to the Romans, St. Paul alludes to a "rule" or "standard": <u>typos didachēs</u> (Rom 6:17). And in 1 Corinthians he gives the essential content of this "form" "into" which they have been "handed": "I hand on to you what was handed on to me: that Christ died according to the Scriptures, that He rose according to the Scriptures ..."(1 Cor 15:3-4). Finally, the Pastorals repeatedly insist on a fidelity to "the faith" <u>(hē pistis)</u> to be handed on by means of <u>instruction</u>[2] by those sent by the Apostles. Now, the all-important pivotal phase in that instruction is the dialogal discourse called "katēchēsis," which follows on the "kērygma" just as the "foundation" follows repentance (Heb 6:1-2), or just as the watering follows the seeding of the Word (1 Cor 3:6-8) -- and which in turn follows the superstructure, or the increase, of the <u>knowledge</u> of the faith.

I

This "catechesis," or instruction in the knowledge of the faith, was destined to be the classic activity of what would be called a millennium later the "<u>magisterium</u>" of the Church.[3] For the teaching office -- then as now -- was directed primarily to those who were already converted to the faith and now needed to grow, not in some kind of "<u>gnōsis</u>" concerning the faith, but in the faith itself. Just as this classic teaching function pre-supposed "<u>metanoia</u>" as the fruit of evangelization, so in turn it was presupposed by "<u>gnōsis</u>" as the fruit of that more elaborate and particularized study of the faith which would later be called "theology."[4] And just as those <u>being taught </u>in this "school" of the Church were the <u>ordinary faithful</u> (i.e., neither the pagans outside nor the "specialists" inside), so those <u>doing the teaching</u> were the <u>ordinary pastors</u> (i.e., neither the itinerant "prophets"[5] nor the contemplative "theologians"): the bishops, with their presbyters and deacons.[6] These basic categories of "the teaching," "the teachers" and "the taught" became clearly delineated as the classic activity of the teaching Church in the course of the second century. By the end of that century this activity had attained what we can call its classic form, viz., the catechumenate.

Before describing this classic form, however, we must look more closely at what this teaching and these teachers really were. The content of the teaching was fundamentally, of course, the Word of God: His revelation in Christ, put into human words, and indeed summarized into as few words as possible to facilitate human memory and human understanding. This was the Symbol or Creed, and what it summarized were the words coming from the Apostles as the original witnesses of Christ and instruments of the Holy Spirit. As the instruments of the Holy Spirit they (with certain other "Apostolic men" of their designation)[7] had written various things -- collections of Jesus' sayings and deeds, letters to some communities and persons among the faithful, some narrative accounts and even some prophecies. By the end of the second century there had emerged, mainly as the result of the recognized need for a fixed body of teaching (corresponding to its fixed summary already in place, viz., the Creed), a "canon" or "rule" of "Scripture."[8] These twenty-seven Apostolic writings now constituted a "canon," as directly inspired and authoritative as the very "Scripture" recognized and appealed to by Christ and the Apostles; indeed, they would soon be called the "new Testament" -- in contradistinction to the "Old Testament."[9]

Antedating this canon of Scripture, both logically and chronologically, was another "canon," that rule concerning the teachers whose teaching comprised the Scriptures, viz., the "canon" or "rule" of the Apostolic Tradition. The original Apostles not only left in writing some of the things they witnessed; they also left living persons in their place, no longer as the first-hand witnesses of Christ and founders of the Church (that was no longer possible), but as the authorized carriers -- guardians and interpreters -- of their witness and foundation, and to hand on to others what had been handed on to them, to the end of time. Thus, in summary, the "teaching" was the Apostolic Tradition, i.e., as a material content, whether written (the Scriptures) or unwritten, whether summarized (the Creed) or unsummarized. The "teachers" were the bishops of the entire -- or Catholic -- Church, personifying the "successio Apostolica." And, of course, to complete the paradigm of this integral reality: the "taught" were the ordinary body of the faithful, formalized as such by that gift of the Holy Spirit disposing for and accompanying the faith itself: the "sensus fidei."[10]

By the end of the second century the Church, which already since the beginning of that century was calling herself -- and was being recognized by others as -- the "Catholic Church,"[11] had securely in place the basic pattern of this primary exercise of her magisterium or teaching function, viz., the catechumenate. Thanks mainly to the genius of two individuals, Tertullian (c.160 - c.220) in the West and Origen (c.184 - c.254) in the East, we can discern the development of the catechumenate as an institution, i.e., as a "canonized" activity of the local Church, fitted into the larger context of a "canonized" way of life: the universal (or Catholic) Church's liturgical life within and her missionary enterprise outside.[12] Tertullian's providing the Latins with their basic theological vocabulary,[13] and Origen's providing the Greeks (and indirectly the whole Church) with their first theological systematization[14] only accentuates the significance of the purely catechetical in their respective achievements. For catechesis, the elementary systematic teaching of the faith, though clearly distinct from evangelization (and apologetics) on the one hand, and from homiletics (and theology) on the other,[15] nevertheless is closely related to them in the living milieu of the historical Church.

Following the providential contributions of "genius" at its beginning, the third century saw what must have been a quiet but solid strengthening of the catechetical tradition. This strengthening was itself providential, for it was taking place at the very time when the Church was facing the increasingly severe challenge of the Roman Empire. Without this inner strength stemming largely from the catechumenate and its effective recruitment of new militant Christians, the Church would not have been able to exploit the immense opportunity offered her so suddenly a hundred years later by

Constantine's edict of peace. As it was, the fourth century ushered in the "golden age of the Fathers," when from East and West there flourished such an array of great bishops as has not been seen in the Church before or since. What should be noted here, of course, is that catechesis was, very often directly or at least indirectly, the main object of their pastoral concern. Among the many illustrious Fathers of the fourth and fifth centuries who contributed to the catechetical tradition, we will limit our consideration here to but four of them: Sts. Cyril of Jerusalem and John Chrysostom in the East, and Sts. Ambrose and Augustine in the West.[16]

St. Cyril (c.315-387), named for his see of Jerusalem, to distinguish him from his better-known namesake a century later in Alexandria, is remembered mainly from his Catecheses, a complete set of nineteen instructions for those preparing for baptism through the course of Lent,[17] and for his Mystagogica, another complete set of five instructions given directly to the newly baptized in the course of the Paschal octave.[18] The Catecheses is concerned almost exclusively with the explanation of the Creed:

> Now the one and only faith that you are to take and preserve in the way of learning and professing it is that which is now being committed to you by the Church as confirmed throughout the Scriptures. . . . This doctrine I want you to commit to memory word for word, and say it over to one another as much as you can, not writing it on paper but using memory to engrave it on your heart.[19]

In the Mystagogica he turns to the sacraments. The entire series is intensely Scriptural: each instruction flowing from and elaborating on a given text-- from both the Old and New Testaments on the Creed, from the New Testament exclusively on the sacraments.[20] Already a place of pilgrimage in the fourth century, Jerusalem grew in prestige under the guidance of her great bishop and the protection of the de facto Christian Empire; and the praxis of her catechesis, performed at the very site of the Death and Resurrection of the Lord, had a profound influence on all the Churches of the East and the West.[21]

Some fifty years after Cyril, we have from Antioch a similar series of catechetical instructions given by a priest of that church, who would later be called to the see of Constantinople: St. John Chrysostom (c.344-407).[22] The series consists of eight instructions, of which only two precede the conferral of baptism on the catechumens; the remaining six are directed to the newly baptized as exhortations to remain faithful to and grow in the sacramental grace that is now theirs. Although the basic pattern -- Scriptural and liturgical -- is the same as Cyril's, the emphasis is different. John Chrysostom is, characteristically, more interested in the moral life, and in very concrete and even homely aspects of it too, than in what is called elsewhere (but not here) the "mystagogic."[23] There is thus a certain mutual complementarity in the catechetical tradition as emanating from these great Churches of the East, the greatness of their ecclesiastical leadership in the Patristic age matching that of their Apostolic origins. The moral and the mystical, the creedal and the sacramental, are all represented -- and modeled -- in this truly "classic" catechesis.

What we have said of the East in the fourth and fifth centuries applies equally to the West. The two greatest exemplars of the catechetical, as of so many other aspects of the Patristic heritage, are St. Ambrose and his protégé St. Augustine. Ambrose of Milan (c.340-397) has three brief but very influential catechetical works: the Explanatio Symboli, the De Mysteriis and the De Sacramentis. The "Explanation of the Creed" is just that: a single instruction, given probably on Palm Sunday to the catechumens preparing for baptism on the Easter Vigil.[24] Following their baptism are the several instructions constituting the other two works. De Mysteriis is a cursory explanation to the newly baptized of what they have received: the three sacraments of initiation and full membership in the Church:

> Speaking of the mysteries before they were received would have betrayed them, not portrayed them.[25]

De Sacramentis is a somewhat more amplified development of the same topic in which is now included an explicit instruction on prayer, i.e., the Lord's Prayer.[26] The rich epigrammatic quality of these two little masterpieces certainly contributed to their enduring importance as authoritative expositions of the catechetical tradition in the West.

St. Augustine's (354-430) position in the catechetical tradition is uniquely great. Although he never specifically described the rites of Christian initiation (as St. Ambrose did), nor composed a course of catechetical instruction (as St. Cyril did), nor even left a series of exhortations on the Christian life as adapted to the needs of the newly baptized (as St. John Chrysostom did), Augustine in a sense accomplished all these purposes -- and more -- in what he did reserve, in his immense output, to what was strictly catechetical. Two of his works are pre-eminently important to the catechetical tradition (and to this present study): the Enchiridion and the De Catechizandis Rudibus. In the Enchiridion Augustine presents a "manual" of the Christian life, based on the triad of faith, hope and charity.[27] The reference to catechesis as such is not made explicit; yet substantively it overlaps the content of St. Cyril's Catecheses and St. Ambrose's Explanatio Symboli. That is to say, it is based on the Creed as its main outline. Moreover, its inclusion of the Lord's Prayer as a kind of "appendix" makes it similar in that respect to Ambrose's De Sacramentis.

As for De Catechizandis Rudibus, its very title identifies it as specifically catechetical.[28] However, unlike any of the works so far mentioned in this chapter, it does not really give -- explicitly or even implicitly -- the "syllabus" of the catechumenate as such. Rather, it gives a sort of introduction to the catechumenate by describing how a prospective catechumen should be approached by the catechist, how motivated and induced to enter into the institution itself. It is nevertheless a most important catechetical work -- possibly the most important single such work in the entire Patristic corpus. For its very stress on the pre-institutional aspect of the catechumenate firmly anchors the catechetical tradition as such into the larger Apostolic Tradition in its purest "nuclear" form, viz., the original kerygma of the Twelve with its almost exclusive stress on the sacred history: the "narratio" of the "magnalia Dei."[29] De Catechizandis Rudibus thus looks back to the <u>original ministry of the word</u> from which sprang the <u>classic teaching of the faith</u>, which is the very heart of the "ordinary magisterium" of the Church. In doing so, it serves as the best possible preparation for the study of the catechetical tradition itself -- which, as we have seen, <u>is</u> the "classic teaching of the faith" -- and, moreover, in <u>its</u> "classic" form, viz., the catechumenate of the "golden age of the Fathers."

II

Because the catechumenate spanned the entire process of initiation into the integral life of the faith, it was divided into certain definite periods corresponding to the progressive phases of initiation.[30] The first phase was strictly preliminary; it was called the "pre-catechumenate." It corresponded to that initial reception of the <u>kerygma</u> whereby a pagan turned from his idols and professed a serious desire to learn the doctrine of Christ. These preliminary candidates were called "<u>accedentes</u>": those "approaching" the faith. They were to pursue their inquiry and desire, while the Church for her part pursued the word of evangelization: the proclamation to them of the Gospel, the "good news" of God's power and mercy in Christ.[31]

The pre-catechumenate led to and ended in the first public act of initiation: the rite of "<u>signatio</u>," in which the "accedentes" were "signed" with the Cross and admitted into the ranks of the catechumens.[32] The catechumenate as such thus began; and it would extend for at least one year -- more often longer. In this period the catechumens began as "<u>auditores</u>," for that was their primary function: the "hearing" of a systematic instruction in the faith. This instruction, was, however, never exclusively a "study". Rather, it was closely tied in with sacred worship: the catechumens participated in the Liturgy of the Word -- i.e., the Sacred Scriptures read publicly in the assembly of the faithful as a formal act of worship.[33] They also participated in the ordinary communal life of the Church, observing her fasts and her feasts, performing works of charity, conforming their lives to all her precepts, and receiving her blessings and sacramentals.[34]

The catechumenate -- whatever might be its overall duration -- always ended within a definite time-frame: the season of Lent. This tie-in was detailed and elaborate, clearly conveying the supreme importance attached to the annual celebration of the Paschal Mystery as the time par excellence for the renewal of the Church in her members.[35] On the First Sunday of Lent there took place the solemn liturgical rite of "electio," in which some "auditores" became "electi" (or "competentes"), i.e., the ones officially approved to receive the sacraments of initiation at Easter.[36] They, with their sponsors, were enrolled in an intensive six-week program of "purification" and "enlightenment," ritualized by a series, respectively, of "scrutinia" and "traditiones." There were three "scrutinies," assigned to the Third, Fourth and Fifth Sundays of Lent; and they effected the "purification" of the catechumens by prayers (based on the three respective Sunday Gospels: the Samaritan Woman, the Man Born Blind, and the Raising of Lazarus) and exorcisms.[37] Then came the "enlightenment": the two "handings over" by the bishop to the "chosen (or competent) ones" of the two sources of their "enlightenment" -- the Creed and the Lord's Prayer. This ceremony usually took place on Palm Sunday, and so symbolized the completion, by the official teacher of the faith, of the catechumens' formal instruction.[38] And thus they were ready for their formal profession of faith at the Easter Vigil, and their reception of the sacraments of baptism, confirmation and Holy Eucharist.

Although they were now fully incorporated into the Church, they remained nevertheless in a special category, that of "neophytes," which constituted the third and final period of the catechumenate.[39] Co-extensive with the Paschal season, this period was called "mystagogic"; for what was now stressed, as the culmination of the ascetical ("purification") and the doctrinal ("enlightenment") regime of Lent, was an intensive instruction in the "mysteries," i.e., the sacramental life.[40] With its formal completion at Pentecost, the catechumenate thus reproduced the total cycle of the Church's life of faith and prayer, and in so doing presented the Church with a new generation of her offspring: "filii in Filio, clamantes in Spiritu: Abba Pater!"⁴¹

This brief survey of the catechumenate -- the institutionalized catechesis of the "golden age of the Fathers" -- is an integral part of our study, for this catechesis became in due course <u>classic</u>, i.e., it became <u>the catechetical prototype</u> to which the historic Church would look as to the model for all subsequent catechesis. And when we remember that catechesis is itself the classic function of the Church's magisterium or teaching office, because it is the clearest verification of the "teaching," the "teacher" and the "taught" as realized in the Apostolic Tradition, we see how not only integral to our study, but how <u>central</u> this brief survey has been.

To illustrate this centrality, let us conclude this chapter with a survey corresponding to the one which began it. Just as we saw how the several centuries preceding the "golden age of the Fathers" led up to the classic catechesis that is the catechumenate, so we should now see how the several centuries following that "golden age" led to the dissolution, in its actualized historic sense, of that same classic catechesis.

III

By a paradox that has never ceased to prompt serious reflection on what constitutes the reality of "Christian culture,"⁴² the very factors which in the world at large favored the "golden age of the Fathers" and their catechesis, were also the factors which finally terminated it. Speaking very generally, we can identify them as these two: the Constantinian peace of the Church, and the barbarian migrations into the Roman Empire. The advantages offered by the peace were obvious: not only was the Church free to pursue her mission; she was actually favored by the secular power.⁴³ As for the barbarians, they, too, offered an opportunity for practically unlimited evangelization and catechesis, especially because of their predisposition to recognize the superiority of the "Roman" order of things.

Yet, as we know, neither the new peace nor the new peoples proved to be an unmixed blessing. On the contrary, more than one Father in that age may have been tempted to see in them an unmixed curse. For the peace not only brought the opening to worldly ambition on the part of ecclesiastics; it also removed the penalties which made being a Christian a matter of life or death. "Purification" and "enlightenment" took on a different meaning for all too many prospective Christians in the "Christian Empire." And if the peace enervated the Church, the barbarians overwhelmed her. Only with heroic patience and tact would the bishops establish any rapport, and then usually only by personal contact, with some of the barbarian chiefs.[44] The results, generally, were mass conversions, which -- like the peace -- were ambiguous at the best. In any case, their effect on the catechumenate was obvious. It can be said that, depending on one's point of view, the catechumenate became either unnecessary or impossible because of the mass conversions.

If one of the most important activities (if not the most important activity) of the Fathers was thus "outdated" by the course of world events, the need for such an overall teaching and pastoral role as such in the Church was, of course, not affected. That is why, after the fifth century, there were still great men in the East and the West maintaining the Apostolic Tradition and adapting it to the new exigencies of the age. As outstanding representatives of this later Patristic period we may cite St. John Damascene (c.645 - c.750) in the East and St. Gregory the Great (c.540-604) in the West.[45] They followed the "golden age" by about the same distance in time as Origen and Tertullian preceded it. And just as the genius of the second/third centuries made possible the catechumenate of the fourth/fifth centuries, so the different but radically kindred genius of the sixth/seventh centuries would make possible the survival of the catechumenate in its essential qualities and so make it to be truly "classic" for all the subsequent centuries of the Church's history.

What are these essential qualities salvaged and secured by the "genius" of Gregory the Great? The first was fidelity to "<u>the faith</u>" as such, i.e., to its <u>formulation</u> in the Creed as deriving from the Apostles and as defined by the sacred Councils of the Universal Church.[46] This "orthodoxy" was the first condition for membership in the Church -- the One Church Catholic. Indeed, her oneness and catholicity were founded on this one universal adherence to the one Creed -- so formulated that all, even unlettered barbarians, could give an account of what they were adhering to. It was not, then, some elitist philosophy -- or even less, some elitist "mystique" -- which "kept the faith" intact. It was, rather, the simple popular profession of the faith as memorized in the Creed.

The second essential quality was equally evident in the character and work of St. Gregory, and equally important. The unquestionably "intellectual" character of orthodoxy, with its insistence on formulas and assent, was, nevertheless, anything but "intellectualist." It was, in fact, just the opposite. Alongside the "<u>explanatio</u>" of the Fathers -- the explaining of the revealed Word to the catechumens -- was the "<u>exhortatio</u>"-- their urging the catechumens to live this Word they were learning. For the Word, first and last, was "Life." The integration of the moral with the dogmatic, the "pastoral" with the "doctrinal," the "<u>orthopraxis</u>" with the "<u>orthodoxia</u>," was simply assumed as being of the very essence of the Gospel.[47] Once more, the role of St. Gregory in this respect was providentially outstanding. More than Augustine, more even than Ambrose or John Chrysostom, Gregory embodied the "down-to-earth" realism of the faith which the post-classic world of the West so desperately needed.

Thirdly and lastly, there was the quality of "order": the unmistakable sense of "Catholic balance" which was so eminently "Gregorian." In this respect St. Gregory was the worthy heir and transmitter to posterity of the entire Patristic tradition. Combining the pastoral and doctrinal offices in the Church, the Fathers also had -- far more often than not -- the fulness of the priestly office as well; the vast majority of them were <u>bishops</u>. The episcopal office was itself an instance of "balance": the Apostolic powers of teaching, governing and sanctifying, wielded by the bishop as the one accredited "steward of the mysteries," the one authoritative custodian and expounder of the faith. His role in the catechesis was, as we have seen, cumulative and crucial; his "tradition" of the Creed and the Lord's Prayer was not merely symbolic. It was in his name and under his guidance that the presbyters and the ministers, clerical and lay, performed their respective roles of sanctifying, teaching and governing, and -- more specifically -- catechizing. The bishop thus held in balance, as it were, the manifold charisms and activities of the Church in her diversity of members: such charisms as the prophetic, the theological, the liturgical, the charitable, the ascetical, the mystical, the catechetical. And he did so, not as some mere coordinator but as a charismatic in his own right, i.e., as holding by divinely instituted succession the Apostolic charism of <u>authority</u>, by which all these other charisms were authenticated and authorized.[48] Certainly, not all the bishops in those early centuries were "Fathers" in this plenary and practical sense. In fact, all too many bishops -- then as now -- exemplified the faith mainly by the demands they made on the faithful to believe in their office despite their person. Yet there were enough bishops in the providence of God -- and culminating in the person of Gregory the Great of the Holy See of Rome -- to establish a credibility and a precedent.

The result was <u>the classic catechesis of the Catholic Church: the ancient catechumenate</u>, which, by virtue of its essential qualities of orthodoxy and orthopraxis and comprehensive balance, would in spirit survive the end of the ancient classical world. If in those first centuries of her history the Church in her magisterium had been given a "canon" -- the Creed and Scriptures of her Tradition -- as the "<u>rule of faith</u>," so, too, by analogy, she was given, in her ordinary exercise of that magisterium in her catechesis, a "canon" -- certain writings of the "Fathers"-- as the "<u>rule for the teaching of the faith</u>." Despite the limits of this analogy, we can say that the "classic catechesis" had become just that: the way to teach the faith in <u>any</u> place or time.

NOTES

1. *Didachē* occurs twenty-seven times, and *didaskolos* fifty-nine times, in the New Testament. *Katēchēsis* occurs only as a verb (in various forms) four times, and as an adjective (also variously) four times.

2. Among some sixteen occurrences in the three Pastoral Epistles, the following are perhaps the most emphatic on the "objectivity" of "*the* faith" 1 Tim 4:1; 4:6; 6:10; 2 Tim 2:18; and Tit 1:4.

3. See Yves Congar, "Pour une histoire semantique du terme 'Magistère'," *Revue des sciences philosophiques et théologiques*, 60 (1976) 85-98.

4. See Pierre Batiffol, "Theologia, Theologi," *Ephemerides Theologicae Lovanienses*, 5 (1928) 205-20.

5. See Damian Van den Eynde, *Les normes de l'enseignement chrétien dans la littérature patristique des trois premiers siècles* (Gembloux-Paris, 1933), pp. 59-61. "Prophet" is a New Testament term, occurring frequently in St. Paul's Epistles.

6. *Ibid.*, pp. 62-67.

7. The term "apostolic men" (*apostolici viri*) is used by Vatican II, *Dei Verbum*, 18 (*AAS*, 58:826).

8. Van den Eynde, *op.cit.*, pp. 110-13.

9. Clement of Alexandria was the first to use the terms "Old Testament" and "New Testament." *Ibid.*, p. 111.

10. See *Lumen Gentium*, 12 (*AAS*, 57:16); *Dei Verbum*, 8 (*AAS*, 58:821).

11. "Catholic" first occurs in St. Ignatius of Antioch's *Letter to the Smyrneans*, 8.

12. Tertullian's *De Baptismo* (*PL* 1:1197-1221) is the first systematic exposition of the sacrament, and (by implication) of the preparation necessary for its reception.

    Origen is usually credited with the first organized "school." "Origène est le premier catéchète que nous connaissions de façon précise." Jean Daniélou, *La catéchèse aux premiers siècles* (Paris, 1968), p.29.

13. E. g., "sacramentum," "Trinitas," etc.

14. Viz., *Peri archōn* (*De principiis*), *PG* 11:115-414.

15 Daniélou has a nicely balanced summary on this point:
"La catechèse est tout d'abord un exposé à la fois complet et élémentaire du mystère chrétien. Par son caractère complet, elle se distingue du kérygme. La foi est maintenant éveillée et il faut instruire de tout son contenu le catéchumène qui se prépare au baptême. Par son caractére èlèmentaire, la catéchèse se differencie de l' homélie. On ne se préoccupe pas d'y répondre aux questions difficiles, ni de s'étendre sur des détails d' exégèse. La catechèse va a l'essentiel, elle donne la substance meme de la foi, laissant de côté les approfondissements spirituels et spéculatifs. Ce caractère complet et élémentaire apparait dans ces schémas antiques de la catéchèse que sont les symboles." op. cit., p.15.

16 These are the four saints named by John Paul II in his survey of the history of catechesis, Catechesi Tradendae, 12 (AAS, 71:1287).

The other notable catechetical works of the fourth and fifth centuries are the following:
A. Theodore of Mopsuesta's catechetical homilies (preserved only in a Syrian translation, an English translation of which occurs in Vols. 5 and 6 of Woodbrooke Studies: Christian Documents Edited and Translated (by A. Mingana, Cambridge, 1932-33). PG 66 contains but two fragments: Ex libro ad baptizandos (cols. 1013-16), and Exemplum expositionis Symboli depravati (cols. 1015-20).
B. Proclus of Constantinople's mystagogical homilies (from Palm Sunday through Pentecost), PG 65:771-808.
C. Gregory of Nyssa's Oratio catechetica magna, PG 45:9-106.
D. Rufinus of Aquilea's Tractatus de Symbolo, PL 21:335-86.
E. Nicetus of Ramesiana's Ad competentes, PL 52:865-74.
F. Quodvultdeus' three homilies on the Creed (attributed to St. Augustine), PL 40:637-68.

17 PG 33:331-1060.

18 PG 33:1065-1128.

19 Pistin de en mathēsi kai epaggelia ktēsai kai pērēson monēn, tēn hypo tēs Ekklēsias nuni soi paradidomenēn, tēn ek pasēs Graphes ōchurōmenēn. Epeidē gar ou pantes dunantai tas Graphas anaginōskein, alla tous men idiōteia, tous de ascholia tis empodizei pros tēn gnōsin; hyper tou mē tēn psychēn ex amathias apolesthai, en oligois tois stichois to pan dogma tēs pisteos perilambonomen. Hoper kai ep' autēs tēs lexeōs mnēmoneusai hymas boulomai, kai par' heautois meta pasēs spoudēs apaggeilai, ouk eis chartas apographomenous, all' en chardia te mnēmē stēlographountas ... PG 33:520-21.

20 It may be useful to list the topics in the "catechetical" series with their corresponding Scriptural texts:
The "Procatechesis" or Introduction (Cant 2:12);

1. Conversion (Is 1:16);
2. Confession (Ez 18:20);
3. Baptism (Rom 6:3-4);
4. "Ten dogmas" (Col 2:8);
5. Faith and the Creed (Heb 11:1);
6. The unity of God (Is 45:16-17);
7. God the Father (Eph 3:14);
8. The omnipotence of God (Jer 32:18-19);
9. God the Creator (Job 38:2);
10. The One Lord Jesus Christ (1 Cor 8:5-6);
11. The Only-Begotten Son of God (Heb. 1:1);
12. The Incarnation (Is 7:10);
13. The Crucifixion and Burial (Is 53:1);
14. The Resurrection (1 Cor. 15:1-4);
15. The Second Coming of Christ (Dan 7:9-13);
16. The Holy Spirit (1 Cor 12:1-4);
17. The Holy Spirit (cont'd) (1 Cor 12:8); and
18. The Catholic Church and the Resurrection of the Body (Ez 37:1).

The topics in the "mystagogical" series with their corresponding Scriptural texts are the following:
Introduction: on the recently baptized (1 Pet 5:8);
1. The ceremonies of baptism (Rom 6:3-14);
2. The sacred chrism (1 Jn 2:20-28);
3. The Body and Blood of the Lord (1 Cor 11:23); and
4. The sacred liturgy of Holy Communion (1 Pet 2:1).

21 Etheria (or Elgeria), a pilgrim from Spain in the 380s, wrote for her "sisters" a detailed description of the Lenten and Holy Week ceremonies conducted in Jerusalem. See John Wilkinson's edition, <u>Elgeria's Travels</u> (London: S.P.C.K., 1971).

22 See Antoine Wenger's edition of St. John Chrysostom, <u>Huit catéchèses baptismales inédites</u> (Paris: Cerf, 1957).

23 St. John Chrysostom points to specific details, e.g., women's jewelry (Cat.1), excessive drinking over the Easter holidays (Cat. 5), taking in the horse races (Cat. 6), the farmers in from the country (Cat. 8).

24 <u>PL</u> 17:1193-96. It is interesting to note the similarity between St. Ambrose's conclusion to his <u>Explanatio Symboli</u> and that of St. Cyril's in the passage cited earlier (see above, note 19): "Illud sane monitos vos volo esse, quoniam Symbolum non debet scribi, quia reddere illud habetis. Sed nemo scribat. Qua ratione? Sic accepimus ut non debeat scribi. Sed quid! Teneri. Sed dicis mihi, quomodo potest teneri, si non scribitur. Magis potest teneri, si non scribatur. Qua ratione? Accipite. Quod enim scribes, securus quasi relegas, non quotidiana meditatione incipis recensere; quod autem non scribis, times ne amittas, quotidie incipis recensere. Magnum autem tutamentum est; nascuntur stupores animi et corporis, tentatio adversarii qui nunquam quiescit, tremor aliquis corporis, infirmitas stomachi; Symbolum

recense intra te, maxime recense intra teipsum. Quare consuetudinem facias et cum solus, ut fortius recenseas ubi sunt fideles." Ibid., col. 1160.

25 "Nunc de mysteriis dicere tempus admonet, atque ipsam sacramentorum rationem edere: quam ante baptismum si putassemus insinuandam nondum initiatis, prodidisse potius quam edidisse aestimaremur. Deinde quod inopinantibus melius se ipsa lux mysteriorum infuderit, quam si eam sermo aliquis praecururrisset." PL 16:406.

26 "Nunc quid superest, nisi oratio? Et nolite putare mediocris esse virtutis scire quemadmodum oretis. Apostoli sancti dicebant ad Dominum Iesum: 'Doce nos orare...' Tunc ait Dominus orationem: 'Pater noster'..."PL 16:469.

27 Enchiridion ad Laurentium sive de Fide et Spe et Caritate, PL 40:231-90. See below, Chapter II, pp.28-30.

28 PL 40:309-48.

29 St. Augustine explains the "narratio" two times in the De Catechizandis Rudibus. Out of the twenty-seven chapters and fifty-five numbers into which this book is divided, three chapters (II-IV) and five numbers (4-8) are devoted to his first discussion of "narratio," and eleven chapters (XIV-XXIV) and twenty-five numbers (20-44) to the second -- for a total of fourteen chapters and thirty numbers.

30 That there are phases in the fieri of an individual Christian is a truth somewhat analogous to the fact that there are phases in the fieri of the Church herself (see Lumen Gentium,2-4), or that there are three sacraments of "Christian initiation" and that there is a progression among them. There are no more "instant Christians" than there are "anonymous Christians." See Mk 4:26-30; 8:22-26. As part of the post-conciliar liturgical renewal, the revival of the ancient catechumenate was envisaged. See Rite of Christian Initiation of Adults (Washington, D.C.: United States Catholic Conference, 1974), and Missale Romanum (Vatican City: Typis Polyglottis Vaticanis, 1971), "In conferendis sacramentis initiationis Christianae," pp. 729-38.

31 The continuation of the specifically "evangelical" into and accompanying the specifically catechetical was always true in the real order of things. It is particularly true in the present cultural milieu of the Church in the West.

It should be noted that for convenience and continuity we are using only the Latin (i.e., not the Greek) terms for the successive stages of the catechumenate.

32 See Rite of Christian Initiation of Adults (RCIA), 68-97 (pp. 17-27).

33 Before the liturgical changes in the wake of Vatican II, what we now call the "Liturgy of the Word" was known as the "Mass of the Catechumens" -- in contradistinction to the "Mass of the Faithful," i.e., the "Liturgy of the Eucharist."

34 See <u>RCIA</u>, 99 (p. 28).

35 It is at least as historically true to say that Lent was fitted into the catechumenate, as to say that the catechumenate was fitted into Lent! See Dom E. Flicoteaux, O.S.B., <u>Le sens du Carême</u> (Paris: Cerf, 1956).

36 See <u>RCIA</u>, 133-51 (pp. 36-43).

37 See <u>Missale Romanum</u>, pp. 729-32; <u>RCIA</u>, 152-80 (pp. 43-55).

38 See <u>RCIA</u>, 181-92 (pp. 55-60).

39 In summary, the three periods of the catechumenate are:
A. The <u>auditores</u>: from the <u>signatio</u> to the First Sunday of Lent.
B. The <u>competentes</u> (or <u>electi</u>): from the First Sunday of Lent to Easter.
C. The <u>neophyti</u> (or <u>illuminati</u>): from Easter to Pentecost.

If the pre-catechumenate (i.e., the <u>accedentes</u>) is included, there are four periods.

40 See above, note 25, p.22. This practice of reserving the explanation of the sacraments until after they were received, although not universal (St. John Chrysostom departs from it), was "classic." It was a significant instance of the dictum: "credo ut intellegam."

41 Vatican II, <u>Gaudium et Spes</u>, 22 (<u>AAS</u>, 58:1044).

42 For both range and depth in this study of the history of Christian culture, the work of Christopher Dawson is invaluable. His assessment in particular of the transition from the ancient to the medieval, in terms of loss and gain for Catholicism, is a frequently recurring theme. See, e.g., <u>The Historic Reality of Christian Culture</u> (New York: Harper and Row, 1960), Chapter 3, "The Six Ages of the Church."

43 The classic eulogist of the Constantinian peace was, of course, Eusebius of Caesarea, "the father of Church history." See his <u>Ecclesiastical History</u>, X, 1-3 (<u>PG</u> 20:842-47).

44 The most spectacular instances of this were the conversion of Clovis, king of the Franks, by St. Remigius in 496, and the conversion of Ethelbert, king of the Jutes, by St. Augustine of Canterbury in 529.

45 St. John Damascene was more closely a contemporary of St. Bede or St. Isidore in the West than he was of St. Gregory. However,

because of the slower dissolution of the classical culture in the East than in the West, the parity in this respect between Damascene and Gregory, as representing their respective "Christianities," is justified.

46 St. Gregory compared the first four Councils to the four Gospels. See his letter to the Patriarch of Constantinople, Registri Epistolarum, I, 25 (PL 77:478).

47 Lampe's Patristic Greek Lexicon (Oxford: Clarendon Press, 1961) lists "orthodoxia" but not "orthopraxis" (p. 972). Liddell and Scott's Greek-English Lexicon (9th edition, Oxford: Clarendon Press, 1961) lists, besides "orthodoxia," "orthopragia," but not "orthopraxis" (p. 1249).

48 See Vatican II, Lumen Gentium, 12 (AAS 57:17).

CHAPTER TWO

THE COMPONENTS OF THE CLASSIC CATECHESIS

In the centuries that followed the pontificate of St. Gregory the Great the memory of the classic catechesis perdured unbroken. Its actualization in the catechumenate of the Fathers had disappeared, due to the great cultural changes which ended the age of classic antiquity and ushered in the new age which would later be called "medieval." But despite the disappearance of its classic actualization, catechesis continued -- as it had to if the Church herself was to continue -- in terms of its essential content. That essential content was, of course, equated with the Apostolic teaching taken as a whole; and by the time of the Fathers it had come to be "articulated" in a manner similar to the articulation of the Creed.[1] But this newer Patristic articulation was broader in content than the Creed taken in an exclusive sense. For the Creed itself was but one of four "articles" or parts of a larger whole: the whole of the Apostolic Tradition.

Nearly a thousand years after St. Gregory the Great, this four-fold division of catechesis was thus described in the Preface of the Roman Catechism:

> ...our fathers in the faith wisely apportioned the entire thrust and meaning of the doctrine of salvation within the framework of four parts, viz., the Apostles' Creed, the sacraments, the Decalogue and the Lord's Prayer.[2]

The "fathers in the faith" ("<u>maiores nostri</u>") are not identified, which is itself significant. For it suggests the universality of its tradition. To the authors of the Roman Catechism -- as to all their contemporaries -- there was no time or place where this four-fold content of catechesis did not obtain.[3] But, as in so many other respects, the initial articulation of this tradition in the Latin West can be credited to St. Augustine (354-430). Rodriguez, in his recent authoritative commentary on the origins of the Roman Catechism, succinctly expresses this credit:

> Above all, what comes through is a clear outline of the basic structure of the Catechism, based on the four classic components of catechesis so closely linked with the Augustinian tradition.[4]

I

The Augustinian locus classicus occurs, as one would expect, in his De Catechizandis Rudibus:

> This love should be your purpose in view of which you direct all that you say. Whatever you recount as history you should so recount that he, to whom you speak, on hearing will believe, on believing will hope, on hoping will love.[5]

The "narratio," i.e., the statement of the Good News as unfolded in history, is the revelation to which the hearer responds in faith; and because of this faith and through this faith he hopes, and because of this hope and through this hope he loves. This great Pauline triad (1 Cor 13:13) is thus taken over by St. Augustine as the matrix of his catechesis. And in three subsequent passages in his discourse he develops this initial point by indicating, at least implicitly, the content of the three components.

The first passage is brief and elliptical, but clear enough: "As a finish to the narration, hope in the resurrection should be set forth."[6] If hope follows faith, then faith (which is not mentioned here explicitly) must be essentially connected with the "narratio." What is narrated is what is believed. The contents of the two acts -- the catechist's "history" and the catechumen's "believing" -- are implicitly identified. The "narratio" is no mere introduction or mise en scène; it is an essential component, the first essential component, of catechesis. And hope, too, is here given its essential content: "resurrectio," i.e., our resurrection, following on and modeled after Christ's resurrection. This is the terminal point of the Creed. Out of the sacred history will issue this final event: the resurrection of the body and life everlasting. The acquisition and development of this infused habit of confident desire for this ultimate consummation is the second essential component of catechesis.

If faith is related to "narratio" and hope to "resurrectio," what is that to which charity is related? St. Augustine's answer, in our second passage, is in the same manner as in the previous one: it is less categoric than rhetorical. Yet, for all that, it is sufficiently clear.

> ...fifty days after His resurrection He sent them the Holy Spirit (as He had promised). With that love poured in their hearts, they were able, not only without difficulty but with joy, to fulfill the law. That law had been given to the Jews in ten commandments called the Decalogue. They are condensed into two commandments: that we love God with all our heart, all our soul and all our strength, and that we love our neighbor as ourselves. For on these two commandments the whole Law and the Prophets depend, as Our Lord made clear in the Gospel by both His words and His example.[7]

The operative term here is "lex." Charity is verified by -- indeed, it is practically identified with -- the Commandments: "Thou shalt love the Lord thy God ... thou shalt love thy neighbor ..." (In fact, not only is love identified with law; law is identified with love -- there is no other law!) This is the life of the Christian in its simplest statement: it flows from faith founded on a reality from the past, it is sustained by hope moving toward a future good, and it lives in the present by love.

In a third passage St. Augustine describes the essential conclusion to the catechetical process: the reception of the catechumen into the Church by means of the sacraments.

> After his instruction the catechumen is asked whether he believes what he has been told and intends to observe it. Upon his response he is to be solemnly sealed and recognized as a member of the Church. The sacrament which he receives has been well explained to him; it is a visible sign of a divine reality, and in that sign the invisible reality is honored. What is visible has been sanctified by solemn blessing, and must not be treated as something in common use. What it signifies must be explained, so that he knows what has been placed in him, and what likeness to what reality he bears.[8]

Immediately following this description of the sacrament as a reality at once visible and invisible, he refers to the Sacred Scriptures as having a similar characteristic.

> At this same time he should be told that if in the Scriptures he should hear anything which sounds merely earthly, he should believe (even if he does not understand) that something spiritual is signified which pertains to holy living and the future life. He thus quickly learns that whatever he hears in the sacred books which cannot refer to the love of eternity and truth and holiness and to the love of the neighbor, he recognizes as having been said or done only figuratively. And thus he will try to understand, so that he can refer (everything in Scripture) to that two-fold love.[9]

Like the sacraments, then, the Scriptures exist on two levels. They both have an outer corporal reality which at once veils and leads to an inner spiritual reality. And this inner reality, which he says pertains to moral rectitude and eternal glory ("<u>ad</u> <u>sanctos mores futuramque vitam</u>"), the newly baptized Christian must believe is there in the sacred text, even if he cannot as yet recognize it as such. (If likewise, we cannot as yet recognize the relevance of Scripture to this discussion of catechetical components, we will be able to do so if we but continue to follow the pedagogy of St. Augustine as our prime mentor in the catechetical tradition.)

Turning now to his <u>Enchiridion de Fide et Spe et Caritate</u> (written some twenty years after his <u>De Catechizandis Rudibus</u>), we see a development of this same Augustinian view of the structure of Christian doctrine. And what makes his presentation here even more impressive is that it is set in the same context as that of his earlier work, viz., the Christian doctrine proper to the beginner. Early in this little treatise he reminds his reader of the two formulas given to the catechumens as a kind of summary of his instruction, viz., the Creed and the Lord's Prayer.

> Now you have the Creed and the Lord's Prayer. What can be more quickly heard or read? What can be more easily memorized? To a human race weighed down by its misery from mortal sin and needing the divine mercy, the prophet proclaimed God's time of grace: "And everyone who calls upon the Lord's name will be saved" (Joel 2:32). Hence you have prayer. And the Apostle

recalling this same prophetic proclamation of grace, immediately adds: "How can they call on one in whom they have not believed?" Hence you have the Creed. In these two sets of words you have three things: faith believes, hope and love pray. But since nothing happens without faith, faith also prays. That is why it is said: "How can they call on one in whom they have not believed?" (Rom 10:14)[10]

There is a correlation, then, between the two formulas -- the Creed and the Lord's Prayer -- on the one hand, and the three virtues -- faith, hope and charity -- on the other. Later in the treatise he returns to this correlation:

From this confession of faith, which is briefly summarized in the Creed, and which is the milk of earthly symbol for the beginner but the solid food of spiritual truth for the strong, there comes hope -- the good hope of the faithful, accompanied by holy love. Yet of all that which is believed by faith, what is hoped for is only that which is in the Lord's Prayer. For, as the sacred writer tells us, "cursed is he who put his hope in man" (Jer 17:5). Thus whoever puts his hope in himself is locked into this curse. And so we must seek from the Lord our God that which we hope for, whether by our good deeds or by what we gain by them.[11]

After a passing reference once more to the two levels of understanding latent in the Creed (because of the two levels in the Scriptures, from which the Creed is derived), Augustine explains the precise coordination of faith and hope, as corresponding respectively to the Creed and the Lord's Prayer. He does not forget charity as also part of his schema; but for the moment he leaves it aside until he has put faith and hope clearly in place.

But then, almost immediately he turns to charity:

Now charity is, as the Apostle says (1 Cor 13:13), greater than faith and hope in whatever thing it is found, in the same degree that it is a better thing in itself. For what determines the goodness of a person is not what that person believes or what he hopes for, but what he loves. The one who loves rightly necessarily believes and hopes rightly. The one who does not love believes pointlessly, even if what he believes is true; and he hopes pointlessly, even if what he hopes for was taught him as leading to true happiness. This believing and this hoping have value only because they enable him to love.

> Although hope cannot really exist without love, yet it is quite possible not to love that without which one cannot attain what he hopes for. For example, one can hope for eternal life (which is something one cannot but love), and yet not love the righteousness without which that eternal life cannot be attained. The faith in Christ which the Apostle commends is the faith that works by love (Gal 5:6); what one does not yet have by love he asks for, that he may receive it; he seeks that he may find it; he knocks that it may be opened to him (Mt 7:7). Thus faith begs for what the law commands. Without the gift of God, i.e., without the Holy Spirit by Whom charity is poured into our hearts (Rom 8:5), the law can command, but it cannot help; indeed, it can make a liar out of the one whose ignorance cannot be excused. Where divine charity is absent, only carnal desire sits enthroned.[12]

This magnificent text (which anticipates St. Thomas' thesis on charity as the form of all the virtues) repeats what he said in <u>De Catechizandis Rudibus</u>: charity is our fulfillment of the law of God -- the law He gave us in the Decalogue. The Commandments are thus an essential component of catechesis, just as essential as the Creed and the Lord's Prayer. In fact, any instruction which is limited to the Creed and the Lord's Prayer and leaves out the Commandments is "pointless" ("<u>inaniter credit ...inaniter sperat</u>").

In the next paragraph St. Augustine presents a kind of summary of his treatise. He puts all human history into four successive stages: "<u>ante legem</u>" -- from Adam to Moses, "<u>sub lege</u>" -- from Moses to Christ, "<u>sub gratia</u>" -- the Christian life in this world, and "<u>in pace plena et perfecta</u>" -- the Christian life hereafter.

> In whatever one of these four ages the grace of rebirth should encounter a man, there would be accomplished the remission of all his previous sins. Of whatever guilt he contracted by his birth he would be absolved by his rebirth. So efficacious is the Spirit Who breathes where He wills (Jn 3:8) that certain ones will feel not so much an enslavement under the Law as rather a divine assistance provided by the Law.
>
> ...Before a man can be capable of living under a command, he must first live according to the flesh. But once he has received the sacrament of rebirth, nothing will impede him if he should then depart from this earthly life. For so did Christ die and rise again, that He might be Lord of the living and the dead (Rom 19:9). The kingdom of death has no claim on him who is free among the dead (Ps 87:6).[13]

The point he makes is that in any one of the four stages man's destiny as willed by God is essentially the same, viz., the same life of faith, hope and charity to which he is called. However, the "adiutorium divinum," which alone enables man to fulfill that destiny comes to him only by "regeneratio," which is conferred only by a "sacramentum": baptism. Thus St. Augustine's catechetical conclusion in the Enchiridion is the same as in the earlier work; and that is: faith, hope and charity are dependent for their full realization on the sacraments -- and therefore, implicitly, by instruction in them. And so the immemorial practice of the Church is confirmed by the reasoned reflection of her greatest theologian. Formal catechesis finds its culmination and completion in the Mystery of Christ's death and resurrection; for in the individual catechumen's reception of baptism, confirmation and Holy Eucharist this Mystery is truly renewed.[14]

Along with the De Catechizandis Rudibus and the Enchiridion stands a third work from the pen of Augustine which we must cite as a literary source of the Latin tradition regarding the structure of catechesis. In his sermon De Symbolo ad Catechumenos, dating from the very last years of his life, we have the final words of the great Doctor on a subject he must have considered as the most fundamental and important of his ministry.

> Receive, my sons, the rule of faith, called the Creed. On receiving it, write it in your heart, and every day recite it among yourselves. Before you fall asleep, before you proceed to anything, gird yourselves with your Creed. No one writes down the Creed just to be read; he stamps it on his soul, lest forgetfulness should lose what diligence had given him. Your book is your memory. What you will hear is what you will believe; and what you will believe is what you will recite. As the Apostle says, "Belief comes from the heart and justifies us; profession of faith comes from the mouth and saves us" (Rom 10:10). This, then, is the Creed: something stamped in your heart, something recited on your lips. The words you have heard, scattered all across the Sacred Scriptures, are here gathered up and reduced to a tight unity. With the burden of our sluggish memory thus eased, every one should be able effectively to say and to practice what he believes.[15]

Is Augustine thinking here of a parallel with the Old Testament? The shema of Deuteronomy was for the Israelite his constant companion through life -- sleeping and waking, it was ever before his mind (Deut 6:4). For it was his very life: this faith of Israel in the One True God. For the Christian this same faith, now fulfilled and perfected in the New and Eternal Testament, is capsulated ("collecta et ad unum redacta") in the Apostles' Creed. This Creed is his constant conscious possession, to be treasured in his heart and proclaimed in his speech ("recensuri ... reddituri"), for it is the "rule of faith" ("regula fidei") by which he begins to live the eternal life.

This essential beginning of the divine life, thus "ruled" by the Creed, is essentially dependent on the sign divinely instituted to impart this life, viz., baptism. To this decisive point Augustine turns as he nears the end of his sermon. He has briefly explained the articles of the Creed in succession, until he reaches "the remission of sins." There he interjects the following comment:

> You have the Creed perfectly in your possession when you are baptized. Once you are baptized, hold fast to a life of goodness by keeping God's commandments, and thus you will preserve your baptism always. We are cleansed once by baptism; we are cleansed daily by prayer.[16]

The Creed, to be "perfectly" possessed, requires baptism. Baptism, to be ultimately efficacious, requires the observance of the Commandments. Observance of the Commandments, to be the daily realization of the effects of baptism, requires prayer. Nowhere can there be found a more succinct resume of the four components of the classic catechesis.

Before he returns to the last two articles of the Creed -- "the resurrection of the body and life everlasting"-- St. Augustine makes a further comment on baptism as the remission of sins:

> The sins which God first forgives are those only of the baptized. When are they forgiven? When they are baptized. Later on, God forgives the sins of those who pray and do penance -- of those, that

is, who were already baptized. For how can anyone say "Our Father" who has not yet been born in baptism?[17]

Far from being an interjection or even an aside, then, this repeated reference to baptism -- and therefore to the moral life, and therefore to prayer -- is essentially related to the Creed! For not only are there three other components to catechesis besides the Creed; they are, together with the Creed, organically inseparable. The remission of sins is professed in the Creed, and initially effected in baptism. But before they can reach the resurrection of the body and life everlasting, the baptized must strive to live the Commandments; and that striving has its necessary prayer, the prayer proper to those reborn who are still pilgrims and penitents: the Our Father.

II

The "tradicion agustiniana" dominated the thought and practice of a near thousand years in the Latin Church. Following St. Gregory the Great by some two centuries (which was about the same interval between Gregory and Augustine) came one of the most representative thinkers and pastors of the early Middle Ages: Rabanus Maurus (c.776-856).

In a three-volume work entitled De Ecclesiastica Disciplina, Rabanus touches on our subject in several passages in Book II, "De Catechismo et Sacramentis divinis."[18] His reliance on Augustine is evident, and is frequently acknowledged. The first problem he addresses is that occasioned by the practice -- by that time practically universal -- of infant baptism. How is it possible for a person incapable of conscious belief to have saving faith?

> Although infants because of their age are incapable of conscious conversion and belief, nevertheless we believe that they are converted to God because of the sacrament of conversion, and that they have faith because of the sacrament of faith which they receive. ...Even though he does not yet have that faith which exists because of the believer's will, the infant is nevertheless made a member of the faithful because of the sacrament of faith. For just as they respond (through their sponsors) to the faith, so they are

> counted among the faithful: not by their own perception of the reality of faith, but by their reception of the sacrament of faith. When later with the age of reason he begins to understand, he does not repeat his reception of the sacrament, but simply ratifies by his mind and will what had already been willed for him.[19]

Two points in particular are to be noted here. First, a profound awareness of the mysterious reality of baptism as an <u>efficacious</u> sign. It is the "sacrament of conversion" and the "sacrament of faith"; in both respects it effects what it signifies, so that the person baptized is eo ipso a member of the "faithful" ("<u>fidelem facit</u>"). Although Rabanus takes into explicit consideration neither the relationship between faith as a personal elicited act and baptism as an act received, nor the relationship between the baptismal sponsors, the person baptized and the Church as a whole, yet he asserts -- not as a current opinion but as the firm traditional faith -- the <u>objective</u> function and efficacy of the sacrament (and, by implication, its necessity for salvation).

On the other hand -- and this is his second point -- the relationship between baptism and faith is still intrinsic to the sacrament. It is, after all, the "sacrament of faith"; and so, even with the baptized infant, the "agenda" regarding the faith must be fulfilled. This means <u>instruction</u> in the faith, once the child has reached the age of reason ("sapere"), so that his reception of the sacrament can now be willed ("consona ...voluntate"). Here is the basic instance, then, of the intrinsic coordination between two of the four catechetical components: the Creed (faith) and the sacraments (baptism).

In a subsequent passage Rabanus Maurus discusses a second and broader relationship, but one equally intrinsic and equally attested by tradition.

> When one has been given the divine sacraments and made a member of the faithful and a sharer in the truth of the Christian name, he must give evidence by his deeds of his professed faith, and strive by his manner of living to be pleasing to God Who so graciously called him to the Catholic faith and willed his insertion into the Body of Christ. He must earnestly pray that God Who thus put him among the elect will enable him to reach the Beatific Vision. Hence it is necessary that he learn thoroughly the Lord's

> Prayer, i.e., not merely to recite it but to understand it, and thus fulfill what St. Paul said about "praying with the spirit and praying with the mind; singing with the spirit and singing with the mind" (1 Cor 14:15).[20]

Here the relationship is between faith/sacrament on the one hand, and good works/prayer on the other. He does not explain these relationships, nor does he even label them as such. We cannot say, therefore, that the author is aware of precisely the number of components -- any more, indeed, than Augustine himself was. Yet, materially, the four are here: all four and only four. And the very fact that they are not explained is itself evidence of their being, in Rabanus' mind, but the unquestioned data of tradition.[21]

The catechetical tradition, so classically formulated by St. Augustine and so effectively witnessed to by Rabanus Maurus, continued on through the following centuries to reach its definitive systematization in the High Middle Ages: the great era of Scholasticism. Outstanding among the men of the "twelfth century renaissance" who established the methodology and the very spirit of the Schools (and especially that of Paris) was Peter Abelard (1079 - 1142). It may be well to cite him as our next witness, for if ever there was a time when a tradition so identified with its Patristic cadre as was the classic catechesis could be displaced by one more "rational," it was in the early twelfth century in Paris, where with unheard-of audacity and prestige Abelard was sweeping all before him.[22]

The relevant texts from Abelard are few and brief. But as we saw in the case of Rabanus Maurus, this paucity of words can be itself revealing. Abelard begins his Introductio ad Theologiam as follows:

> Responding as best I can to the request of my students, I have written a kind of summary (summa) of sacred learning, as an introduction to the divine Scriptures. As they zealously pursued under my tutelage their secular philosophical studies, and found ever greater pleasure in their reading, they concluded that this talent of mine could be even more happily spent delving into the sacred page and the reasons of faith, than in plumbing the wells -- as they put it -- of philosophy. ...[23]

After setting the scene with this Prologue, he gets to his (and our) matter immediately.

> There are, as I see it, three things in which man's salvation consists, viz., faith, charity and sacrament. As for hope, I put it as a species under the genus faith.[24]

This terse resume must have seemed highly satisfactory to its author, for Abelard repeats it <u>verbatim</u> in his later and even more abbreviated work entitled <u>Epitome Theologiae Christianae</u>.[25] Remarkable, from our point of view, are two points: 1) the persistence of the Pauline/Augustinian triad as the fundamental matrix of Christian doctrine -- as evidenced by Abelard's need to explain what happened to hope; and 2) the unequivocal inclusion of "sacrament" in that triad. Abelard's "revision" of the traditional triad reveals his penetrating grasp of the <u>real</u> content of the classic catechesis as Augustine treated it. His restless genius <u>had</u> to come up with a new formulation, but substantially it is identical with the tradition as he found it.

Abelard's substantial fidelity is confirmed by his treatment of the Apostles' Creed and the Our Father in the opening paragraphs of his <u>Expositio Symboli quod dicitur Apostolorum</u>:

> The holy fathers have taught us, my brethren, that both the symbol of Faith called the Apostles' Creed and the Lord's Prayer should be known by all Christians generally, and indeed should be so memorized that they can be at any moment recited. For in the one our confession of faith is succinctly expressed, and in the other we are taught what things we are to ask of God....
>
> ... It should be noted that no one may present an infant for baptism until in the presence of the priest he has first recited the Creed and the Lord's Prayer....[26]

Although he does not link the Creed and the Lord's Prayer to faith and hope respectively, and although he makes no allusion to their context in the moral life (both of which points Rabanus Maurus had made), Abelard does insist on their comprehensiveness -- providentially rendered in a brevity of form within the reach of all, and on their integral, indeed intrinsic, connection with baptism. These latter two points are not only a faithful echo from Augustine; they are a clear anticipation of Aquinas.

III

At the peak of the Scholastic movement stands St. Thomas Aquinas (c. 1225-1274), and at the peak of his gigantic literary production stands -- alongside his <u>Summa Theologiae</u> -- his <u>Compendium Theologiae</u>. Like the <u>Summa</u>, the <u>Compendium</u> is an unfinished work, interrupted by his death. Thus they both reflect the full maturity of his genius. But if the <u>Summa</u> contains Thomas' final thought on a scale of awesome grandeur, the <u>Compendium</u>, in contrast, contains the same thought in perfect miniature. Only eighty-five pages in the Parma edition, it is usually listed among his collected works as "<u>Opusculum I</u>."[27] That this last little treatise from the great Master of the School should be on catechesis is movingly significant, for both its finality and its brevity seem to corroborate the thesis here expounded. Catechesis itself must be brief and definitive if its essential pastoral role in the Church is to be achieved.

"Brevity" is in fact the very term St. Thomas selects to set the theme of his discussion. With consummate skill, literary as well as theological, he describes the great "economy" itself as God's "brevity":

> The Word of the eternal Father, holding in His immensity all things, and willing that man cut down by sin should be restored to the heights of divine glory, willed His own abbreviation -- not by putting aside His majesty but by assuming our lowliness. And lest anyone should be excused from grasping the doctrine of His heavenly word, because of the very bulk of the Sacred Scriptures containing it, He summarized the doctrine of our salvation in brief form.
>
> For man's salvation consists in 1) the knowledge of the truth (lest the human mind be darkened by error), 2) the willing of the proper end (lest the pursuit of improper ends lead to the loss of true happiness), and 3) the observance of justice (lest the life of vice lead to corruption).
>
> The necessary knowlege of the truth of our salvation is contained in a few articles of faith. As St. Paul said to the Romans, "The Lord fulfills His word briefly on the earth" (Rom 9:28), which word is the word of faith which we preach.[28]

This first "brevity" is now echoed by a second and a third. If the faith can and must be "abbreviated" in a Creed, if it is to be readily learned, there must be corresponding "abbreviations" to those gifts of God following on faith, by which we learn to hope in Him and love Him. For these three -- faith, hope and charity -- are the "compendium" of all sacred learning.

> God has rectified our human intention by giving us a brief prayer. By teaching us to pray He has shown us how our intention and our hope should be directed. And as for our justice, which consists in the observance of the law, He has summarized it under one commandment of charity. "The fulness of the law is love" (Rom 13:10).
>
> Thus St. Paul puts the whole perfection of our present life under these three headings of faith, hope and charity. "Now there remain these three, faith, hope and love" (1 Cor 13:13). As St. Augustine says, it is by these three virtues that God is worshipped. Therefore, my dear Reginald, since the doctrine of the Christian religion is summarized by these three, I intend in this present work to treat of them.
>
> We will treat first of faith, then hope, and finally charity. This is the order that the Apostle follows and reason requires. For love cannot be right unless the proper end is set by hope; and hope cannot thus be set unless truth is known. Faith is necessarily first: by it we know the truth. Then comes hope: by it we set our intention in the proper direction. Finally comes charity: by it our affections are wholly directed and controlled.[29]

Here, then, is the perfect reprise of St. Augustine's Enchiridion. Following the same order deriving from St. Paul, Aquinas proceeds to an explanation of the Creed, article by article.[30] "Faith" is for him what it was for Augustine: that which is "articulated," briefly yet comprehensively, in the Creed.

Part II of the Compendium Theologiae is introduced as follows:

> As according to the Prince of the Apostles we are exhorted to render an account not only of our faith but also of our hope, so, following what we have offered as a brief exposition of Christian faith, let us now do something similar regarding hope.

> It is to be noted that any knowledge can satisfy some human desire, since man naturally desires to know and is satisfied by that knowlege. But in the kind of knowledge called faith man's desire is not satisfied, for faith is an imperfect knowledge. What is believed is not seen, as the Apostle says: "It is the evidence of things that are not seen" (Heb 11:1). Hence, even with faith there remains the spiritual impulse to see the truth of what one believes, and to secure that whereby he can enter into that truth. Now among the things we believe is that God provides for all human needs. Hence there arises in the soul of the believer the impulse called hope whereby he may attain the goal he naturally desires as learned from faith. Following faith, then, the next requisite for the perfection of the Christian life is hope.[31]

St. Thomas thus develops the Augustinian (and Pauline) correlation between the two habits: hope follows on faith as desire follows on knowledge. This desire for God must take that form appropriate to man's nature: he must <u>pray</u>. This is the subject matter of Chapter II of this Second Part of the <u>Compendium</u>.

> Because in the order of divine providence there is given to each created thing the mode of attaining its end according to its own proper nature, there has been given to man an appropriate mode of attaining what he hopes from God, according, that is, to his condition as man. It is a human condition that in seeking something from someone -- especially if that person is a superior -- the one so hoping should make use of a petition as a means of obtaining what he hopes for. Prayer is therefore instinctive on the part of man, whereby he seeks to obtain from God what he hopes for.[32]

Prayer, then, is the "confession" of hope. And just as the confession of faith has, in the providence of God for His smallest rational creatures, taken an "abbreviated" form, so too there has been provided for us an "abbreviated" form of prayer.

Finally, in Chapter III we are told what form that prayer must take.

> Since therefore, after faith, hope also is required for our salvation, it was fitting that besides being the author and finisher of faith by instituting heavenly sacraments, our Saviour should also bring us hope by giving us a form of prayer.
>
> By prayer our hope is lifted up to God, and taught by Him what to ask for. God would not have us pray to Him unless He was already disposed to hear us. No one asks of another for what is not his hope -- his hope is in effect his prayer. Thus we are taught by God to

> exercise our hope by asking, and to perfect our asking by learning what our petitions should be. Our study, therefore, of what is contained in the Lord's Prayer will tell us what comprises true Christian hope; i.e., it will tell us whom we are to pray to, and why, and for what. Our hope must be in God, just as our prayer must be. As the Psalmist says: "Hope in Him (i.e., God), all you people; pour out before Him (i.e., in prayer) your hearts." (Ps 61:9).[33]

The Lord's Prayer is, therefore, even more clearly an instance of God's providence toward us than is the Creed itself.

In the course of this Second Part of the Compendium Theologiae, in Chapter XI, where he was treating of the second Petition of the Our Father ("adveniat regnum tuum"), St. Thomas died. What he left unfinished, viz., the remainder of Part II on hope and the whole of Part III on charity, we can, fortunately, reconstruct from his other works. Completing Part II we have his "Opusculum V": In Orationem Dominicam videlicet Pater Noster Expositio.[34] And replacing Part III is "Opusculum III": In Duo Praeceptis Caritatis et in Decem Legis Praeceptis Expositio.[35] The latter is particularly valuable, for, as the title itself makes clear, St. Thomas' treatment of charity is exactly in line with the format of the Compendium. He begins this Expositio on charity as follows:

> Man needs three kinds of knowledge for his salvation: knowledge of what to believe, knowledge of what to desire, and knowledge of what to do. The first knowledge is taught us in the Creed, where we learn of the faith; the second, in the Lord's Prayer; the third, in the Law.[36]

The correspondence between faith and the Creed, and between hope and the Our Father, are by now clear enough. The third correspondence, between charity and "the law," calls for the further explanation which is precisely the object of his little book.

St. Thomas' emphasis on law in this treatise on charity is at least as strong as St. Augustine's, as we saw in both the De Catechizandis Rudibus and the Enchiridion.[37] The connection between the two Doctors on this point is, in fact, almost verbal. For just as Augustine develops his understanding of law in the context of "four ages," so

Aquinas develops law in terms of "four laws." For, immediately following the opening passage cited above occurs this sentence:

> We now come to the knowledge of what to do. And here we find that we must treat of a four-fold law.[38]

The "four laws" are: the law of "nature" founded on creation, the law of "concupiscence" resulting from sin, the law of "Scripture" recorded by Moses, and the law of "Christ" or "the Gospels" or "grace." It may be noted that for St. Thomas they are not, strictly speaking, "four laws" ("<u>quattuor leges"</u>); they are, rather, a "four-fold law" ("<u>quadruplex lex</u>"). Nevertheless, what emerges from St. Thomas' division is an even more cogent emphasis on the Decalogue than St. Augustine's, for what corresponds to Augustine's fourth "age" is not only Thomas' fourth "law" but his third "law" as well. For Thomas the Decalogue is, even <u>formaliter,</u> as proper to the New Testament as it is to the Old. It is not merely the law of Moses; more definitively it is the law of Christ.[39]

Following this introductory consideration on law as the context of the Commandments, St. Thomas returns to the theme of the <u>Compendium Theologiae</u>, viz., the utility -- indeed the necessity -- of "brevity " in our exposition of sacred doctrine.

> It is obvious that not everyone can study a body of knowlege. That is why Christ gave us a very brief law: so brief that everyone could learn it, and no one could be excused from its observance because of ignorance. This is the law of divine love.[40]

Now the reason why there can be brevity in the "knowledge of things to be done" is that all goodness in human action is specified and measured by only one law: the law of the love of God.

> It should be clear that this law is the proper norm for all human actions. For just as among things made by man that which is good and right is what conforms to a standard, so too that human action is right and virtuous when it conforms to the standard of divine love.[41]

St. Thomas does not go on to say -- perhaps it was so obvious that it required no explicit mention -- that we now have a perfectly symmetrical triad in the "abbreviations" of our three knowledges. "Abbreviated faith" is the Creed, "abbreviated hope" is the Lord's Prayer, and "abbreviated love" is the law of love.

After describing the efficacy and sufficiency of this law of love, by virtue of which it more than fulfills its function of ruling the whole of our lives, Aquinas finally comes to its factual formulation.

> As we have already said, the entire law of Christ depends on charity. And charity depends on two commands: the first commanding love for God, the second, love for the neighbor. Now when God gave the law to Moses, He put it in the form of ten commandments, written on two stone tablets. On one tablet were the three commandments pertaining to our love for God; on the other were the seven pertaining to our love for the neighbor. On the two commands of love thus promulgated was based the entire law.[42]

Just as St. Thomas was more explicit than St. Augustine in identifying the Decalogue with the law of the Gospel, so he is likewise more explicit in drawing out the parallel between our knowledge of it and our preceding two knowledges regarding faith and hope. He does this by presenting an analysis of each of the Ten Commandments in a manner exactly like his analysis of each of the twelve Articles of the Creed and each of the seven Petitions of the Lord's Prayer. And with this presentation he concludes the "<u>Opusculum</u>" which, as the effective equivalent of "Part III," completes his <u>Compendium Theologiae</u>.

Thus far we have examined the teaching of St. Thomas on the structure of sacred doctrine, especially as it pertains to catechesis, i.e., in the "abbreviated" form most suitable for beginners. We have seen that he is totally faithful to the "<u>tradición agustiniana</u>" -- that he has, in fact, deepened and reinforced it. But thus far we have seen nothing in his writings (except one passing allusion -- so passing, in fact, that we did not call attention to it at the time)[43] that would suggest his adherence to what was, in final analysis, not a three-fold but a <u>four-fold</u> structure in the traditional catechesis.

St. Augustine, as we have seen, added to the triad -- Creed, Lord's Prayer, Commandments -- a <u>fourth</u> component, which was not so much an "addition" from outside as it was a kind of "binder" from inside, giving the other three components a unity and a dynamism they could not otherwise have. This fourth component was "baptism": the sacramental culmination -- and finality -- of the catechetical process.[44] And, as we have also seen, this four-fold <u>schema</u> was, at least to some extent, further developed in the subsequent tradition, as evidenced by Rabanus Maurus and Abelard. Is there any similar evidence of this tradition in St. Thomas?

In spite of the fact that by the thirteenth century the reality of the classic catechumenate of the Fathers was but a distant memory, St. Thomas was quite aware of the intrinsic sacramental aspect of catechesis. He firmly defends the thesis that in principle catechesis must precede baptism -- and therefore, by implication, must include some instruction in it.

> In the doctrine of the faith there are certain things which are basic and must be explicitly believed by all, e.g., the doctrines of the Trinity, the Incarnation and Redemption, the final Judgment, and the Providence of God. Instruction in these doctrines is called catechesis. As for other doctrines, instruction in them can come later, i.e., after baptism.[45]

Again, with more explicit reference to the baptism of infants, which historically occasioned the question of their relative sequence:

> Catechesis is, as it were, a certain disposition for baptism. Now dispositions must be proportioned to that for which they dispose. In the case of adults, therefore, where one's own faith and volition are required for baptism, so too one's own catechesis is required, i.e., one must himself be convinced of and profess the Christian religion. In the case of infants, on the other hand, where one's baptism is effected solely by the faith of the Church and the merits of Christ, one's instruction in the faith is likewise taken care of by another. That is to say: those truths in which the infant will one day be instructed must now be affirmed by the infant's sponsors, to whom that charge of eventual instruction is given. In place of the infant, the sponsors make his affirmation and profession of the faith.[46]

When St. Thomas addresses the same question, "utrum catechismus debeat praecedere baptismum," in his Summa Theologiae, he is more succinct:

> Baptism is the sacrament of the faith, since it is a certain profession of the Christian faith. Since reception of the faith presupposes instruction in it (as St. Paul says to the Romans 10:4, "How can they believe what they have not heard? And how can they hear what was not proclaimed?"), it is fitting that catechesis precede baptism.[47]

So intrinsic and intimate, in fact, is this connection between faith and the "sacrament of the faith" (and, by extension, the "septenarium" and the sacramental system as a whole) in the thought of St. Thomas that we can understand why he seems to treat them as one entity rather than two.

Moreover, there is evidence that he does consider the sacraments as proper matter for explicit instruction, similar to and following the instruction in the articles of the Creed. Besides the obvious prominence he gives to the sacraments in his Summa Theologiae,[48] there is his formal juxtaposition of the articles and the sacraments in one of his works "Opusculum IV": In Articulos Fidei et Sacramenta Ecclesiae Expositio.[49] It is true, he prefaces the second part, on the sacraments, with a certain disclaimer:

> We must now consider the sacraments of the Church. We could study them as a single thing -- contained, that is, under one article of the Creed -- since they all pertain to one reality: the effect of grace. But since you have posed a special question concerning the sacraments, we will treat them as a topic apart from the Creed.[50]

This demurrer on his part only heightens the appreciation on our part of the importance he attaches to the catechetical tradition. In spite of the development in sacramental theology since Augustine's time (e.g., regarding the "septenarium, "the "ex opere operato," etc.) -- or indeed because of it -- Aquinas is almost archaic in his fidelity to the outward format of the Augustinian catechesis. What we said earlier regarding Augustine is equally applicable to Thomas: the

44

sacraments are not an "addition" from outside, but rather a "binder" from within.

In light of this discussion we can at last return to that allusive passage we cited earlier but left without comment. We can now see how, as so often occurs in the writings of the Angelic Doctor, a whole landscape can be lighted up by a small detail. In Chapter III of Part II of the Compendium Theologiae we recall this sentence:

> Since therefore, after faith, hope also is required for our salvation, it was fitting that besides being the author and finisher of faith by instituting heavenly sacraments, our Savior should also bring us hope by giving us a form of prayer.[51]

Whether the correct reading is "reserando" or "reservando,"[52] in either case the emphasis is not on the verb but on the noun. St. Thomas, by putting the term "sacramenta" (which by the thirteenth century has a very specific meaning) between "fides" and "spes" has in effect put the sacraments within the Pauline/Augustinian triad, in the sense that not only is faith radically unrealizable without them, but that hope too -- and charity -- are in some analogous manner intrinsically dependent on them.

All three knowledges -- of what to believe, of what to desire, and of what to do --- look, then, to this knowledge: the knowledge of the "signs" Christ has chosen to "release" -- or "reserve" -- for our instruction. In a manner interestingly reminiscent of both Rabanus Maurus and Abelard,[53] we have here -- verbally and really -- the intimation of the four components, on all of which -- and on only which -- the classic catechesis is structured. It only remained for the authors of the Roman Catechism to make explicit and authoritative what had been in substance handed down to them by their "maiores."

NOTES

1. For the division of the Creed into "articles," see Henri de Lubac, La Foi Chrétienne: essai sur la structure du Symbole des Âpôtres (Paris: Aubier, 1950), Chap.1, "Histoire d'une légende" (pp.23-59), in which he discusses the origin of the twelve-fold articulation corresponding to the twelve Apostles, and dismisses it in favor of the three-fold articulation corresponding to the Three Persons of the Trinity. For the ratio of "articulus," see S.T., II-II, 1,6.

2. "...sapientissime maiores nostri totam hanc vim et rationem salutaris doctrinae in quattuor haec capita redactam distribuerunt: Apostolorum Symbolum, Sacramenta, Decalogum, Dominicam Orationem," (Praef.,12;p.6) (The two numerals are, respectively, the "Rovillian number" designating the section in the Preface, and the number designating the page in the first Manutian edition of 1566. See below, Chapter VI, note II, p. 157). All subsequent citations from the Roman Catechism in this study will follow this format.

3. E.g., Carranza, after listing and describing the same four parts of catechesis, makes this conclusion: "Este Catechismo y Doctrina cristiana que hicieron los Padres de la Iglesia, conservó muchos años la religión en su limpieza primera. Esta tenemos por regla (después de la Escritura Santa, donde ella se ha sacado) todos los cristianos..." Comentarios sobre el Catecismo Cristiano (Madrid:BAC, 1972), Vol. I, p. 126.

4. "...sobre todo, se tiene un diseño claro de la estructura general del Catecismo, configurada en torno a las cuatro piezas clásicas de la catequética de entonces, tan estrechamente vinculada a la tradición agustiniana." Pedro Rodriguez and Raul Lanzetti, El Catecismo Romano: Fuentes e Historia del Texto de la Redaccion (Pamplona: Ediciones Universidad de Navarra, 1982), p. 128.

5. "Hac ergo dilectione tibi tanquam fine proposito, quo referas omnia quae dicis, quidquid narras ita narra, ut ille cui loqueris audiendo credat, credendo speret sperando amet." IV, 8 (PL 40:316). The final clause in this passage is quoted in the opening paragraph of Vatican II's Dei Verbum (AAS, 58: 817).

6. "Narratione finita, spes resurrectionis intimanda est." VII, 11(PL 40:317).

7. "...completis a resurrectione quinquaginta diebus, misit eis Spiritum Sanctum (promiserat enim), per quem diffusa caritate in cordibus eorum, non solum sine onere, sed etiam cum

iucunditate legem possent implere. Quae data est Iudeis in decem preaeceptis, quod appellant Decalogum. Quae rursus ad duo rediguntur, ut diligamus Deum ex toto corde, ex tota anima, ex tota mente; et diligamus proximum sicut nos ipsos. Nam in his duobus praeceptis totam Legem Prophetasque pendere, ipse Dominus et dixit in Evangelio (Mt 22:37-40) et suo manifestavit exemplo. " XXIII,41 (PL 40:339-40).

8   "His dictis, interrogandus est an haec credat, atque observare desideret. Quod cum responderit, solemniter utique signandus est et Ecclesiae more tractandus. De sacramento sane quod accipit, cum ei bene commendatum fuerit, signacula quidem rerum divinarum esse visibilia, sed res ipsas invisibiles in eis honorari; nec sic habendam esse illam speciem benedictione sanctificatam, quemadmodum habetur in usu quolibet: dicendum etiam quid significet et sermo ille quem audivit, quid in illo condiat, cuius illa res similitudinem gerit." XXVI,50 (PL 40;344-45).

9   "Deinde monendus est ex hac occasione, ut si quid etiam in Scripturis audiat quod carnaliter sonet, etiamsi non intelligit, credat tamen spiritale aliquid significari, quod ad sanctos mores futuramque vitam pertineat. Hoc autem ita breviter discit, ut quidquid audierit ex Libris canonicis, quod ad dilectionem aeternitatis et veritatis et sanctitatis, et ad dilectionem proximi referre non possit, figurate dictum vel gestum esse credat; atque ita conetur intelligere, ut ad illam geminam referat dilectionem." ibid.

10 "Nam ecce tibi est Symbolum et Dominica Oratio; quid brevius auditur aut legitur? quid facilius memoriae commendatur? Quia enim de peccato gravi miseria premebatur genus humanum, et divina indigebat misericordia, gratiae Dei tempus propheta praedicans ait, 'Et erit omnis qui invocaverit nomen Domini salvus erit' (Joel 2:32); propter hoc oratio. Sed Apostolus cum ad ipsam gratiam commendendam hoc propheticum commemorasset testimonium, continuo subiecit, 'Quomodo autem invocabunt in quem non crediderunt?' (Rom 10:14); propter hoc Symbolum. In his duobus tria illa intuere: fides credit, spes et caritas orant. Sed sine fide esse non possunt, ac per hoc et fides orat. Propterea quippe dictum est: 'Quomodo invocabunt in quem non crediderunt?"' II, 7 (Pl 40:234).

11 "Ex ista fidei confessione, quae breviter Symbolo continetur, et carnaliter cogitata lac parvulorum est, spiritaliter autem considerata atque tractata cibus est fortium, nascitur spes bona fidelium, cui caritas sancta comitatur. Sed de his omnibus quae fideliter sunt credenda, ea tantum ad spem pertinent quae in Oratione Dominica continentur. 'Maledictus' enim 'omnis,' sicut divina testatur eloquia, 'qui spem ponit in homine' (Ier 17:5), et per hoc et in se ipso qui spem ponit, huius maledicti vinculo innectitur. Ideo nonnisi a Domino Deo petere debemus, quiquid speramus nos vel bene operaturos vel pro bonis operibus adepturos." XXX, 114 (PL 40:285).

12 "Iam vero caritas, quam duabus istis, id est, fide et spe, maiorem dixit Apostolus (1 Cor 13:13), quanto in quocumque maior est, tanto melior est in quo est. Cum enim quaeritur utrum quisque sit homo bonus, non quaeritur quid credat aut quid speret, sed quid amet. Nam qui recte amat, procul dubio recte credit et sperat; qui vero non amat, inaniter credit, etiamsi sint vera quae credit; inaniter sperat, etiamsi ad veram felicitatem doceantur pertinere quae sperat; nisi et hoc credat et speret, quod sibi petenti donari possit ut amet.

"Quamvis enim sperare sine amore non possit, fieri tamen potest ut id non amet sine quo ad id quod sperat non potest pervenire. Tanquam si speret vitam aeternam (quam quis non amat?) et non amet iustitiam, sine qua ad illam pervenit. Ipsa est autem fides Christi, quam commendat Apostolus, quae per dilectionem operatur (Gal 5:6), et quod in dilectione nondum habet, petit ut accipiat, quaerit ut inveniat, pulsat ut aperiatur ei (Mt 7:7). Fides namque impetrat quod lex imperat. Nam sine Dei dono, id est, sine Spiritu Sancto, per quem diffunditur caritas in cordibus nostris (Rom 5:5) iubere lex poterit, non iuvare; et praevaricatorem insuper facere, qui de ignorantia se excusare non possit. Regnat enim carnalis cupiditas, ubi non est Dei caritas." XXXI, 117 (PL 40:286-87).

13 "In quacumque autem quattuor istarum velut aetatum singulum quemque hominem gratia regenerationis invenerit, ibi ei remittuntur praeterita universa peccata; et reatus ille nascendo contractus, renascendo dissolvitur. Tamque multum valet quod Spiritus ubi vult spirat (Jn 3:9), ut quidam secundum illam servitutem sub Lege non noverint, sed cum mandato incipiant adiutorium habere divinum....

"Antequam possit autem homo capax esse mandati, secundum carnem vivat necesse est; sed si iam sacramento regenerationis imbutus est, nihil ei oberit si tunc ex hac vita migraverit. Quia ideo Christus mortuus est et resurrexit, ut et vivorum et mortuorum dominetur (Rom 14:9); nec tenebit regnum mortis eum, pro quo mortuus est ille liber in mortuis (Ps 87:6)." XXXI, 119-20 (PL 40:288).

14 See above, Chapter I, p.14.

15 "Accipite, filii, regulam fidei, quod Symbolum dicitur. Et cum acceperitis, in corde scribite, et quotidie dicite apud vos; antequam dormiatis, antequam procedatis, vestro Symbolo vos munite. Symbolum nemo scribit ut legi possit; sed ad recensendum, ne forte deleat oblivio quod tradidit diligentia, sed vobis codex vestra memoria. Quod audituri estis, hoc credituri; et quod credideritis, hoc etiam lingua reddituri. Ait enim Apostolus: 'Corde creditur ad iustitiam, ore autem confessio fit ad salutem' (Rom 10:10). Hoc est enim Symbolum, quod recensuri estis et reddituri. Ista verba quae audistis, per divinas Scripturas sparsa sunt; sed inde collecta, et ad unum

16 "Habetis Symbolum perfecte in vobis quando baptizamini. ... Cum baptizati fueritis, tenete vitam bonam in praeceptis Dei, ut baptismum custodiatis usque in finem....Semel abluimus baptismate, quotidie abluimus oratione."VII, 15 (PL 40:636).

17 "Ipsa peccata quae primum dimittit, nonnisi baptizatis dimittit. Quando? Quando baptizantur. Peccata quae postea orantibus dimittuntur, et paenitentibus, quibus dimittit, baptizatis dimittit. Nam quomodo dicunt 'Pater noster' qui nondum nati sunt?" VIII, 16 (ibid.).

18 Book I, entitled "De sacris ordinibus," is practically a paraphrase of De Catechizandis Rudibus, and a resume of De Civitate Dei.

19 "Quamvis ... parvuli pro aetate non possunt intelligere ipsam conversionem ad Deum atque credulitatem, credimus tamen eos ad Deum converti propter conversionis sacramentum , et fidem habere propter fidei sacramentum.... Itaque parvulum, etsi nondum fides illa quae in credentium voluntate consistit, iam tamen ipsius fidei sacramentum fidelem facit. Nam sicut credere respondentur, ita etiam fideles vocantur; non rem ipsam mente annuendo, sed ipsius rei sacramentum percipiendo. Cum autem sapere homo coeperit, non illud sacramentum repetit, sed intelligit, eiusque voluntate consona etiam voluntate cooptabitur." (PL 112:1217)

20 "Cum autem sacramentis divinis quis imbutus fuerit, et fidelis effectus Christiani nominis et verae religionis existit particeps, necesse est ut fidem quam professione tenet, operibus probet, et toto nisu per sanctae conversationis studium contendat placere illi qui eum per suam gratiam ad fidem Catholicam convocavit, et unitum corpori suo inserere voluit. Hocque quotidie sacris precibus instanter deposcat, ut ipse qui, eum cum caeteris electis in filiorum numerum ascribi voluit, sua opitulatione faciat eum pervenire ad conspectum gloriae eius sempiternae. Unde necesse est ut Orationem Dominicam pleniter discat quatenus eam non voce tantum proferat sed intelligat, ut fiat quod Apostolus docuit dicens: 'orabo spiritu, orabo et mente; psallam spiritu, psallam et mente' (1 Cor 14:15)." (PL 112:1221)

21 There is a further text from Rabanus Maurus which, for a purpose to be better seen later in our study, is well worth transcribing here:
"Est autem Symbolum signum per quod agnoscitur Deus, quodque proinde credentes accipiunt, ut noverint qualiter contra diabolum fidei certamina praepararent. In quo quidem pauca sunt verba, sed omnia continentur sacramenta. De totis enim Scripturis, haec breviatim collecta sunt ab Apostolis; ut quoniam plures credentium littera nesciunt, vel qui sciunt praeoccupatione saeculi Scripturas legere non possunt, haec corde retinentes, habeant sufficientem sibi scientiam salutarem.

Est enim breve fidei verbum, et olim a Propheta praedictum: 'Quoniam verbum breviatum faciet Dominus super terram.' Quod hoc tenore recitatur." (PL 112:1225)

22 Fortunately, the matter we here discuss and the texts we here cite have nothing to do with the controversies surrounding the name of Abelard, all of which were occasioned in one way or another by the "audacity and prestige" alluded to.

23 "Scholarium nostrorum petitioni, prout possumus, satisfacientes, aliquam sacrae eruditionis summam, quasi divinae Scripturae introductionem conscripsimus. Cum enim a nobis plurima de philosophicis studiis et saecularium litterarum scriptis studiose legissent, et eis admodum lecta placuisset; visum illis est, ut multo facilius divinae paginae intelligentiam, sive sacrae fidei rationes nostrum penetraret ingenium, quam Philosophicae abyssi puteos, ut aiunt, exhausisset. ..." (PL 178:979)

24 "Tria sunt, ut arbitror, in quibus humanae salutis consistit, fides videlicet, caritas et sacramentum. Spem autem in fide, tanquam speciem in genere, comprehendi existimo." I,1 (PL 178:981).

25 PL 178:1695.

26 "Institutum, fratres, a Patribus sanctis habemus tam Symbolum fidei, quod dicitur Apostolorum, quam Orationem Dominicam ab omnibus communiter Christianis debere sciri, et memoriter retineri, ut promptius quaerant frequentari. In illo quippe fidei confessio breviter est expressa; in ista instruimur a Domino postulare necessaria....

"Illud etiam observandum, ut nullus suscipiat infantem in baptismo a sacro fonte, antequam idem Symbolum et Orationem Dominicam coram presbytero decantet. ..." (PL 178: 617,619)

27 The citations from St. Thomas' works in this chapter are taken from the Parma edition (New York: Musurgia, 1950).

28 "Aeterni Patris verbum sua immensitate universa comprehendens, ut hominem per peccatum minoratum in celsitudinem divinae gloriae revocaret, breve fieri voluit nostra brevitate assumpta, non sua deposita maiestate. Et ut a caelestis verbi capessenda doctrina nullus excusabilis redderetur, quod pro studiosis diffuse et dilucide per diversa Scripturae sanctae volumina tradiderat, propter occupatos sub brevi summa humanae salutis doctrinam conclusit.

"Consistit enim humana salus in veritate cognitione, ne per diversos errores intellectus obscuretur humanus; in debiti finis intentione, ne indebitos fines sectando, a vera felicitate deficiat; in iustitiae observatione, ne per vitia diversa sordescat.

"Cognitionem autem veritatis humanae saluti necessariam est quod Apostolus ad Romanos (9:28) dicit: 'Verbum abbreviatum faciet Deus super terram'; et hoc quidem est verbum fidei, quod praedicamus." (Pars I) Cap.1 (Vol . XVI, p.1).

29 "Intentionem humanam brevi oratione rectificavit; in qua dum nos orare docuit, quomodo nostra intentio et spes tendere debet, ostendit. Humanam iustitiam, quae in legis observatione consistit, uno praecepto caritatis consummavit. 'Plenitudo legis est dilectio' (Rom 13:10).

"Unde Apostolus (1 Cor 13:13) in fide, spe et caritate, quasi in quibusdam salutis nostrae compendiosis capitulis, totam praesentis vitae perfectionem consistere docuit, dicens: 'Nunc autem manent fides, spes, caritas.' Unde haec tria sunt, ut beatus Augustinus dicit, quibus colitur Deus. Ut igitur tibi, fili carissime Reginalde, compendiosam doctrinam de Christiana religione tradam, quae semper prae oculis possis habere, circa haec tria in praesenti opere nostro versatur intentio.

"Primum de fide, secundo de spe, tertio de caritate agemus. Hoc enim et apostolicus ordo habet, et ratio recta requirit. Non enim amor rectus esse potest, nisi debitus finis spei statuatur; nec hoc esse potest, si vertitatis agnitio desit. Primo igitur necessaria est fides, per quam veritatem cognoscas; secundo spes, per quam in debito fine tua intentio collocetur; tertio necessaria est caritas, per quam tuus affectus totaliter ordinetur." ibid.

30 (Pars I) Capita 2-246 (ibid., pp. 1-77).

31 "Quia secundum principis Apostolorum sententiam admoneamur ut non solum rationem reddamus de fide, sed etiam de ea quae in nobis est spe, post praemissa, in quibus fidei Christianae sententiam breviter prosecuti sumus, restat ut de iis quae ad spem pertinent, compendiosam tibi expositionem faciamus.

"Est autem considerandum, quod in aliqua cognitione desiderium hominis requiescere potest, cum homo naturaliter scire desiderat veritatem, qua cognita eius desiderium quietatur. Sed in cognitione fidei desiderium hominis non quiescit; fides enim imperfecta est cognitio, ea enim creduntur quae non videntur; unde Apostolus eam vocat 'argumentum non apparentium' (Heb 11:1). Habita igitur fide, adhuc remanet animae motus ad aliud, scilicet ad videndum perfecte veritatem quam credit et assequendum ea per quae ad veritatem huiusmodi poterit introduci. Sed quia cetera fidei documenta unum esse diximus ut credatur Deus providentiam de rebus humanis habere, insurgit ex hoc in animo credentis motus spei, ut scilicet bona quae naturaliter desiderat, ut edoctus ex fide per eius auxilium consequatur. Unde post fidem ad perfectionem Christianae vitae spes necessaria est." Pars II, Cap. 1 (ibid., p.77).

32 "Quia vero secundum divinae providentiae ordinem unicuique attribuitur modus perveniendi ad finem secundum convenientiam suae naturae, est etiam hominibus concessus

congruus modus obtinendi quae sperat a Deo secundum humanae conditionis tenorem. Habet enim hoc humana conditio ut aliquis interponat deprecationem ad obtinendum ab aliquo, praesertim superiori, quod per eum se sperat adipisci; et ideo indicta est hominibus oratio per quam homines a Deo obtineant quod ab ipso consequi sperant." Cap. 2 (ibid.)

33   "Quia igitur ad salutem nostram post fidem etiam spes requiritur, opportunum fuit ut Salvator noster sicut auctor et consummator nobis factus est fidei reserando caelestia sacramenta; ita etiam nos in spem vivam induceret, nobis forman orandi tradens, per quam maxime spes nostra in Deum erigitur, dum ab ipso Deo edocemur quid ab ipso petendum fit. Non enim ad petendum induceret nisi proponeret exaudire: nullusque ab alio petit nisi de quo sperat, et ea ipse petit quae sperat. Sic igitur dum nos docet a Deo aliqua petere, in Deo nos sperare admonet, et quid ab eo sperare debeamus ostendit per ea que petenda esse demonstrat. Sic igitur prosequentes ea quae in Oratione Dominica continentur, demonstrabimus quiquid in spem Christianorum pertinere potest: scilicet in quo spem ponere debeamus, et propter quam causam, et quae ab eo sperare debemus. Spes quidem nostra debet esse in Deo, quem etiam orare debemus, secundum illud Psalmi (61:9): 'Sperate in eo,' scilicet Deo, 'omnis congregatio populi; effundite coram illo' scilicet orando 'corda vestra.'" Cap. 3 (ibid., p.78).

34   Vol. XVI, pp. 123-32. It is followed by "Opusculum VI" : In Satutationem Angelicam vulgo Ave Maria Expositio (pp. 133-34), and "Opusculum VII" : In Symbolum Apostolorum scilicet "Credo in Deum" Expositio (pp. 135-51). All three Opuscula are usually dated 1273.

35   This work is likewise dated 1273.

36   "Tria sunt homini necessaria ad salutem: scilicet scientia credendorum, scientia desiderandorum, et scientia operandorum. Primum docetur in Symbolo, ubi traditur scientia de articulis fidei; secundum in Oratione Dominica; tertium autem in Lege." Vol XVI, p. 97.

37   See above, pp. 29-30.

38   "Nunc autem de scientia operandorum intendimus; ad quam tractandam quadruplex lex invenitur." loc. cit.

39   Significantly, St. Thomas calls his third law "Scripture" (i.e., not the Old Testament only). He contrasts the law of Moses with the law of Christ on three counts: whereas Moses' law was 1) for slaves, 2) promising temporal rewards, and 3) difficult to fulfill, Christ's law is 1) for sons, 2) promising eternal rewards, and 3) easy to fulfull. (ibid.).

40   "Sed manifestum est quo non omnes possunt scientiae insudare; et propterea a Christo data est lex brevis, ut ab omnibus posset

sciri, et nullus propter ignorantiam possit ab eius observatione excusari; et haec est lex divini amoris." ibid.

41 "Sed sciendum quod haec lex debet esse regula omnium actuum humanorum. Sicut enim videmus in artificialibus quod unumquodque opus tunc bonum et rectum dicitur quando regulae coaequatur; sic etiam quodlibet humanum opus rectum est et virtuosum quando regulae divinae dilectionis concordet." ibid., p. 98.

42 "Sicut iam dictum est, tota lex Christi dependet a caritate. Caritas autem pendet ex duobus praeceptis; quorum unum est de dilectione Dei, reliquum de dilectione proximi; et de istis duobus iam dictum est. Nunc autem sciendum quod Deus dando legem Moysi, dedit decem praecepta in duobus tabulis lapideis scripta; quorum tria in prima tabula scripta pertinent ad amorem Dei, septem vero scripta in secunda tabula pertinent ad amorem proximi; et ideo tota lex fundatur in duobus praeceptis." ibid., p.102.

43 Viz., "...opportunum fuit ut Salvator noster sicut auctor et consummator nobis factus est fidei reserando caelestia sacramenta..." ibid., p. 78. See above, note 33, p.52.

44 See above, p. 31.

45 "...in doctrina fidei quaedam dicuntur quae sunt fidei communia rudimenta, ad quae credenda explicite omnes tenentur, sicut est fides Trinitatis et Incarnationis et Passionis et divini iudicii et providentiae Dei de factis hominum; et talis instructio catechismum dicitur; de aliis autem debet instrui post baptismum temporis processu." In Sent. IV, 6,2,1.

46 "Catechismus est quasi quaedam dispositio ad baptismum. Dispositiones autem debent proportionari illis ad quae disponunt; unde in adultis, in quibus in baptismo requiritur propria fides et propria voluntas, requiritur etiam quod ipse per se catechizetur, et per se confiteatur, et Christianam religionem profiteatur. In puero autem cuius baptismum operatur tantum ex fide Ecclesiae et merito Christi, fit instructio mediante alio; unde eadem quibus instruendus est, proponuntur praesente anadocho, cui committitur in his instruendis; et ipse loco eius confessionem et professionem facit." ibid., 6,2,3.

47 "...baptismus est fidei sacramentum, cum sit quaedam professio fidei Christianae. Ad hoc autem quod aliquis fidem accipiat, requiritur quod de fide instruatur, secundum illud ad Romanos (10:4): 'quomodo credant quem non audierunt? Quomodo autem audient sine praedicante?' Et ideo ante baptismum convenienter praecedit catechismus." III, 71, 1. Later in this same article there is a charming amplification of St. Thomas' view of infant baptism: "...sicut mater Ecclesia ...accomodat pueris baptizandis aliorum pedes ut veniant, et aliorum cor ut credant,

ita etiam accomodat eis aliorum aures ut audiant et intellectum ut per alios instruantur." ibid., ad 3.

48 There is no formal treatise "de Ecclesia" in the Summa. In the "Tertia Pars" St. Thomas moves directly from Christ to the sacraments.

49 Vol. XVI, pp. 115-22. This work is dated 1261-68.

50 "Nunc restat considerandum de Ecclesiae sacramentis; quae tamen omnia comprehenduntur sub uno articulo, quia ad effectum gratiae pertinent. Sed quia specialem de sacramentis fecistis quaestionem, de his seorsum agendum est." ibid., p.119.

51 "Quia igitur ad salutem nostram post fidem etiam spes requiritur, opportunum fuit ut Salvator noster sicut auctor et consummator nobis factus est fidei reserando caelestia sacramenta; ita etiam nos in spem vivam induceret, nobis formam orandi tradens..." . See above, note 33, p.52, and note 43, p.53.

52 "reserando" in the Parma edition, with "reservando" noted as a variant. Busa (S. Thomae Aquinatis Opera Omnia, Stuttgart: Frommann, 1980; Vol. III, p. 631) prefers "reservando" without variant.

53 See above pp. 33-36.

CHAPTER THREE

THE CLASSIC CATECHESIS AND SACRED SCRIPTURE

In the preceding chapters we have looked at the content of that catechesis (Chapter II) which in the Age of the Fathers had become institutionalized in the catechumenate (Chapter I), which in turn had issued from the catechetical tradition going back to the Apostles. The content of the classic catechesis, which survived the Age of the Fathers and the ancient catechumenate, and continued on without any interruption into the Middle Ages, was four-fold: the Creed, the Our Father, the Commandments and the sacraments. This four-fold content we examined, especially in the works of St. Augustine and St. Thomas Aquinas; and, as we have seen, the continuity of that content was maintained. More important and more enduring, then, than any particular mode of its presentation -- e.g., even the ancient catechumenate itself -- was this four-fold content. In its essentials, the classic catechesis consisted of these four elements, and these only.

What we must now note is that this classic catechesis with its four constituent elements never existed apart from the Sacred Scriptures. We can say without exaggeration that from the beginning the Bible was the prime catechetical "textbook." That that was so for St. Augustine should be obvious to anyone reading his <u>De Catechizandis Rudibus</u>. It is equally obvious to one reading the <u>Summa Theologiae</u> of St. Thomas, where "sacred doctrine" and "sacred Scripture" are practically synonyms,[1] that for him too catechesis and the Bible are intimately intertwined. We have already seen how in the Scriptures themselves the existence of a <u>didachē</u> was repeatedly affirmed, a <u>didachē</u> which was itself the very <u>raison d'être</u> of the Apostolic writings.[2] Although that <u>didachē</u> is not to be identified with the Scriptures as such -- for what the Apostles were mandated to "hand on" was something not to be read but to be heard[3] -- yet the Apostles did not hesitate to ground the authenticity of their tradition on an appeal to "the Scriptures." As we learn from St. John, the precedent for this was set by Christ Himself (see Jn 5:39; Lk 24:44). The very first Christian kērygma, St. Peter's sermon on Pentecost, was materially but a commentary on three texts from the Old Testament (Acts 2:14-39; Joel 3:1-5; Ps 15:8-11; Ps 109:1); and the very first formulation of a "creed," St. Paul's recitation to his Corinthians of the Paschal Mystery, affirms it as true "according to the Scriptures" (1 Cor 15:3-4). The "Scriptures" in question were, of course, the only Scriptures that Christ and the Apostles knew: the Old Testament. And there was no "New Testament" recognized as "Scripture" until long after the Apostles and the "Apostolic men" who wrote the New Testament were dead.[4] Yet the primordial fact that there was a "Scripture" known to the Apostles and used by them in their "handing on" of the Good News -- in that unique and supreme prototype of all catechesis -- is immensely significant for our study.

If we remember that the catechetical tradition thus began with a "Scripture," we can better understand why the appearance of the catechumenate as an institution and the appearance of the Apostolic writings as a "New Testament" were contemporaneous events.[5] There is surely more than coincidence in this parallel development. And going even further, there is more than coincidence in the fact that the most famous teacher in the most famous catechetical school -- Origen in Alexandria -- was at the same time a famous exegete of Sacred Scripture, among the most famous and influential in the entire history of the Church. Indeed, the full implications of this correlationship in Origen's lifework can almost be considered as the thesis of this present chapter.[6] But even apart from Origen and the magnitude of his contribution to our topic, it can be argued that in the very nature of the case the catechumenate and the canon of Scripture were two co-ordinates of prime importance to the Catholic Church of the late second and early third centuries. For in the catechumenate was concretized the Church's essential teaching, whereby she was (humanly speaking) assured of that recruitment to the body of her faithful which was her future. And in the New Testament was canonized that same essential teaching, whereby the Church had (humanly speaking) a direct line of contact with her origins in the now fast receding past.

With these data firmly in place by the early third century, it is easy to see how the classic catechesis of the Fathers in the fourth and fifth centuries was not only Scripturally oriented but, we may say, Scripturally saturated. Already, of course, the immemorial liturgy of the Eucharist -- whatever its local diversities, which would eventually become the great patriarchal rites -- had as its nucleus the "action" of the Lord as narrated in the Synoptics and St. Paul. And the homilies of the Fathers, complementing the liturgy of the Word and introducing the liturgy of the sacraments, were, as it were, but evocative glosses on the wisdom and righteousness of the Biblical texts:

> The wondrous depth of your words, whose surface before us attracts our little minds. But what wondrous depths, my God, what wondrous depths! It is a very terror to peer into it: a terror of exaltation, a trembling of love.[7]

How the Church understood the meaning of Scripture had, then, a profound effect on the whole of her life and teaching, and especially so on her catechesis. That catechesis, consisting essentially of four elements: the Creed, prayer, the Commandments and the sacraments, had to have some special relationship with the Scriptures as understood by the Church. That there had to be a special relationship of some sort was clear from the very nature of the two things in question. The Church's catechesis was the primary exercise of her magisterium: here was her teaching office in its most "ordinary and universal" function.[8] Similarly, the Church's Scriptures were the privileged source of her teaching: here were the very words of her Lord and His prophets and apostles, the words which she could now make her very own.

Just as there was a parallel development of the classic catechesis and the canon of Sacred Scripture in the third century, so, by a kind of analogy, another parallel development can be detected a thousand years later. By the thirteenth century there occurred another double "canonization": under the greatest Scholastics (and especially St. Thomas Aquinas) a consensus was reached that the classic catechesis does indeed have certain essential parts -- four in number, and that the

Sacred Scriptures do indeed have certain different meanings -- four in number.

The purpose of this present chapter is to ponder a question: is there a connection between these two sets of four? In the preceding chapter we reviewed the development of the four parts of catechesis, from the heyday of the catechumenate (St. Augustine) to the high Middle Ages (St. Thomas). In the present chapter we will, within the same general historical parameters, pursue a similar development: that of the senses, or meanings, of Scripture. With this brief review in place, we should then hopefully be in some position to address the question we have posed.

I

That there had to be a meaning in Scripture different from what the words themselves conveyed, and that this difference of meaning was recognized by the Church from the very beginning, is clear from the words of Christ Himself: "You search the Scriptures,...it is they that bear witness to me" (Jn 5:39). The Apostles took this "Christian" interpretation of the "Scriptures" (i.e., the Old Testament) so for granted that it was for them the basic premise of their entire kerygma.[9] By the third century, with the appearance of a "New Testament" alongside the "Old Testament" in the one set of "Writings" which were divinely authored, the distinction implicit from the beginning became explicit. There were two senses to the Sacred Writings, corresponding -- in some inchoate manner at least -- to the two authors: the Holy Spirit and the particular prophet or apostle He used as instrument in a particular book, and to the two Testaments: the Old and the New. These two pairings overlapped, of course: the whole Bible was equally divine and human. Being truly and totally human, the Scriptures meant, first of all, what the words said -- the words, that is, not necessarily of the copyist nor of the translator, but of the original inspired human author.

The only real difficulty about the proper understanding of this first "literal" sense of the Biblical writing occurs when there is a discrepancy between what the word itself <u>as a word</u> means, and what the <u>human author means</u> when using it.[10] In other words, is the metaphorical sense the literal sense? One tendency among the Christian exegetes of the early centuries was to leave the human author out of account and concentrate exclusively on the <u>word</u>. This excessively narrow interpretation of "literal" meant that if Scripture was to make any sense at all, it would often have to have a purely symbolic meaning. Such a view, because it leaves out of account the human author, leaves the field wide open for meanings to be read into the text by the reader himself.[11] This tendency, furthered by a neo-Platonism which denigrated the corporeal, the time-bound, the "letter"-- and which was exemplified in the work of the prestigious Alexandrian school under the great Origen -- definitely affected the subsequent course of exegesis in the Church.

However, two points in this regard must not be forgotten. First, the literal sense (also called, significantly, the "historical" sense) was always accorded the <u>primacy in time</u> in the reading of Scripture. One had always to <u>begin</u> there, if there was to be any hope of attaining the reality of Scripture at all.[12] This point was no mere truism for the early Church. Her greatest enemy, precisely because it was so seductively "spiritual," was Gnosticism, which found the Scriptural "letter" an embarrassment, if not a scandal. The Church defended the Old Testament in its entirety; yes, the very "carnality" of the Old Law was part of the <u>oeconomia</u> effected and revealed by the One True God. There could be no true continuity between the two Testaments if the literal, historical sense were not recognized and revered as the Word of God.[13]

The second point complements the first. For all its primacy and reality in time, the literal sense cannot be the <u>only</u>, nor can it be the <u>highest</u>, sense if Scripture is indeed more than a mere human work. The very fact of the New Testament's existence as an integral part of Scripture points to this truth. For the New Testament is justified not only by its <u>continuing</u> the Old Testament but by its <u>transcending</u> it. There would be -- could be -- no New (and Eternal!) Testament if the total meaning of the Old Testament were in itself something self-contained, if it ended in itself. David, Moses, Abraham, Adam were historical realities in themselves; yet there was more to them than just that. They were "figures", "types"of what was to come after them in time but before them in <u>meaning</u>, viz., Christ and His Church. Without this living "spirit" whereby the Old Testament is essentially <u>relative</u> to the New Testament, its "letter" taken absolutely is absolutely dead. This was the second great polemic the Church had to engage in in her earliest years: defending her identity as distinct from the Synagogue -- as precisely the <u>New</u> Testament.[14] To sum up this paradox of two Testaments in one Economy, of two meanings in one Sacred Scripture, we can say that the <u>literal</u> meaning of the New Testament vis-a-vis the Old is the "spiritual" meaning of the Scriptures taken as a whole.[15]

This "spiritual" meaning of the Scriptures, the elaboration of which was to be perhaps the greatest enduring legacy of the Fathers, (and especially so in their catechesis), was given different names in the course of time. The two terms most frequently used were "typical" and "allegorical." Both are warranted by Scripture itself: St. Paul spoke of Adam as a "type" (Rom 5:14) and of the two wives of Abraham as an "allegory." (Gal 4:24). Both terms were used interchangeably by the Fathers, and their practice was continued by the Scholastics. But though the term (the "letter"!) might vary, the meaning itself -- at least the root of the meaning -- remained unique and constant.[16] It was simply : "Christ."

Examples of this simple yet inexhaustible hermeneutic abound in the writings of the Fathers, thus echoing faithfully the writings of the Apostles, i.e., the New Testament itself:

> In Lia, who was the elder sister, we recognize the blindness of the synagogue; in Rachel we see the beauty of the Church. And yet, regarding those who were in one respect types of our Lord and Savior, not all the things which they are reported as having done are to be taken in the typical sense. For a "type," by its very definition, denotes only a part of its total truth. If the total were "typical," it

would cease to be a "type." The truth of history, i.e., the truth of what actually happened, must also be taken into account. [17]

This statement by St. Jerome (c. 340 - 410) is all the more impressive, for among all the Fathers he was perhaps the greatest champion of the literal sense. St. Augustine's eloquence on this point is well known:

> Not all those who are called Christians move on to Christ, but only those for whom the veil is removed: the veil which in the exclusive reading of the Old Testament remains in place. For those who remain in the Old Testament, because of that veil, there is no true understanding of either the Old or the New Testament. For those who move on to Christ, by the removal of the veil in the New Testament, there is true understanding of both Old and New (2 Cor 3:14-16). Would that those blind opponents of the Law and the Prophets would move on to Christ, so that for them nothing would veil the Gospel itself.[18]

And for perhaps the most "typical" statement of all, we can turn to St. Gregory the Great:

> "It was written inside and out." The book of Sacred Scripture as written on the inside is allegory; as written on the outside it is history. As read on the inside it is spirit; as read on the outside it is the plain sense of the letter, proportioned to those who are still weak. On the inside it promises invisible realities; on the outside it disposes of visible realities by the rightness of its commands. On the inside it holds forth heavenly things; on the outside it orders earthly things -- which, whether as held for use or as mere passing actions, are in themselves but objects of scorn. Indeed, those things which on the outside the Scripture enjoins are evident; while those things which on the inside it speaks of can never be fully grasped.[19]

Yet, for all their fecundity and felicity of thought, none of the Fathers came up with a really adequate principle of intelligibility for distinguishing between the "literal" and the "spiritual." What St. Gregory called "intus" and "foris" suggest the distinction finally made by St. Thomas, which gives us at last this principle:

... words signify things, while one thing can be the figure of another thing. The Creator, as author of things, not only can arrange for words to signify things, but also can arrange for things to signify other things. Accordingly, in Sacred Scripture the truth is indicated in two different ways. In one way, things are signified by words, things are signified by other things, and this constitutes its spiritual sense.[20]

While the understanding of the typical sense was being refined and the range of its applicability tested, there emerged another spiritual sense -- again in the Alexandrian ambiance, and again with some Alexandrian ambiguities. This subdivision of the spiritual sense could, like the typical or allegorical, claim a Pauline credential: his tripartite division of "spirit" (<u>pneuma</u>), "soul" (<u>psychē</u>) and "body" (<u>sōma</u>) (1Thes 5:22). As opposed to the "pneumatic" (i.e., the "spiritual" in its proper Christian sense), the "psychic" represented the values of the natural man. It was in this sense that Origen was said to have followed Philo, over-allegorizing the Scriptures and applying them to what was essentially a pagan ethic.[21] But this third sense -- properly called "tropological" or "moral" -- need not have this reductively non-Christian meaning. It could equally apply to the imperfect Christian, i.e., one still living ambiguously on both the "carnal" and the "spiritual" levels, and therefore needing nourishment from the Scriptures that would be somewhere between the "milk" for the beginners and the "meat" for the strong.[22] In fact, by the time of St. Gregory the Great, a tendency had set in which saw the "moral" sense as the most spiritual sense of Scripture, i.e., surpassing the typical as being more personal and pastoral.[23] Generally, however, it was seen as a valid application of the "Christian" sense of the Scriptures, willed by the Holy Spirit and directed to the building up of the <u>individual</u> members of the Body by perfecting their life of <u>virtue</u> modelled on the exemplar which is Christ.

Just as the typical (or allegorical) sense -- the "Christian" sense <u>par excellence</u> -- led into the tropological (or moral) sense as a further specification (or actualization) of its <u>spiritual</u> potential, so too it led into another and yet further plane of the "spiritual": the plane which by definition is the furthest possible. This fourth and ultimate sense of Scripture was called the "anagogical" or "eschatological," for what it referred to was the heavenly reality itself, the <u>patria</u> of pure and total reality.[24] Beyond all signs or figures of any kind as necessary for the viator but useless to the comprehensor, this reality is the Triune God in Himself and with His community of the Blessed. This reality is revealed as a definite meaning of the Scriptures; it is indeed its final revelation, in the sense not only of ultimate realization but also of final causality. "Last in execution," it was "first in intention." And so the great circle is complete: from Genesis to the Apocalypse, from the Creation as literal history to the Resurrection and eternal life as the supreme "anagogue," at which all words and all other symbols cease.

Although there was some fluctuation over those thousand years as to the precise order -- and even the precise number -- of these Scriptural senses (for occasionally now one, now two, of the "spiritual" senses would be subsumed under another),[25] yet in the main the four-fold structure and sequence here outlined remained constant. No one knows whence came the famous diptych of the schools:
> Littera gesta docet, quid credas allegoria,
> Moralis quid agas, quo tendas anagogia.[26]

Its very anonymity bespeaks its age. Certainly much older than the schools as such, it goes back to the earliest monastic origins in the West, and with some justification is associated with the name of John Cassian (360-434), Augustine's contemporary. For Cassian, speaking on "spiritual knowledge" in one of his famous Collationes, had this to say:

> It should be noted that while practical knowledge is as diverse as there are different skills and studies, theoretical knowledge is ultimately reduced to two kinds: historical interpretation and spiritual understanding. Thus when Solomon spoke of the varied graces of the Church, he added "all her charges are doubly clothed" (Prov 31:27). Now spiritual knowledge can be subdivided into three kinds: tropology, allegory and anagogy. As again in the book of Proverbs we read: "Write these down three times in the storehouse of thy heart" (Prov 3 and 32).
>
> Historical knowledge, first of all, concerns visible realities in time. E.g., "Abraham had two sons, one by the slave girl, the other by the freeborn wife. The son of the slave girl had been begotten in the course of nature, but the son of the freewoman was the fruit of the promise" (Gal 4:22-23). Allegorical knowledge concerns that which follows in this example, i.e., the historical realities are said to prefigure as signs the reality of something else: "All this is an allegory: the two women stand for the two covenants. One is from Mt. Sinai and brings forth children to slavery; this is Hagar. That mountain is in Arabia, and corresponds to the Jerusalem of our time,

which is likewise in slavery with her children" (Gal 4:24-25). Anagogical knowledge rises to even higher spiritual realities, i.e., to those heavenly secrets of which St. Paul goes on to speak: "But the Jerusalem on high is free born, and it is she who is our mother..." (Gal 4:26). Tropological knowledge finally, is the explanation of the spiritual in terms of morality: the amending of our life, and our personal guidance here and now. When, in other words, we wish to take both these testaments as norms of practical conduct, we understand by "Jerusalem" or "Sion" the individual human soul, as in Ps 147 we pray: "Praise the Lord, Jerusalem."

The four knowledges we have described here thus converge in one word, so that the one same "Jerusalem" can be understood in four different ways.[27]

Nearly a millennium after Cassian and an exact millennium after Origen, this classic doctrine of the four senses of Scripture found in the thirteenth century two statements with which we can conclude our summary description of it. The first is from a sermon of the great Innocent III (c. 1160-1216), where he elaborates on the favorite example, "Jerusalem":

> You know, dearly beloved, that the word "Jerusalem" can be used in four different ways, according to the four different kinds of theological knowledge, viz., the historical, the allegorical, the tropological and the anagogical. For there is a Jerusalem which is at once above and below, internal and external. Or, if you will, heavenly and earthly, spiritual and corporal. That which is above is in heaven; that which is below is on the way to heaven; that which is internal is in the soul; that which is external is in Syria. The Jerusalem above is the Church Triumphant, about which St. Paul says: "What is above is our mother." The Jerusalem below is the Church Militant, about which Isaiah says: "Arise, be enlightened, O Jerusalem." The Jerusalem within is the faithful soul, about which it is written: "I will give salvation to Sion, and in Jerusalem my glory." The Jerusalem outside is the pitiful city, about which it was said: "Jerusalem, Jerusalem, you kill the prophets."
>
> The four-fold Jerusalem bespeaks a four-fold peace: the peace of the sinners, the peace of the penitents, the peace of the just, and the peace of the blessed; the peace of the sinners in their vices, the peace of the penitents in their virtues, the peace of the just in their grace, the peace of the blessed in their glory."[28]

The second statement is from St. Thomas, where, as in so many other instances, we have a theological resume incomparable for its precision and balance:

> ...the author of Sacred Scripture is God, Who has the power not only of giving meanings to words (which man can also do), but of giving meanings to things as well. In every science words have meaning, but what is special to this science (of what is divine) is that the things meant by words have also a meaning of their own. That first meaning whereby words signify things is what we call the first meaning of Scripture, viz., the historical or literal meaning. That second meaning whereby the things signified by words in turn signify other things is called the spiritual meaning. It is based on the literal meaning, and presupposes it.
>
> The spiritual meaning is subdivided into three. As the Apostle says, the old law is a figure of the new law (Heb 7:9); and, as St. Denis says, the new law is a figure of the future glory. Also, in the new law that which is done in the head is a sign of what should be done in the members.
>
> Accordingly, as what falls under the old law signifies what falls under the new, the spiritual sense is called the allegorical sense; as what Christ did (or what represented Christ) signifies what we ought to do, the spiritual sense is called the moral sense; and as what signifies what pertains to eternal glory, the spiritual sense is called the anagogical sense. [29]

II

From St. Thomas, then, we have a definitive theology of the four meanings of Sacred Scripture, just as from him we have a definitive theology of the four components of catechesis. [30] In both respects his work was not original; he was dealing with materials which in their basic terminology and configuration were essentially the same as what St. Augustine dealt with. Yet his work was definitive in the sense that these materials, now tested by a near-thousand years' experience, were remoulded by his genius into a form that we can now assuredly call "classic." What St. Thomas did not do, however, (and there is no hint that it had ever occurred to him as something to do) was: <u>correlate the two data</u>. Is there any connection between these four senses of Scripture and these four components of catechesis? Before addressing this question in the light of the Roman Catechism (which is <u>the</u> thesis of this study), let us address it on its own terms, and thereby come up with a workable hypothesis.

We begin with the first sense of Scripture: the literal or historical meaning, derived from the words themselves as conveying the meaning intended by the human author. The very juxtaposition of "historical" with "literal" as synonymous throws some initial light on the matter. For what is seen here by the author, and intended by him that we see it too, is reality as "event." What is <u>formal</u> here is the "timed-ness" of a thing: its motion and termination in time. The essential grammatical form of its verbalization is that of verbs in the past tense: "it came to pass," "it happened," "he said," etc. Applied now to catechesis, this literal or historical sense is perfectly realized in the <u>Creed</u>. For the Creed is essentially a series of statements of <u>historical events</u>. Even the latter part where the events are not past but present or future (viz., from "is seated at the right hand of God" to the end) is not really outside this purview, because one's belief in these truths (i.e., that they are happening or will happen as an "event", i.e. not as a mere symbol) is based on the implied affirmation that these truths <u>have been</u> revealed -- and precisely within the ambit of the same Creed taken as a whole.[31]

The literal or historical sense of Scripture -- which, in its formal respect, is the same as the literal or historical sense of any writing -- not only <u>puts us in touch with</u> the Creed (it does the same for us regarding all the other parts of catechesis); it also <u>identifies</u> the Creed for us. Without the literal or historical sense, we would not understand the Creed as the Church understands it.[32] And just as the literal or historical sense comes <u>first</u> (without it, we would not only be unable to appropriate any further sense; we would not even know that a further sense exists!), so the Creed comes <u>first</u>. For without the Creed there may be some vague "fiduciality," but there is no faith. And without faith there may be some natural virtue, but there is no Christian life.

Now what that faith, affirmed and specified by the Creed, leads us to is Christ, Who is the Word made flesh. This reality into which we are led is the "mystery of faith" in its truest, profoundest sense. Not "mystery" as something impossible or at best difficult for our knowing except by revelation, but "mystery" as something hidden but now made manifest to our living by actual participation. In this sense the real "mystery of faith" professed and proclaimed in the Creed becomes realized in the sacraments.[33]

Whereas in the Creed the events of faith, for all their splendor, are far removed from us in time and space, they are in the sacraments here and now surrounding us, within us -- or rather, we are within them! What was once but "word" is now a "thing," concrete and real. Both in its humbleness and in its exaltedness, the sacramental "thing" is the Christian religion at its very heart. And in fact, without this "thingness" in it, Christianity itself fades into non-reality, back into the dead "letter" of a book, back into a "history" that is no longer alive.

Such, then, is the "mystery" of the spiritual sense of the Scriptures, i.e., that primordial level of the spiritual sense called the typical or allegorical (or "symbolic" or "real"), as corresponding to the catechesis of the sacraments. The sacraments are to the Creed what the spiritual sense is to the literal, as the "inside" is to the "outside," as the "Word" is to the "flesh." This last analogy is pure paradox. It would seem that the "Word" is the Creed and the "flesh" the sacraments; and superficially that is true. Yet, such is the "mystery of faith" that the exact opposite is the spiritual or "real" -- as opposed to the literal or "carnal"-- truth. For the "flesh" is what is time-bound and purely human; the Word alone is eternal and divine (see Jn 6:63).

The analogies mentioned in the preceding paragraph simultaneously suggest and obscure a relationship between the Creed and the sacraments which we cannot in honesty ignore. The clear implication of the typical sense as developed by the Fathers was that it was somehow identified with the New Testament precisely as opposed to the Old. If that is so, i.e, if the New Testament, the whole New Testament and nothing but the New Testament, is the "spiritual sense," then how can the division between the Creed and the sacraments be analogous to the division between "letter" and "spirit"? The answer, it seems to me, lies in that further dimension of the New Testament intimated by Our Lord Himself, both in His actions and in His words. In His actions Christ chose to live, in effect, His entire earthly life "<u>sub lege</u>" in the Old Testament.[34] For the <u>reality</u> of the New Testament began only with His death. (Mt 26:28; 27:51; Heb 9 <u>passim</u>). Likewise in His words His intent was to speak openly in "parables," while reserving the "mystery of the kingdom" to His disciples in secret (See Mt 13:11). The "New Testament," therefore, with which the spiritual sense --- i.e., the typical sense of the reality (the "inside") as distinguished from the prefiguration of that reality (the "outside") -- is identified, is, quite simply, the <u>Church</u>, i.e., the "<u>Christus Totus</u>," the Risen Lord with His members living by the grace of His Spirit.

The Church, by the sure instinct of that same Holy Spirit, understood the consequent distinction between Creed and sacrament from her earliest days. The Creed could be -- and was -- preached openly to the whole world, whereas the sacraments were reserved for those alone who believed. Even within the catechumenate itself this distinction was observed. The Creed was given to the catechumens to be learned before they were baptized; and only then, as baptized neophytes, were they taught the sacraments.[35]

Once we have postulated the alignment of the first two senses of Scripture with two components of catechesis -- viz., the literal sense with the Creed, and the typical sense with the sacraments -- the second half of our paradigm falls into place almost by itself. The third Scriptural meaning, the tropological or moral, obviously aligns with that part of catechesis which teaches morality, viz., the Commandments. As we saw, this third sense is best seen as a spin-off of the second; it makes little if any sense to construe it as more "spiritual" than the typical sense. In fact, if anything, the more prevalent danger has been to consider it as something less.[36] The Ten Commandments have been dismissed as "Old Testament," an anachronism in our new "spiritual" dispensation. The adequate response to such proposed "improvements" to catechesis as the substitution of the

Beatitudes for the Decalogue, as being more "Christian," is to cite what Christ Himself, and the primitive Church in its first Pentecostal fervor, enjoined as the proper moral code.37 This total harmonization of the tropological with the typical in one comprehensive "spiritual" sense -- or, in other words, the total harmonization of the Ten Commandments with the sacraments as co-ordinate components of catechesis -- avoids both extremes: the minimization of moral teaching to the level of mere ethics, and its maximization into some imagined mysticism that can dispense with the ministry of the Church and her sacraments.

This leaves the final sense of Scripture and the final component of catechesis: the anagogical or eschatological sense, and the component called prayer -- or, more properly, the Our Father. To the Father -- through the Son and the sacraments of His Church, in the Holy Spirit and the good works of His grace -- the great trajectory of the Christian life finds here its one termination and total fulfillment. The final meaning of the Word of God can only be prayer, and the final prayer can only be "Abba, Father!" Clearly distinct from all that preceded it, this final reality is nothing but that: sheer reality, the face-to-face vision of God "sicuti est" (1 Jn 3:2). Compared to this, even the earthly reality of the New Testament, viz., the Church and the sacraments, is but a sign, a figure or type!

This comparison has, in fact, prompted the temptation to see the Sacred History, the Scriptures, as consisting not of two Testaments only, but of three.38 For, compared to the "heavenly Jerusalem," the Church of the "New Testament" is as time-bound and passing as the "earthly Jerusalem" of the Old. Such a view is tempting, but it is a mistake. The New Testament is the "Eternal Testament." The sacraments are signs, yes, but not signs only (the sacramentum tantum, as in the Old Testament). They are also reality (the sacramentum et res) -- indeed the identical reality, substantially, as the "reality only" (the res tantum) of heaven.39 And so, for all their distinctness, the fourth and final meaning and the fourth and final component are inseparably joined with what precede them. For the sacraments and the works of charity and the movement toward heaven are essentially one in the unity of the one faith as expressed in the one Creed, just as the typical, the tropological and the anagogical are essentially one in the unity of the one Spirit Who is the Author of the one "letter" called Sacred Scripture.[40]

III

In our brief summary of the four components of the classic catechesis as aligned with the four senses of Scripture, it may have been noticed that no explicit mention has been made of that triad which, in the preceding chapter, we posited as the fundamental seminal structure of catechesis as seen by both St. Augustine and St. Thomas, viz., the triad of the <u>theological virtues</u>.[41] True, there was an equation made between the first virtue, faith, and the first component, the Creed. But from there on, it seemed, that original paradigm (viz., faith = Creed, hope = prayer, charity = Decalogue) was discreetly set aside. And no wonder; for consider the difficulties it posed! First, we were apparently forced to align faith -- which is every bit as "spiritual" as hope and charity -- with the first sense of Scripture, viz., the literal, non-spiritual sense. Secondly, there was the obvious embarassment of having one component (and one Scriptural sense) too many! If hope went with prayer, and charity with the commandments, where did that leave the sacraments? And finally, what about the proper sequence? If prayer went with the anagogical, it would be last; and so hope would follow charity, rather than precede it as it should. Altogether, then, a rather awkward situation and a demonstration of the limited usefulness, and the possible dangers of such neat paradigms in theology.

On reflection, however, the situation is not one of disarray. In fact, the reflection called for by the seeming confusion can yield added light to our understanding of the "economy" behind our paradigm. First, as a general principle, the three virtues adequately cover all four components and senses; that is to say, no <u>fourth</u> virtue is necessary (or possible). But that also means necessarily that the virtues cannot be aligned with the components and senses on any exclusive one-to-one basis. Consider each virtue in turn.

Faith is aligned with <u>both</u> the Creed and the sacraments.[42] It is therefore "spiritual" and "New Testament," as much so as hope and charity are. However, its relation to the <u>first</u> sense of Scripture is neither accidental nor regrettable. It is a salutary reminder of faith's uniquely specific function, viz., to discern the "inside," which it does precisely by going beyond -- or rather, <u>into</u> -- the "outside"!

Hope is likewise aligned with <u>two</u>: with prayer (and the anagogical), which is obvious; but also with the sacraments (and the typical). Its tie-in with the sacraments is parallel with faith's, viz., the "mutual causality" which is so integral to and characteristic of the "economy" as a whole.[43] Moreover, hope's sacramental connection puts it in direct sequence with faith, which is essential to its intelligibility. If, therefore, in one sense hope follows charity, it certainly does not follow charity in every sense.[44]

Finally charity as the greatest virtue, has the greatest realm. It is coextensive with the entire spiritual sense, and therefore with the sacraments, the commandments and prayer. This general alignment does not affect its special alignment with the moral sense and the Decalogue; that remains unchanged. But what is now gained is the perspective, the context of that alignment. Charity co-exists with faith and hope in the sacraments and in the typical sense of Christ and His Church.[45] And likewise charity co-exists with hope in prayer and the "lifting up" to heaven. Indeed, it is the perfection of hope, and so the "end"-- i.e., the fourth sense and the fourth component -- is more perfectly seen as loved than as hoped for.[46] And in some analogous fashion, as also being the perfection of faith, charity also shares in that first and lowly sense of Scripture and that first and elementary stage of catechesis. For, being <u>love</u>, it pervades <u>all</u>; for, after all, "love" is a name proper to God (1 Jn 4:8,16).

Our purpose in this present chapter was to show how the classic catechesis with its four constituent elements was profoundly, pre-eminently Scriptural, in its origins, in its orientation, in its modalities, in its very words. True, the Fathers, and the Scholastics after them, added further words. But the net effect of all their words was but to deepen our understanding of that "word" that was uniquely divine: the "<u>sacra pagina</u>" of Scripture. The manifold inter-related meanings of the sacred writings not only provided the <u>matter</u> of catechesis; they constituted its very <u>form</u>. There were added formularies in the course of the centuries, filtering out from the immeasurable vastness of the Tradition in its widest sense, and finding their way into the catechetical syllabus.[47] But, as we have seen, the fundamental outline of the classic catechesis held firm. How well it was being <u>taught</u> was, of course, another matter.

Very shortly after the "golden age" of the Scholastics, medieval Christendom began to show unmistakable signs of decline, even of rupture. The eventual break-down in the sixteenth century took the form of open repudiation of the Catholic Church and the establishment of new churches. The ultimate justification for this revolutionary turn of events was made by the revolutionaries' appeal to Scripture. The "<u>sola Scriptura</u>" of the Protestants was a formidable challenge to a Catholic Church that for over a millennium had grounded her future -- her recruitment and preservation of the faithful -- primarily on that most ordinary use of her <u>magisterium</u> called catechesis, and had grounded that catechesis primarily on Scripture! How would the Catholic Church, at last alerted to the challenge, respond?

NOTES

1   S..T., I, 1. See Thomas Gilby, O.P. (ed.) Christian Theology (Volume I of Summa Theologiae), Appendix 5: "Sacra Doctrina," pp.58-66.

2   "All scripture is inspired by God and profitable for teaching (pros didaskalian), for reproof, for correction, and for training in righteousness , that the man of God may be complete, equipped for every good work." (2 Tim 3:16-17)

3   "...fides ex auditu..." (Rom 10:17)

4   Van den Eynde, op. cit., p.21.

5   Ibid., p.315.

6   Properly extrinsic to this importance of Origen for our study, yet providentially appropriate to an appreciation of his genius, is the truly monumental work of Henri de Lubac, S.J. His Histoire et Esprit: l'intélligence de l'Ecriture d'après Origène (Paris: Aubier, 1950), and its brilliant abridgement entitled L'Ecriture dans la Tradition (Paris: Aubier, 1966), have provided invaluable insights for this chapter.

7   "Mira profunditas eloquiorum tuorum, quorum ecce ante nos superficies blandiens parvulis, sed mira profunditas, Deus meus, mira profunditas! Horror est intendere in eam: horror honoris, et tremor amoris." Confessions, XII, 14 (PL 32:832).

8   Vatican I, Dei Filius, cap.3 (DS 3011). See above, Chapter I, note 3 (p. 19).

9   See above, p. 56. Perhaps the most formal statement of this "Christian" premise of the Apostolic kērygma was St. Peter's identification of the entire history he had narrated as being God's "plan and foreknowledge" (boulē kai prognōsis) (Acts 2:23).

10 That the intention of the human author, along with the meaning of the words he employs, determines the literal meaning of Scripture was really settled by the Scholastics (see, e.g., St. Thomas, In Epist. ad Gal., IV, 7; Parma Edition:Vol. XIII, pp.421-22). However, the most authoritative statement is probably Pius XII's in his Encyclical Divino afflante Spiritu, even though his reference to this particular point is oblique: "Hanc litteralem verborum significationem omni cum diligentia per linguarum cognitionem iidem eruant, ope adhibita contextus, comparationisque cum assimilibus locis ...ut auctoris mens luculenter patescat. ...exegeta, sicut litteralem, ut aiunt,

verborum significationem, quam hagiographus intenderit atque expresserit, reperire atque exponere debet." (AAS 35:310,311)

As for the further question, "whether there can be more than one literal sense in any given text of Scripture," a further distinction of the term "literal sense" -- as used, e.g., in St. Thomas, De Potentia, IV, 1 (Parma, Vol.VIII, p.79) -- seems to be in order. But that question does not concern our present study. See the Pontifical Biblical Institute's Institutiones Biblicae, Vol I (1951), pp. 370-71.

11 Thus, paradoxically, there is a de facto rapprochement between two seemingly diametrical opposites: the old-fashioned fundamentalism which concentrates on the word to the exclusion of the author, and the radical "new hermeneutic" which concentrates on "what does it mean to me?"to the exclusion of what it may have meant to the author, are equally subjective, equally non-literal in their approach to Scripture. See R. E. Brown, "Hermeneutics," The Jerome Biblical Commentary (Englewood Cliffs, N.J.: Prentice-Hall, 1968), pp. 614-15.

12 St. Jerome: "...Et primum iuxta consuetudinem nostram, historiae fundamenta iaciamus." In Ezech., VII, 24 (PL 25:229). "Et cum historiae habuerint fundamenta, tunc spiritualis intelligentiae culmen accipiunt: ut vere Christus de Virgine natus sit, vere Lazarum mortuum suscitavit ... licet secundum tropologiam quotidie de anima virginali nascatur sermo divinus, quotidie peccato mortui ... de sepulchro iubeantur exire ..." In Amos, III, 9 (PL 25:1090).

St Gregory the Great: "aliquando autem qui verba accipere historiae iuxta litteram negligit, oblatum sibi veritatis lumen abscondit; cumque laboriose invenire in eis aliud intrinsecus appetit, hoc quod foris sine difficultate assequi poterat, amittit." In Iob, "Epistola missoria," 4 (PL 75:514).

St. Thomas Aquinas: "...sensus spiritualis semper fundatur super litteralem, et procedit ex eo. "Quodlibet. VII, 6, 14, ad 1. "...spiritualis expositio semper debet habere fulcimentum ab aliqua litterali expositione S. Script., et ita vitatur omnis erroris occasio. "ibid., ad 3. "...non est propter defectum auctoritatis quod ex sensu spirituali non potest trahi efficax argumentum; sed ex ipsa natura similitudinis, in qua fundatur spiritualis sensus." ibid., ad 4.

Hugh of St. Victor: "Cum igitur mystica intelligentia non nisi ex iis quae primo loco littera proponit colligatur, miror qua fronte quidam allegoriarum se doctores iactitant, qui ipsam adhuc primam litterae significationem ignorant. Nos inquiunt: Scripturam legimus, sed non legimus litteram. Quomodo ergo Scripturam legitis, et litteram non legitis? Si enim littera tollitur, Scriptura quid est? " De Scripturis et Scriptoribus Sacris Praenotatiunculae, V (PL 175:13).

13   The most conspicuous instance of this Gnostic dichotomy of "letter" and "spirit" was Marcion, whose repudiation of the entire Old Testament and reconstruction of the New Testament accelerated the orthodox response admirably exemplified in St. Irenaeus' doctrine of "recapitulation."

The perfect concatenation of the two Testaments is beautifully described by St. Bede: "...ut eo cunctis vera ac sine scrupulo dubietatis suscipienda quae scriberet intimaret, quo haec a prophetis Sancto Spiritu impletis antea praescita ac praedicta esse monstraret, simulque uno eodemque Evangelii sui principio et Iudaeos qui legem ac prophetas susceperant, ad suscipienda etiam Evangelii sacramenta quae ipsorum prophetae praedixerant instituit, et Gentiles qui per omnia Evangelii praeconia ad Dominum venerant, ad auctoritatem quoque legis et prophetarum suscipiendam venerandamque provocat, ne si qui iuxta haereticos aut Vetus solummodo Testamentum, aut solummodo Novum suscepisset, alienus a testimento Dei remaneret." In Marci Evangelium, I, 1 (PL 92:134).

14   See de Lubac, L'Ecriture dans la Tradition, "L'Acte du Christ," pp. 133-47. Especially: "Hors de mesure avec la 'création perpétuelle' qu'on pouvait observer jusque-là est la 'nouvelle creation' qui l'achève. Reconnaissons toutefois que le cas est unique, hors de toute vraisemblance comme de toute analogie. Il n'y a pas, dans l'histoire humaine deux 'plénitudes du temps.' Il n'y a pas davantage, dans l'histoire de la révélation, toute une série de testaments échelonnés: après l'Ancien Testament, il n'y a plus que le Nouveau. S'il y a bien eu plusieurs passages, il n'y en a cependant qu'un, le dernier au double sens du mot, qui mérite à jamais le nom de 'Pâques.'" p. 135.

15   "...le sens spirituel de l'Ecriture, strictement entendu, n'est autre que celui de Nouveau Testamant. Il est ce Nouveau Testament lui-même: (Lex) spiritualiter intellecta, Evangelium est (La Loi spirituellement comprise, c'est l' Evangile). Il n'existerait donc pas sans le Christ et ne serait pas perçu sans la conversion au Christ." ibid., p. 48.

16   The term "typological" (and "typology") is actually post-Patristic. Their word was "typicus" (and "typus"). Moreover, it sometimes lends itself to an application considerably more restricted than what the Fathers gave it. Curiously, the term "allegorical" (and "allegory") runs the opposite risk; it is often too broadly -- and arbitrarily -- applied, ending up as a mere accommodated meaning. For a very penetrating and balanced discussion of this problem of terminology, see de Lubac, op. cit., pp. 24-27.

17   "In Lia quae maior erat, caecitatem intellegimus synagogae, in Rachel pulchritudinem Ecclesiae; et tamen qui ex parte typi fuerunt Domini Salvatoris, non omnia quae fecisse narrantur, in typo eius fecisse credendi sunt. Typus enim partem indicat; quod si totum praecedat in typo, iam non est typus, sed historiae veritas appellanda est." In Osee, III, 11 (PL 25:916).

18 "Non ...omnes qui Christiani appellantur, ad Christum transeunt; sed quibus aufertur velamen, quod in lectione Veteris Testamenti manet. Qui enim sunt in Vetere Testamento, impediente velamine nec Vetus intellegunt nec Novum; qui autem transeunt ad Christum, remoto velamine per Novum, intellegunt et Vetus et Novum (2 Cor 3:14-16). Utinam ut isti caeci oppugnatores Legis et Prophetarum, sic transeant ad Christum, ut non sint in eis in quibus obvelatum est ipsum Evangelium. "Contra Adversarium Legis et Prophetarum, II, 7 (PL 42:655).

There is also, of course, his famous epigram: "...in Veteri Testamento est occultatio Novi, in Novo est manifestatio Veteris." De Catechezandis Rudibus, IV, 8 (PL 40:315). A variant of this epigram occurs in his Quaestiones in Hepteteuchen, II, 73 (PL 34:623): "Novum in Vetere latet, et in Novo Vetus patet." This latter is quoted in Vatican II's Dei Verbum, 16 (AAS 58:825).

19 "'Qui erat scriptus intus et foris.' Liber enim sacri eloquii intus scriptus est per allegoriam, foris per historiam. Intus per spiritum intellectus, foris autem per sensum litterae simplicem, adhuc infirmitatibus congruentem. Intus, quia invisibilia promittit; foris, quia visibilia praeceptorum suorum rectitudine disponit. Intus, quia coelestia pollicetur, foris autem quia terrena contemptibilia qualiter sint, vel in usu habenda, vel in exterioribus actionibus iubet. Et ea quidem quae foris praecepit patent, sed illa quae de internis narrat plene apprehendi nequeunt." In Ezech., I, 10 (PL 76:883).

20 "...verba significant res, et una res potest esse figura alterius. Auctor autem rerum non solum potest verba accomodare ad aliquid significandum, sed etiam res potest disponere in figuram alterius; et secundum hoc in sacra Scriptura manifestatur veritas dupliciter. Uno modo secundum quod res significantur per verba, et in hoc consistit sensus litteralis. Alio modo secundum quod res sunt figurae aliarum rerum, et in hoc consistit sensus spiritualis." Quodlibet. VII, 6, 14 (Parma: Vol.XIX, p. 563). See also S. T., I, 1, 9-10.

21 "...à ce courant [viz., the authentic typology of Adam derived from Scripture] qui constitue celui de la tradition ecclésiastique et catéchètique, nous voyons chez certains Pères de l'Eglise, Clément, Origène, Ambroise, Grègoire de Nysse, un autre se mêler qui cherche dans les chapitres II et III de la Gènese, non le rappel d'un événement historique destiné à fonder l'éspérance dans un autre événement analogue, mais une philosophie de l'homme exprimée d'une manière allégorique. Ce courant, proprement philosophique, est tout à fait autre chose que la typologie. Il remonte à Philon. ...Or ce sont des réalités absolument hétérogènes. L'allégorie en effet n'est pas un sens de l'Ecriture: c'est la philosophie et la morale chrétiennes presentées sous une imagerie biblique, comme les stoïciens presentaient la leur sous une imagerie homérique. ...Nous sommes donc en presence d'une ligne exégétique très

déterminée, qui reste toujours proche de sa source, qui est Philon, et qui est plus juxtaposee que fondue avec l'éxègèse traditionelle. C'est plus tard que cette fusion s'accomplira davantage. Mais ce qui importe pour nous, c'est de reconnaitre qu'il s'agit d'une interprétation étrangère à la tradition commune de l'Eglise, qui se rattache à l'enseignement des didascales et qui doit donc etre absolument distinguée de l'exégésè typologique. C'est un véritable abus de mots que de ranger, sous la même étiquette de sens spirituel, opposé à sens litteral, cette allégorie morale à côté de la typologie: celle-ci réprésente en effect le prolongement authentique du sens, littéral; l'autre lui est parfaitmanent etrangère; la première est de l'exègèse, la seconde n'en est pas. C'est Origène le premier qui, dans sa puissante synthèse, a rapproché ces diverses interprétations. Mais elles constituent des courants hétérogènes, qu'il juxtapose artificiellement." Jean Daniélou, <u>Sacramentum Futuri; études sur les origines de la typologie biblique</u> (Paris, 1950), pp. 45,48,52.

For a gentle rejoinder to Daniélou's indignation, see de Lubac, <u>op. cit.</u>, pp. 150-166, where he defends Origen. The following passage will suffice: "... tout revient ... à se demander si le troisième élément consitutif de l'homme est compris par Origène à la manière de la Bible ou à la manière des Grecs. C'est pour une part affaire d'appréciation personelle. Ici comme en bien d'autres cas que nous offre la Patristique -- songeons par example à la doctrine de l'image et de la ressemblance -- deux influences se combinent, dans une mesure qu'il est sans doute impossible de doser avec exactitude. Il faut d'ailleurs se garder de prendre pour contamination doctrinale et corruption de l'Ecriture toute intégration d'un élément de reflexion naturelle à la donnée révélée. Pareille intransigence serait peu conforme à la doctrine catholique des rapports de la raison et de la foi. Elle équivaudrait à nier dans l'ordre de la pensée toute union de la nature et du surnaturel. Contraire à la tradition la plus constante, elle supposerait une grave unintelligence du christianisme lui-même, qui serait pris ainsi, bon gré mal gré, pour une doctrine parmi d'autres, luttant contre les autres en quelque sorte sur le même plan, comme si elle était faite pour ainsi dire du même grain humain; alors que la Révélation nous apporte une Vérité concrete incommensurable à toutes les pensées élaborées par l'homme et une Force divine capable de tout <u>convertir</u>. Des lors, n'est-il pas à craindre que l'idéal qu'on semble se forger d'un christianisme pur ne soit encore qu'un système humain, avec toutes ses partialités?" <u>ibid.</u>, pp. 155-56.

22 It has been somewhere suggested that this "median" food (i.e., between "milk" and "meat") was the vegetable diet of young Daniel and his three companions at the court of the Persian king (see Dan 1:1-21).

23 "Sciendum vero est, quod quaedam historica expositione transcurrimus, et per allegoriam quaedam typica investigatione perscrutamur; quaedam per sola allegoricae moralitatis

instrumenta discutimus; nonnulla autem per cuncta simul sollicitius exquirentes, tripliciter indagamus. Nam primum quidem fundamenta historiae ponimus, deinde per significationem typicam in arcem fidei fabricam mentis erigimus; ad extremum quoque per moralitatis gratiam, quasi superducto aedificium colore vestimus." St. Gregory the Great, In Iob, "Epistola Missoria," 3 (PL 75:513).

An interesting observation on this same subject occurs in Guibert's commentary on Genesis: "Ex his quattuor modis, licet omnis fieri possit, aut certe ex singulis, tamen si quid utilius ad curam interioris hominis pensetur, magis commoda ac intellegibilis in tractando moralitas esse videtur. Allegoria sane dum in propheticis apostolicisque libris disquiritur, paene nihil aliud quam fidem aedificat; quia scilicet dum multifariam (Heb 1:1)... Christiani temporis sacramenta indubie praenuntiata ibidem comperimus. Dei vero gratia iam fides omnium cordis innotuit, non minus tamen imo multo crebrius ea quae mores eorum instituere possint, dicere convenit. Facilius enim et securius de virtutum natura disserimus quam de fidei sacramentis de quibus valde moderate aliquibus loquendum est, disputamus. Error namque minus intelligentibus ex nimis profunda praedicatione generari potest; ex morali autem institutione maxime solet acquiri discretionis utilitas." Ad Commentarium in Genesim. Introd. (PL 156:26).

24 "...prout...significant ea quae sunt in aeterna gloria est sensus anagogicus." S.T. , I, 1,10. The very fact that the anagogical is always listed last (just as the literal or historical is always listed first) clearly indicated the rank: it is the ultimate meaning -- the literally "heavenly" meaning -- of Sacred Scripture.

Incidentally, St. Thomas notes that the anagogical sense, when found in the New Testament, cannot be anything other than "literal" in its meaning (Quodlibet.,VII, 6,15,ad 5). So, in a sense, with this re-joining of the literal and the anagogical, the circle is complete -- just as St. Augustine may be intimating when he put the anagogical not last but first in his famous line (in Genesi ad Litteram, 1), which St. Thomas quotes in his "Sed contra" (loc cit.): "In omnibus libris sanctis oportet intueri quae ibi aeterna intuentur, quae ibi facta narrantur, quae futura praenuntiatur, quae agenda praecipiuntur."

25 Thus, e.g., St. Gregory the Great combines the "moral" with the "contemplative" (i.e., anagogical): "Legentis enim spiritus, si quid in eis scire morale aut historicum quaerit, sensus hunc moralis historiae sequitur. Si quid typicum, mox figurata locutio agnoscitur. Si quid contemplativum, statim rotae quasi pennas accipiunt, et in aere suspenduntur, quia in verbis sacri eloquii intelligentia coelestis aperitur. 'Quocumque ergo ibat spiritus, illuc eunte spiritu et rotae pariter levebantur, sequentes eum.' Rotae enim spiritum sequuntur, quia verba sacri eloquii, ut saepe iam dictum est, iuxta sensum legentium per intellectum crescunt.

"In una eademque Scripturae sententia alius sola historia pascitur, alius typicam, alius vero intelligentiam per typum contemplativam quaerit. Et fit plerumque, sicut dictum est, in una eademque sententia cuncta simul tria valeant inveniri." In Ezech., I, 7 (PL 76:844).
Hugh of St. Victor does the same; he seems to use "anagogen" and "tropologia" interchangeably (see De Scripturis et Scriptoribus Sacris Praenotatiunculae, 3 (PL 175:11)).

26   "What happened is the literal sense; what you are to believe, the allegorical;
What you are to do is the moral sense, where you are to go, the anagogical."

For a masterful survey of this topic, see de Lubac, "Sur un vieux distique: la doctrine du 'quadruple sens,'" Mélanges Ferdinand Cavallera (Toulouse: Institut Catholique, 1948), pp. 347-66.

27   "Sciendum ...est quod practica erga multas professiones ac studia derivatur, theoretica in duas dividitur partes, id est, in historicam interpretationem et intelligentiam spiritalem. Unde etiam Solomon cum Ecclesiae multiformam gratiam enumerasset, adiecit: 'omne enim qui apud eam sunt, vestiti sunt duplicibus' (Prov 31). Spiritalis autem scientiae genera sunt tria: tropologia, allegoria, anogoge. De quibus in Proverbiis ita dicitur: 'Tu autem describe ea tibi tripliciter, super latitudinem cordis tui' (Prov 2 et 32).

"Itaque historia paeteritarum ac visibilium agnitionem complectitur rerum (sic: Gal 4:22-23). Ad allegoriam autem pertinent quae sequuntur, quia ea quae in veritate gesta sunt, alterius sacramenta formam praefigurasse dicuntur (sic: Gal 4:24-25). Anagoge vero de spiritalibus mysteriis ad sublimiora quaedam et sacratiora coelorum secreta conscendens ab Apostolo ita subicitur (sic: Gal 4:26-27). Tropologia est moralis explanatio ad emandationem vitae et institutionem pertinens actualem, velut si haec eadem dua testamenta intelligamus practice et theoreticam disciplinam hominis velimus accipere; vel certe si Ierusalem aut Sion animam hominis velimus accipere: secundum illud 'Lauda, Ierusalem, Dominum' (Ps 147).

"Igitur praedictae quattuor figurae in unum ita si volumus confluunt, ut una eademque Ierusalem quadrifariam possit intelligi ..." Collationes, XIV, 8 (PL 49:962-64). This same text reappears, word for word, in Rabanus Maurus' In Epist. ad Galatas, XV, 4 (PL 112:331).

28   "Scitis, carissimi, quod Ierusalem quattuor modis accipitur, secundum quattuor theologicos intellectus: historicum, allegoricum, tropologicum et anagogicum. Est enim Ierusalem superior et inferior, interior et exterior. Coelestis videlicet et terrestris, spiritualis et corporalis. Superior est in patria, inferior est in via, interior est in anima, exterior est in Syria. Superior est

Ecclesia triumphans, de qua dicit Apostolus: 'Illa quae sursum est ...mater nostra.' Inferior est Ecclesia militantium de qua dicit propheta: 'Surge, illuminare, Ierusalem.' Interior est anima fidelis, de qua dicitur, 'Dabo in Sion salutem et in Ierusalem gloriam meam.' Exterior est miserabilis Ierusalem de qua dicitur: 'Ierusalem, Ierusalem, quae occidis prophetas...'

"Est autem pax peccatorum, pax conversorum, pax iustorum, et pax beatorum. Pax peccatorum in vitiis, pax conversorum in moribus, pax iustorum in gratia, pax beatorum in gloria." Sermo IV (PL 217:330).

29 "...auctor sacrae Scripturae est Deus, in cuius potestate est ut non solum voces ad significandum accommodet (quod etiam homo facere potest), sed etiam res ipsas. Et ideo, cum in omnibus scientiis voces significent, hoc habet proprium ista scientia, quod ipsae res significatae per voces, etiam significant aliquid. Illa ergo prima significatio, qua voces significant res, pertinet ad primum sensum, qui est sensus historicus vel litteralis. Illa vero significatio qua res significatae per voces, iterum res alias significant, dicitur sensus spriritualis; qui super litteralem fundatur, et eum supponit.

"Hic autem sensus spiritualis trifariam dividitur. Sicut enim dicit Apostolus (Heb 7;19), lex vetus figura est novae legis; et ipsa nova lex, ut dicit Dionysius (Eccles. Hier., 5), est figura futurae gloriae; in nova etiam lege, ea quae in capite sunt gesta, sunt signa eorum quae nos agere debemus.

"Secundum ergo quod ea quae sunt veteris legis, significant ea quae sunt novae legis, est sensus allegoricus; secundum vero quod ea quae in Christo sunt facta, vel in his quae Christum significant, sunt signa eorum quae nos agere debemus est sensus moralis; prout vero significant ea quae sunt in aeterna gloria, est sensus anagogicus." S.T., I, 1,10.

30 See above, Chapter II, pp. 44-45.

31 See S.T., II-II, 1, 3, ad 3.

32 An example of a prevalent contemporary equivocation as to the literal sense of Scripture and its relation to the Creed is Gerald O' Collins' comment on how "traditional Christology has looked inadequate," viz., "its easy acceptance of that mixture of history, faith and mythical imagery which the old creeds present." He then asserts that the conception, the birth, the suffering and death, the descent into hell, the resurrection and the ascension of Christ cannot all be "history" in the same sense. What Are They Saying about Jesus? (New York: Paulist Press., 1977), pp. 8-9.

33 And the greatest realization of this "mystery of faith" is, of course, the Real Presence in the Holy Eucharist, whereby the

Passion, Death and Resurrection of Our Lord are here and now renewed in the Church.

34 See S.T., III, 40, 4.

35 Regarding the "disciplina arcani," see Tertullian, Apologeticum, 7 (PL 1:358-61), and St. Cyril of Jerusalem, Catecheses, "Monitum post Procatechesis" (PG 33:365).

36 See above, notes 21, 22 and 23, pp. 76-78.

37 See Mt 19:17. For the position of the primitive Church, see below, Chapter VII, note 18, p 188.

38 The most famous exponent of this third and ultimate "Testament," corresponding to the Holy Spirit following the Father (Old Testament) and the Son (New Testament) is, of course, Joachim of Flora. See de Lubac, Exégèse médiévale, Vol. IV, pp. 325-44.

39 See Innocent III's felicitous terminology: "forma visibilis ...veritas corporis ...virtus spiritualis" (DS 783). See below, Chapter VII, note 26., pp. 190-91.

40 De Lubac (op. cit., pp. 264-72) credits St. Bonaventure with "luxuriant richness" in developing the manifold symbolism of the four senses of Scripture -- even to comparing the three spiritual senses with the three Persons of the Trinity, and the one literal sense with the one divine essence.

41 See above, Chapter II, pp. 28-30, 37-38.

42 See, e.g., St. Thomas' habitual expression, "sacramenta fidei." See above, Chapter II, p. 44.

43 Just as faith at once precedes and follows the sacraments --as their pre-condition and their effect -- so hope does something -similar: it disposes us for the sacraments (mainly by prayer) and it is nourished by them in turn. This mutual causality, as applied specifically to prayer, is admirably treated by the Roman Catechism (IV, 2,6-7; pp. 294-95).

The four numerals in this reference to the Roman Catechism designate the following: the Part, the chapter and the section -- i.e, the "Rovillian numbers" -- and lastly the page in the first Manutian edition. See below, Chapter VI, note 11, p. 157.

44 E.g., hope, like faith, can be "informis," i.e., unlike -- and antecedent to -- charity, it can exist apart from sanctifying grace.

45 The normal state of both faith and hope is to be "formatae," i.e., to co-exist with grace and charity. Their co-existence with mortal sin is possible -- and abnormal.

46 "Amor autem quidam est perfectus, quidam imperfectus; perfectus quidem amore est quo aliquis secundum se amatur, ut puta cui aliquis vult bonum, sicut homo amat amicum. Imperfectus amor est quo quis amat aliquid, non secundum ipsum, sed ut illud bonum sibi ipsi proveniat, sicut homo amat rem quam concupiscit. Primus autem amor Dei pertinet ad caritatem, quae inhaeret Deo secundum seipsum; sed spes pertinet ad secundum amorem, quia ille qui sperat, aliquid sibi obtinere intendit.

"Et ideo in via generationis spes est prior caritate. Sicut enim aliquis introducitur ad amandum Deum per hoc quod timens ab ipso puniri cessat a peccato,...ita etiam spes introducit caritatem, inquantum aliquis sperans remunerari a Deo accenditur ad amandum Deum, et servandum praecepta eius. Sed secundum ordinem perfectionis caritas prior est naturaliter; et ideo, adveniente caritate, spes perfectior redditur, quia de amicis maxime speramus...." S.T., II-II, 17,8.

47 See below, Chapter IV, notes 7 and 46. pp. 101-02 and 108.

CHAPTER FOUR

CATECHESIS AND CATECHISMS

In the millennium between Origen and St. Thomas Aquinas the catechetical tradition had undergone many changes, exactly as the Church in all aspects of her life had changed. Underlying the changes, deep and recurring as they were, there remained, however, the identity of the faith. It was the same Church, reading the same Scriptures, handing on with them the traditions of the same teaching which formed her life. The continuity -- and the consciousness of the continuity -- were certainly there. As we have seen in the preceding two chapters, what the Scholastics were systematizing was nothing other than what they had received from the Scriptures: the Scriptures as summarized by the Fathers in the great formularies which formed the core of the tradition -- the Creed, the Commandments, the Our Father, and the formularies combined with actions called the sacraments.

This continuity was not, however, something floating free, unaffected by the enormous historical and cultural changes which marked this millennium. The most important single change affecting the catechetical tradition we have already noted, viz., the disappearance of the catechumenate with the disappearance of the ancient classical world.[1] The effects of that change can hardly be exaggerated. It can almost be said that from it sprang (if only by implication, of course) the very concept of "Christendom," i.e., a social order where "the faith" was co-extensive with the entire population, where "citizen" and "Christian" were practically synonymous. As we know, the new effects of that change on the real life of the Church have been much debated.[2]

Now in the fourteenth century, following St. Thomas by about the same length of time as Constantine followed Origen, another change began to be noted, which would eventually prove to be as momentous for the Church as the change from the ancient to the medieval world. This change would, in fact, be seen as marking the end of the Middle Ages and leading to what would later be called the Modern Age. Just as Christendom had replaced the catechumenate, so Christendom in turn would undergo a shock of internal crisis from which it could not recover. Would there be some equivalent to the ancient catechumenate to stand in its place, and so maintain the continuity of the catechetical tradition -- and with it, the continuity of the Church herself?

Our purpose in the present chapter is to sketch in broad outline the terms and process of this change through the two hundred years between the appearance of the first catechism in the mid-fourteenth century to that of the Roman Catechism in the mid-sixteenth century. The very word "catechism" can serve as our theme. What the catechumenate once was as a specific institution in the catechetical tradition, that is what the catechism would now be: a remarkable witness to what was at once changing and unchanging in the same great tradition. We will first consider the catechism as a new genre, undergoing changes which always accompany newness, and which will extend into the sixteenth century. Then, secondly, we will look at some of the catechisms of the sixteenth century, Catholic and Protestant, leading to and culminating in the Roman Catechism.

I

Until the fourteenth century "catechism" was simply the English transliteration of the Latin derivative for the Greek "katēchēsis." The meaning of the two words was identical. That was St. Thomas' habitual usage of "catechismus."

> ...Baptism is "the sacrament of faith" since it is a profession of faith. Now, for a man to receive the faith he must be instructed in it, as we read in Rom 10:14: "How can they believe what they have not heard? and how can they hear what was not preached?" Therefore, it is fitting that catechesis (catechismus) should precede baptism.[3]

That "catechism" continued, in fact, to mean the same thing as "catechesis" is evidenced by the Roman Catechism itself. It uses both terms interchangeably. In the chapter on Baptism "<u>catechismus</u>" occurs twice:

> ...the priest instructs him in the doctrine of the Christian faith, the profession of which is to be made in Baptism (primum eos Christianae fidei doctrina quam in Baptismo profiteri debent instituit: id autem <u>catechismo</u> efficitur)...
>
> ...In keeping with the catechetical form of this instruction, the person to be baptized is asked questions about the faith (quoniam vero <u>catechismi</u> ratio ex multis interrogationibus constant)...[4]

But in the following chapter, on Confirmation, we have "<u>catechesis</u>":

> According to this opinion, the sacrament of Confirmation would be essentially no more than catechetical instruction itself (ita ut Confirmatio nihil a <u>catechesi</u> differe videatur)...[5]

Of course, the very first occurrence of the term in the Roman Catechism is in its title: "<u>Catechismus ad Parochos.</u>" And here it is using the word in the new and different meaning it began to have in the fourteenth century. "Catechism" now means a <u>book</u>. That is to say, "catechism" is no longer the process itself of instruction, but only the "primer" for that process. It is the tangible, readable <u>instrument</u> of "catechesis." The earliest instance of this new usage of the term seems to have been the <u>Catechismus Vaurensis,</u> a manual of instruction to be used by priests, mandated by a synod held at Lavaur, near Narbonne, in 1368.[6]

The most important name in this period when the catechism first emerges as a <u>book</u> is undoubtedly that of the great chancellor of the University of Paris, Jean Gerson (1363-1429). The measure of his greatness was precisely his pastoral vision. Theologian and ecclesiastic, caught up in the disputes of the schools and the politics of the Schism, he nevertheless recognized the primacy of religious instruction at the most basic level, and devoted as much time as he could to it. Two works of his achieved the status of "catechisms" for many dioceses in France: his so-called <u>Opusculum tripartitum</u> and, smaller and more popular still, his <u>A B C des simples gens</u>.[7]

Both works, and especially the latter, called for "live" instruction, for of themselves these mere booklets were but resumes of doctrine and piety. The role of the parish priest was, therefore, essential to the "catechism." That this was Gerson's firm intent is shown in another work, his Summa Theologica et Canonica.[8] In this large volume, written for the use of those charged with the ministry of the word, he treats of the following topics and in this order: the articles of the Creed, the Decalogue, sins, the sacraments (with prayer included as one of the "good works" listed under the sacrament of penance), the virtues and the Last Things.[9] Gerson's works on the two levels of instruction, popular (mediated by the pastor) and clerical, became the working models for the reform now recognized as critically urgent for the Church, wounded as she was by the experience of Avignon and the Schism, and faced with all sorts of new situations in the fifteenth century.

Among the new situations of the time, the invention of printing would one day be seen as perhaps the most revolutionary. Although its truly revolutionary potential would not be realized until the following century, already in the fifteenth it was having its effect, especially on such things as the catechism, which now, thanks to it, had definitely become a book. The catechism, as a "breve compendium"--of the Creed and the Our Father and some preparation for receiving the sacraments (especially the examination of conscience for Penance, and the "last sacraments" before death) -- became the object of much episcopal concern and legislation. The following synodal decree, in a Spanish diocese early in the century, can be considered typical:

> It is deemed most useful for the salvation of souls that each one of the faithful should know what he ought to believe, viz., the articles of the Creed; what he ought to seek, viz., what Christ taught us to ask for in the Lord's Prayer; what he ought to observe, viz., the Ten Commandments of the Law; what he ought to avoid, viz., the seven capital sins; what he ought to desire, viz., the glory of heaven; what he ought to fear, viz., the pains of hell. Thus is comprised the brief and handy summary of Christian doctrine which, we notice, is not known by all too many people.

By this present decree, therefore, we strictly enjoin on all those in a position of authority in this diocese to arrange with some competent and worthy men for the production of a certain brief compendium, in which all the foregoing matters are accurately and clearly presented for the instruction of the public.

This compendium should be divided into manageable parts, e.g., into some six or seven lessons, which would then be repeated throughout the year on a regular Sunday cycle. Thus will they instruct the people in all they need to know; and thus, with the darkness of ignorance put to flight, will they prepare by God's will an acceptable people. ...[10]

How many such "compendia" were actually produced -- and used -- is hard to say. But toward the end of the century, thanks to the printing press, two works had become particularly well known. In Italy a Libretto della dottrina cristiana, by the Dominican archbishop of Florence, St. Antoninus (1388-1459), was printed in Venice in 1473.[11] Its sub-title indicates its contents: "la quale e utile et molto necessaria che li puti pizoli et zovenzelli limpara per sapere amare servire et honorare idio bendetto et schivare le temptationi et peccati."[12] The emphasis is on the immediate instruction of the young, with direct application to the moral life. Somewhat the same is true of the other catechism, Ein fruchtbar Spiegel oder Handbücheschen der Christenmenschen, by the Augustinian Diedrich von Münster (1435-1515), printed in Cologne in 1470.[13] This random compilation of doctrine and piety, which seems to follow Gerson's in its emphasis on making a good Confession and preparing for death, was very popular. It went through nineteen printings before 1500, and twenty-eight after. "It was probably the most widespread Catholic catechism before and during the early years of the Reformation." [14]

These popular works did more than anything else to establish the catechism as a fixed genre, as permanent as the new technology which produced them, and as effective as the new literacy would allow. They were popular in the literal sense, meant for the "rudes et simpliciores" of both Augustine's and Gerson's predilection, and faithful to the millennial tradition of inculcating a "way of life" more by means of an attitude set in an ambiance of "devotion" than by detailed formulas of the catechetical tradition set in terms of "theology." There were still, of course, the basic formulas of the catechetical tradition -- the Creed, the Our Father, the Decalogue. And there were also the other formulas which had accumulated through the Middle Ages--the capital sins, the virtues, the works of mercy, etc. But the explanation of these was minimal as far as the catechism itself was concerned. That was left to the living teacher, the parish priest, who was expected to be himself instructed by the "summas" or manuals, condensing the work of the theologians in the schools. Both these purposes and endeavors, pioneered by Gerson one hundred years earlier, were to receive a new impulse of development as the sixteenth century began. At once corresponding to and contrasting with Gerson in this regard stands the curiously commanding figure of Desiderius Erasmus of Rotterdam (1466-1536).

The very name of Erasmus evokes contrasts -- the startling contrasts of that crucial moment in the history of the Church. The quiet conviction of the "devotio moderna" and the showy conceits of the Renaissance, the homespun "humanity" of the Gospel and the aristocratic cult of "virtù"-- both strains are found in Erasmus, the quintessential critic and would-be reformer of the Church. Like Gerson, he composed both a catechism for the "simple" and an instructional guide for the cleric. And both works clearly demonstrated what had been accomplished in the catechetical tradition since the end of the Middle Ages -- and what had been far from accomplished. Let us consider first his catechism, and then his "Methodus."

Erasmus' Explanatio, or catechism, must strike most students as a disappointment, especially when they recall that it was written (or at least published) in 1533 -- three years before his death, and sixteen years after Luther's theses at Wittenberg. [15] What could have been the distillation of a full life's work -- a lapidary statement of the essentials of the faith, renewing a love for the embattled Church and summarily dismantling at their roots the new heresies -- was in fact an abstruse disquisition on the basic data: the Creed, the sacraments, the Decalogue and the Our Father; brief enough, but strangely aloof and almost "neutral." The sacraments are significantly situated inside the

88

Creed, i.e., as a corollary to the article on the Church as "communio sanctorum." Yet, far from developing, even modestly, what could be (and in the Roman Catechism would be) an immensely important dogmatic and pastoral point, Erasmus dismisses the entire subject in one paragraph.[16] However, in spite of this momentous missed opportunity, the prestige enjoyed by Erasmus among the Catholic humanists across Europe and in the Roman curia itself remained intact; and fortunately so, for it would prove helpful in salvaging the positive value of his work and in applying it to the real reform of the Church which would at last get underway a decade later at the Council of Trent.

That enduring prestige of Erasmus was based on his earlier work, before Luther was known outside Saxony and while there was still a possibility -- however remote -- of an effective peaceful reform of the Church. That reform would have to begin with the clergy, and it was for them (if not expressly so) that Erasmus wrote his Methodus.[17] "Methodus" was originally but the Latin transliteration of the Greek "methodos," meaning a "pursuit" (of knowledge), some kind of investigation. It did not become a proper Latin word with a proper meaning until the sixteenth century, when the logicians began to use it to designate "systematic arrangement."[18] Erasmus adopted the new term for what we might consider as his up-date of the Gersonian Summa, i.e., the kind of manual really proper to an aspiring "minister of the word." His Ratio seu Methodus was written, he says, in response to many requests that he offer an introduction on how one should use his new translation of the New Testament.[19] For Erasmus "theology" is the study of Sacred Scripture, and in this respect he is hearkening back to an authentic tradition of the Fathers, from which the intervening medieval scholasticism was, in his view, a deviation.[20] For the Scholastics he has, in fact, only disdain. Their excessive preoccupation with logic, with its penchant for "quaestiones" and "sententiae," had distorted their understanding of what theology is really all about. The Scriptures have been so overlarded with commentaries and "glosses" that one has become practically oblivious of the sacred text itself; and the only texts still functioning for the Scholastics as genuine "fontes" are the writings of pagans like Aristotle. Erasmus has, of course, no disdain for erudition as such. Theology needs as auxiliary disciplines the ancient languages, besides a good acquaintance with the arts and sciences in general.[21] And even commentaries have their place; but one must be selective -- there is time for only the best.[22] And, first and last, what is needed in the student is a purification of heart and a love for Christ.[23]

With this "strength of mind and true piety," however, there seems to be for Erasmus scarcely any ecclesial connection. In fact, "ceremonies" are for him but the occasion for "superstition."[24] So, even in this purportedly practical manual for beginners lurk the familiar Erasmian ambiguities. He decries Scholasticism as pagan and dialectical, but he replaces it with stoicism and rhetoric. He praises the spirituality of the Scriptures (which means, if it means anything, that the Scriptures have a spiritual sense), but never once does he mention the sacraments. And as for the "method" itself, only two passages seem to verify the term in anything like a concrete manner. He advises the redaction of a "compendium," but gives no hint as to what it should contain or how it should be used. [25] Then, some hundred and twenty pages later, he suggests using "locos aliquot theologicos" for the compilation of Scriptural texts, presumably for ready reference; but the examples he gives are so casual and disjointed that one wonders what real usefulness they could have, either for comprehensive understanding of Scripture as such or for a basic homiletic approach to the immediate and pressing problem of popular instruction. [26] Yet, the work probably deserves the praise accorded it. It helped focus the attention of the humanists on the serious problems of catechesis at all levels in the Church, it reinforced the sense of urgency to vindicate the use of Sacred Scripture (and, to a lesser extent, of the Fathers also) in the face of the Protestant challenge, and -- it showed, perhaps, how not to put together a truly substantive and effective "methodus" for the training of instructors in the faith.

II

By the time Erasmus got around to his catechism, as we have seen, the long-threatening revolution had burst over Europe, and a Reformation of the Church was underway -- without the Church. Whatever authentic reform might have been effected along the lines of Gerson's or even Erasmus' purposes, it was now too late. In fact, it was now too late for even an unauthentic reform, such as might have been effected under the leadership of some "scholastic" like the systematic and stuffy Wycliffe (1330-1384) -- or of some "charismatic" like the dreamy and unpredictable Hus (1369-1415). For the initiative had been seized -- and the peculiar circumstances of time and place had corroborated the seizure -- by a man of genius, whose impress on all that followed was indelible. Volatile, passionate, master of the common touch, Martin Luther (1483-1546) accomplished within less than a dozen years a rupture within the Church such as she had never known before.

Now that "Christendom" in any effective sense was gone, was there anything left to keep the revolution from devouring itself? to keep intact the very idea of "church"? With the colossal inconsistency which marked his entire career, Luther clearly saw the need for ecclesiastical order. And he saw it as essentially based on what it had always been based: a common identification in one "faith," catechetically formulated and inculcated. As early as 1520, the fateful year that saw the Diet of Worms, his flight to the Wartburg and the publication of the three "position papers" of his revolution -- the <u>Appeal to the German Nobility</u>, the <u>Babylonian Captivity of the Church</u> and the <u>Freedom of the Christian Man</u> -- he wrote a pamphlet entitled <u>A Brief Form of the Ten Commandments, of the Creed and of the Lord's Prayer</u>.

> These three contain fully and completely everything that is in the Scriptures and that ever should be preached and everything that a Christian needs to know, all put so briefly and so plainly that no one can make complaint or excuse, saying that what he needs for his salvation is too long or too hard to remember. 27

So far, Luther's catechesis is anything but revolutionary; even his non-inclusion of the sacraments at this point in his scheme is non-exceptionable.28 But then he goes on to do two things: first, he rearranges the three elements in a manner that had not been done before (at least not for the reasons he now gives); and secondly, he adds the sacraments, but in a manner that likewise was quite new.

> Three things a man needs to know in order to be saved. First, he must know what he ought to do and what he ought not to do. Second, when he finds that by his own strength he can neither do the things he ought, nor leave undone the things he ought not to do, he must know where to seek and find and get the strength he needs. Third, he must know how to seek and find and get this strength... the Commandments teach a man to know his illness, so that he feels and sees what he can do and what he cannot do, and what he can and what he cannot leave undone, and thus he knows himself to be a sinner and a wicked man. After that the Creed shows him and teaches him where he may find the remedy -- the grace which helps him become a good man and to keep the Commandments; it shows him God and the mercy which He has revealed and offered in Christ. In the third place, the Lord's Prayer teaches him how to ask for this grace, get it, and take it to himself. 29

The primacy of the Creed has been superceded by the primacy of the Commandments because existentially -- and pedagogically -- the Christian life begins with the consciousness of sin and human futility. Following that comes the divine remedy as learned in the Creed and sought in prayer. The sacraments, i.e., Baptism and the Lord's Supper, are then <u>added</u> as what we can call "supplements." Being of divine institution, they cannot be ignored. So they are included in the basic catechesis, but only for this "positive" reason, not for any <u>intrinsic</u> connection they may have with the essential triad: "Gebote, Glauben und Gebet." 30 In 1529 Luther embodied the doctrine of his <u>Brief Form</u> in a booklet which probably deserves to be regarded as his greatest work: the famous <u>Small Catechism</u>.31 Not only did it immediately become and permanently remain the single most typical and influential statement of the Protestant faith; it also became -- for all practical purposes -- the first "catechism." There had been of course many earlier catechisms, both Catholic and Protestant,³² but none of them had the impact on the genre that Luther's had. He followed it up with his Large Catechism, incorporating further explanation and exhortation, while maintaining the same structure. But it was his Small Catechism -- even more than his Bible -- which secured his revolution.

It was still within Luther's lifetime that his role as premier Reformer was effectively challenged, and by the time of the last period of the Council of Trent (and the appearance of the Roman Catechism) a greater threat than the revolution in Germany was confronting the Catholic Church. John Calvin (1509-1564) had first written his Institutes of the Christian Religion as a "catechism" in 1536. As he explained to the King of France in his Preface:

> When I first set myself to writing this present book, Sire, nothing was farther from my thought than writing things that would be presented to your Majesty. My intention was only to teach some rudiments by which those touched by any good affection to God might be instructed in true piety. ³³

In the following year he wrote an abridgment of it, entitled Instruction in Faith, which he patterned after Luther's work. But then in 1541, back in Geneva, he issued his own Catechism, which in two respects rivals Luther's in importance in both the history of Protestantism and the history of the catechism.³⁴ First, he changed Luther's arrangement: he returned the Creed to its traditional first place, and the Decalogue to second place (followed by the Lord's Prayer, and the same "appendix" for the sacraments). This change meant that for Calvin the Law was no mere "pedagogue" leading to Christ; it was Christ's Law and meant to be observed! And as for the Creed, it was significantly prefaced by a short disquisition on the "end of man" and the "glory of God."

Secondly, he put an unprecedented emphasis on the formulation of the learner's responses. Whereas the earlier catechisms -- Luther's included--were meant primarily to be teaching aids (i.e., for the teacher), Calvin designed his book primarily for the learner: what the learner must know is not so much a "way of life" as a "formulation of faith." This "confessional" -- we can just as well say this "partisan"-- aspect of catechesis is Calvin's contribution to what became, precisely because of his revolutionary success, the dominant aspect in the vast majority of all subsequent catechisms, Protestant or Catholic.[35] This second point, which surely explains why Calvinism displaced Lutheranism as the Protestant church par excellence, is vividly illustrated by Calvin himself in a letter to the English government of Edward VI in 1548:

> First, there ought to be an agreed summary of doctrine that all ought to preach, which all prelates and curates swear to follow, and no one ought to receive any ecclesiastical charge who does not promise to keep such an agreement. Next, there ought to be a common formula of instruction for little children and ignorant people that serves to make them familiar with sound doctrine, so that they may discern it amidst the lies and corruptions which may be introduced to the contrary. Believe me, Monseigneur, the Church of God will never be preserved without catechesis.[36]

Following the work of Luther and Calvin, and in fact endeavoring to synthesize them, is the famous Heidelberg Catechism of 1563, which we need here only briefly mention. [37] Designed to be the Protestant catechism deriving from both Wittenberg and Geneva, it rearranged the traditional data as a balance between them. Its first part was on the Law, as the witness to man's slavery to sin. The second part was on the Creed, including the sacraments, the ministry and church discipline, all of them considered as the means of man's liberation in Christ. Completing the structure is a third part, designating our grateful return of service of God as set forth in the Commandments and the Lord's Prayer. This two-fold treatment of the Commandments (i.e., both before and after the Creed) is an evident compromise between the Lutheran and the Calvinist views, as is also the central part with its added "churchly" elements balancing the Creed. With the Heidelberg Catechism we have as "classic" a statement of Protestantism as a whole as we could expect, and we have it in 1563 -- the same year in which the Council of Trent finally authorized the "classic" catechism for the Catholic Church.

Although the beleaguered Church of Rome had as yet no comparably official catechism in 1563, there were at least twenty Catholic catechisms in circulation, all directed to the same end: the explanation of the essentials of the Catholic faith, especially those doctrines under attack by the Protestants.[38] The apologetic aspect was, understandably, very prominent in these works; yet they were fundamentally catechetical in their purpose and structure. That is to say, they intended an elementary coverage of the whole of Christian doctrine, and this coverage was more or less in line with the pattern of the classic catechesis as most recently enunciated by Gerson and Erasmus.

The two largest and most prestigious of these catechisms were Frederick Nausea's (c. 1490-1552) Catholicus Catechismus and John Gropper's (1503-1559) Enchiridion Christianae Institutionis.[39] Both were written in the late 1530's or early 1540's by prominent ecclesiastics, both were in Latin and directed to the clergy (i.e., they were not for the students nor put in a question-and-answer form), and both considered their task as but a holding action, pending the arrival on the scene of the definitive catechism of the Council soon to be called by the Church. Limiting our comment to the one point most pertinent to our purpose, viz., their structure, we notice some significant similarities and dissimilarities, as regarding both the catechisms which preceded them and the Roman Catechism which was to follow.

Both Nausea and Gropper retrieve the sacraments from the place relegated them by the Reformers. From being a kind of mere afterthought appended to the triad of "creed-code-cult," the sacraments are put in the same place by both men, viz., in second place, immediately after the Creed. For Nausea it is because of an affinity which he detects between the sacraments and the second virtue, hope.

> ...In behalf of sinners the Mother shows to her Son her pierced heart, and the Son shows to his Father His wounded side. No refusal is possible where such signs of love are shown. It is indeed as the signs and seals of this faith and hope that Christ willed to leave after

Him the seven sacred sacraments, concerning which sacraments we must now speak.[40]

For Gropper, who keeps the traditional connection between hope and prayer, the sacraments are seen as "part of the Creed" and must therefore be treated in immediate sequence to it.

> The first place is given to the explanation of the Apostles' Creed, because this deals with faith, and faith is the entrance-way to God. Next come the sacraments of the Church, which are, as it were, part of the Creed; for they are the most certain symbols or signs of our faith.[41]

If in this respect (as we shall see later) the Roman Catechism more closely resembles Gropper, it departs from Gropper in favor of Nausea in its ordering of Parts Three and Four (viz., on the Commandments and the Our Father), which Gropper reverses.[42]

The pairing we have made in the case of Nausea and Gropper can be even more appropriately made in the case of two other catechisms which must also be described (again, very briefly) as among the more important precursors of the Roman Catechism. These two were written in the 1550's and early 1560's, in Latin and in the vernacular, and in the question-and-answer format. In this respect they were both less similar to Nausea and Gropper than they were to Luther and Calvin. In fact, they were intended as the Catholic response to the two arch-Protestants: answering Luther was Peter Canisius (1521-1597) in Germany, and answering Calvin was Edmond Auger (1530-1591) in France.[43]

Canisius' work was destined to become, beginning in his own lifetime and continuing for centuries, the most widely used catechism in the Catholic world. Its merits were incomparable: written in three versions (the original "Summa" for young collegians, the "Minor" for young adolescents, the "Minima" for beginners) in a style conspicuous for its succinctness, clarity and serenity, it was the greatest single instrument of the Counter-Reformation, unquestionably in the German lands and in Eastern Europe, and perhaps also throughout the entire Church of the West. Its author was eventually canonized and proclaimed a Doctor of the Church: St. Peter Canisius was not only the second Boniface; he was also the second Cyril of Jerusalem.⁴⁴ One measure of his greatness was, precisely, his readiness to adapt the classic catechesis to the needs of his time. He saw that the taproot of Protestantism -- Luther's doctrine of justification by faith alone (i.e., without good works) -- had to be directly disproved and displaced. Accordingly, he recast the structure of catechesis into a dual mould: in the first, which he called "Wisdom," he retained the traditional four-fold content of Creed, prayer, Decalogue and sacraments;⁴⁵ in the second, which he called "Justice," he assembled the various medieval formularies -- the capital sins, the cardinal virtues, the gifts of the Holy Spirit, the Beatitudes, the works of mercy, the Last Things -- all in the perspective of things to do and things to avoid as good works accompanying faith. ⁴⁶

That it was effective in fulfilling its immediate intention -- stopping Protestantism in its tracks, and indeed rolling it back -- is evident. That it was less so in the long run, i.e., as a presentation of Catholic doctrine, prescinding from the particular challenge of a particular heresy, is perhaps equally evident. The key criterion, once more, is how this catechism treats grace and the sacraments. Canisius' seven sacraments are surely more central to his whole structure than Luther's two sacraments are to his. Yet, grace is still perforce more of an aid to live the life of virtue than the very life of virtue itself. To quote from the Preface of the 1560 German edition:

> Everything depends on faith, hope, love, sacraments and justice, if we wish always to be God's children and to reach heaven. Without faith we do not know God; without hope we despair of God's grace; without love neither faith nor hope or trust are of any use to us. Rather, we then remain in darkness -- yes, even in death, as the holy Apostles tell us in Scripture. Without the sacraments, on the other hand, and their correct Catholic usage, the grace of the Holy Spirit is neither given nor held. And, finally, without justice there is nothing that is Christ's; rather, it is but the kingdom of the devil.⁴⁷

The tendencies and tensions resulting from adaptations in structure are evident in Canisius' work. But they are comparatively minor, when compared, that is, with the work of his fellow Jesuit, Edmond Auger.

More sharply and narrowly focused than Canisius' work, Auger composed his catechism as a head-on, almost word-for-word, riposte to Calvin. In this he was brilliantly successful: Calvin's great assets -- logical rigor and rhetorical acumen -- were effectively neutralized. It was the Counter-Reformation at its most literal! Yet, even more than in the case of Canisius, this was effected at a price. The classic catechesis can be -- must be -- adapted from age to age. But this adaptation can go only so far, if the ultimate purpose of catechesis is to be identified and fulfilled. It is one thing to have <u>formularies</u>; it is another to have a "way of life." [48] And specifying that purpose -- more than may be immediately appreciated -- is <u>structure</u>.

We come now to the last work in our modest survey of "catechesis and catechisms" leading up to the Roman Catechism, viz., the <u>Comentarios sobre el Catechismo Christiano</u> of Bartholomew Carranza (c. 1503-1576).[49] Chronologically it comes after Nausea and Gropper and between Canisius and Auger. But logically it is at once considerably closer to Nausea and Gropper than it is to the two later works, and certainly closer to the Roman Catechism than either Canisius and Auger are. Carranza thus occupies a pivotal position in the pre-history of the Roman Catechism. His work is, as it were, the last formal version of the classic catechesis before it went "into committee" -- from 1562 to 1566 at Trent and in Rome.

Bartolomé Carranza de Miranda, a Spanish Dominican and a leading theologian at the Council of Trent (in its first period, 1545-47), wrote his catechism during his stay in England as adviser to Cardinal Pole in the Catholic restoration there under Philip II and Mary Tudor. In 1558 he was made Archbishop of Toledo and returned to Spain, only to encounter trouble with the Inquisition, which lasted until his death. It is ironic that while some fellow Dominicans were sniffing heresy in his catechism before the Inquisition in Spain, other fellow Dominicans were seeing such treasures in the same catechism that they were making it the working model for their new catechism commissioned by the Council and supervised by the Dominican Pope Pius V! What smacked of "heresy" was Carranza's identification of "conversion" with "faith" -- and of "faith" with Christ.[50]

Given this rich -- and clearly Thomistic -- interiorization of "faith" in Carranza's work, it is doubly ironic that he did not follow through with it in his treatment of what St. Thomas consistently calls the "sacraments of faith." For Carranza the sacraments are "works of God" in the sense that, as perceptible signs, they "back up" God's word as spoken. This is how he introduces the sacraments in the Part III of his work to which he assigns them:

> The third part of Christian doctrine comprises the sacraments. To understand what they are, it should be noted that, generally speaking, God has, from the very beginning of history, dealt with mankind in two different ways. First, and more ordinarily, He used words. But secondly, He used bodies, i.e., things perceived by the senses, as signs. It would have been quite sufficient for our instruction if God had simply used words, for there can be nothing more certain in itself as a basis for our faith than a simple word from God. Anticipating our weakness, however, He added to His words certain outward signs; for now, with these two things in combination, our faith in the assurance of God's promises is confirmed. Although God does not always accompany His words with signs, nevertheless in matters of greater importance He does, for that very importance can make it hard for us to base our faith on His word alone.[51]

This description certainly does justice to the reality of the sacrament as sign, but does it do as much for its reality as cause? Earlier, when introducing the Decalogue in his Part II, he says this about sacramental causality:

> In every systematic study there must be some proper procedure and conclusion, which in our ordinary language can be called an outline and summary. For certainly one of the most important aspects of any study is order. Now the Church acts in this way when, to put order into Christian studies, she produces those summaries of her teaching called the catechism. In the first place, the Church at the very time of the Apostles put together and summarized all those items pertaining to faith that were written in the Sacred Scriptures. They were listed in twelve articles, and make up what we call the Apostles' Creed. Secondly (as we have just seen), she summarizes all the laws we need for the ordering of our lives; these are the Ten Commandments. And now, in the third place, all that we need as a

remedy and medicine for our souls God has gathered together in the seven sacraments.⁵²

With this emphasis on the "remedial" and the "medicinal,' Carranza once more misses the opportunity to bring out the full Thomistic evaluation of the "sacraments of faith," and so seems to join those for whom grace is more "actual" than "sanctifying."⁵³

Altogether, then, there is a surprising (and truly ironic) sense of hesitancy on the part of Carranza regarding the sacraments: just how to treat them as "works," and where to put them in his book. This is all the more so when it is recalled that he had before him and used -- as has now been demonstrated ⁵⁴ -- Gropper's work, which (like Nausea's also) put the sacraments in second place, following the Creed. In his decision to put the sacraments in third place -- separated from the Creed, and following the Decalogue -- Carranza was not followed by the authors of the Roman Catechism, who were otherwise so indebted to him. If, as has been suggested, Carranza's sequence -- Creed, Decalogue, sacraments -- is identical with the sequence of the three Parts in St. Thomas' Summa Theologiae, ⁵⁵ the authors of the Roman Catechism seem not to have been impressed. Their fidelity to St. Thomas -- and to the classic catechesis -- would be demonstrated in a more fundamental and important way.

The classic catechesis: this has been our topic, regarded in its various aspects, through four chapters. We come at last to the Roman Catechism itself. If perhaps the center of gravity of this study seems displaced, with the Roman Catechism relegated to a marginal position in it, it is to be hoped that in the three remaining chapters this study will retrieve and confirm the true place of the Roman Catechism in the catechetical tradition. For we would never see that catechism in its reality unless we had first seen -- however cursorily -- that which its authors so clearly saw: that same tradition which now they were bid by the Church to render in as "classic" a form as could be possible in any one given moment of history.

NOTES

1   See above, Chapter I, pp. 15-16.

2   Despite (because of?) the wave of "anti-Constantinianism" in the wake of Vatican II, this debate is far from foreclosed.

3   "...baptismus est 'fidei sacramentum,' cum sit quaedam professio fidei christianae. Ad hoc autem quod aliquis fidem accipiat, requiritur quod de fide instruatur; secundum illud Rom 10: 'Quomodo credent quem non audierunt? Quomodo autem audient sine praedicante?' Et ideo ante baptismum convenienter praecedit catechismus..." S.T., III, 71, 1. See also In Sent. IV, 6, 2.

4   II, 2, 63-64; p.119.

5   II, 3,21; p. 128.

6   Pietro Tacchi-Venturi, S.J., Storia della Compagnia di Gesù in Italia (Roma: Civilta Cattolica, 1938; 2nd ed.), Vol. I, p.336.

7   The Opusculum Tripartitum comprises 1) Le miroir de l'âme (a brief explanation of the Creed, the Decalogue and sacramental confession), 2) Examen de conscience selon des sept péchés mortels, and 3) La science de bien mourir. These three works are found in Glorieux's edition of Gerson's Oeuvres complètes, Vol. VII (Paris: Desclée, 1966), #312 (pp.193-206), #330 (pp.393-400), and #332 (pp.404-07), respectively.

The A B C des simples gens (ibid., # 310, pp. 154-57) consists exclusively of headings, mostly enumerations, of catechetical topics. Since this work represents a kind of culmination of this medieval development, it may be useful to list here the complete contents of Gerson's A B C:
- the five bodily senses
- the seven mortal (i.e., capital) sins
- the contrary virtues
- the seven petitions of the Our Father
- the Hail Mary
- the Credo (i.e., the twelve Articles of the Creed)
- the Ten Commandments of the Law
- the seven virtues
- the seven gifts of the Holy Spirit
- the seven Beatitudes
- the seven spiritual works of mercy
- the seven corporal works of mercy
- the seven orders
- the seven sacraments

- the seven "branches" of penance (viz., fasting, almsgiving, prayer, contrition, confession, satisfaction; there is no seventh)
- the seven endowments of paradise
- the four counsels of Christ (viz., humility, poverty, virginity, charity)
- the principal joys of paradise
- the pains of hell

The edition I consulted was printed in Venice in 1587.

8   This work is not included in Glorieux's Oeuvres complètes. I have been unable to pursue the problem this poses regarding its authenticity. On internal evidence the Summa resembles, in content, order and tone, the two authentic works mentioned previously.

9   The space apportioned to these several topics is as follows:
[I. de Articulis Fidei] pp. 3-31.
II. "de Praeceptis,"pp. 32-40.
III. "de Peccatis," pp. 40-115.
IV. "de Sacramentis," pp. 116-190; 224-310.
"de Oratione," pp. 190-223.
V. "de Virtutibus," pp. 311-391.
VI. "de Novissimis," pp. 393-434.

10 "Saluti animarum plurimum dignoscitur opportunum ut unusquisque fidelis ignoscat, et sciat quod credere debeat, scilicet articulos fidei; quid petere, scilicet quae in oratione dominica Christus nos docuit postulare; quae servare, videlicet decem praecepta legis; quae vitare, scilicet septem peccata mortalia; quid optare, gloriam paradisi et sperare; quid timere, poenas inferni: quod Christianae doctrinae breve et utile epilogum esse censeatur; quae a multis popularibus, ut percepimus, ignorantur.

"Hac igitur constitutione diocesanis omnibus et aliis praelatis ecclesisticis super his iurisdictionem ecclesiasticam habentibus districte praecipiendo mandamus, ut per viros litteratos et probatos dictari et scribi faciant aliquod breve compendium in quo praedicata omnia, quantum populares est scire necesse, districte comprehendantur et clare.

"Quodque compendium sic commode dividatur inter partes ut per sex vel septem lectiones valeat declarari, et sic per totius anni decursum, repetitis vicibus pro cunctis diebus dominicis, populo totaliter faciant explanari et, excussis ignorantiae tenebris, populum acceptabilem, Deo volente, exhibere..." Decree VI of the Synod of Tortosa, 1429: "De modo instruendi populum circa fidem necessariam." Mansi, Sacrorum Conciliorum nova et amplissima collectio, Tom. XXVIII (Venice, 1785), cols, 1147-48.

11 This little work preceded by a few years his Summa Moralis, his chief theological writing which earned for him the (unofficial)

title "Doctor of the Church" and the generally recognized standing as the greatest moral theologian between St. Thomas and St. Alphonsus Ligouri.

12 Cited by Tacchi-Venturi, op. cit., p.337.

13 The full German text (without commentary) in Christopher Moufang's Katholische Katechismen des sechzehnten Jahrhunderts in deutsche Sprache (Mainz, 1881), pp. I-L (i.e.,pp. 1-50). An English translation (entitled Mirror for Christians, by Theodorich Kolde) is included in Denis Janz's Three Reformation Catechisms: Catholic, Anabaptist, Lutheran (New York and Toronto: Edwin Mellen Press, 1982).

14 Janz, p.8. The three main divisions of Diedrich's catechism are: 1) "wie man glauben soll," Chs. 1-22 (Moufang, pp. II-XXVIII), 2) "wie man leben soll," chs. 23-43 (pp. XXVIII-XLVI), 3) "wie man sterben soll," chs. 44-46 (pp.XLVI-L).

15 Dilucida et pia explanatio Symboli quod Apostolorum dicitur, Decalogi praeceptorum et Dominicae Precationis, in Opera Omnia, Tom. V (Leiden, 1704), cols. 1133-96.

16 In "Catechesis V," cols. 1175-76. This "catechesis" on the sacraments concludes with the following comment, as enigmatic as it is Erasmian: "Et quidam Romanus Pontifex Episcopo cuidam Anglo, ni fallor, scitanti quiddam re ritibus mysteriorum, quum nonnulla respondisset, verba, quibus oleum consecrabatur, non ausus est litteris committere, ne forte, quod saepe fit, litteris interceptis arcanum evulgaretur. Haec causa non quidem omnino nulla est. Verior tamen et receptior est, quod in sacramentis per signa quaedam sensibilia, infunditur insensibilis gratia congruens externis signis."

17 Ratio seu Methodus compendio perveniendi ad veram theologiam (Prague, 1786).

18 Bacci, Ant., Lexicon eorum vocabulorum quae difficilius Latine redduntur (Rome: Soc. Lib. "Studium," 1949), p. 317.

19 p. 9.

20 "...videbit illic [i.e., the Fathers] aureum quoddam ire flumen: hic [i.e., the Scholastics] tenues quosdam rivulos, eosque nec puros admodum, nec suo fonti respondentes. Illic tonant oracula veritatis aeternae; hic audis hominum commentula, quae quo propius inspicias, hoc magis similia insomniis evanescunt. Illic recto cursu tendes ad portum veritatis evangelicae; hic inter questionum humanarum anfractus luctans, aut illidens in Scyllam potestatis pontificiae, aut in syrtes scholasticorum dogmatum, aut in symplegadas iuri divini atque humani, nisi mavis hanc Charydim facere. Illic solidis Scripturarum fundamentis innixum aedificium surgit in altum; hic futilibus hominum argutiis, aut etiam adulationibus non minus inanes quam immanes,

superstructa machina, tollitur in immensum. Illic velut in felicissimis hortis affatim tum oblectaberis, tum expleberis, dum hic inter spineta sterilia dilaceraris, ac torqueris. Illic maiestas plena omnium; hic adeo nihil splendidum, ut pleraque sordida, parumque digna dignitate theologica, ut interim a comparatione morum abstineam." ibid., pp. 20-21.

21 Ibid., p. 14.

22 Ibid., p. 151.

23 "Iam quemadmodum fidei et caritatis comes est animi fortitudo veraque pietas..." ibid., p. 98.

24 "...quemadmodum sincera pietas animi puritate nititur, ita superstitio caeremoniis sese venditat. Illam spiritus vocabulo frequenter notat Paulus, hanc carnis..." ibid.

25 "Illud mea sententia magis ad rem pertinuerit, ut tyrunculo nostro dogmata traduntur, in summum ac compendium redacta, idque potissimum ex evangelicis fontibus, mox apostolorum literis, ut ubique certos habeat scopos, ad quos ea quae legit conferat..." ibid., p. 25.

26 " ...ut locos aliquot theologicos aut tibi pares ipse, aut ab alio quopiam traditos accipias; ad quos omnia quae legeris, velut in nidulos quosdam digeras, quo promptius sit, ut videbitur, quod voles vel promere vel recondere..." ibid., p. 146.

27 "...in wilchen drei stucken fur war alles, was in der schrifft steht und immer geprediget werden mag, auch alles, was ein Christen nott ist zu wissen, grundlich und uberklussig begriffen ist, und mit solcher kurtz und leichts vorgasset, das niemant clagen noch sich entschuldigen kan, es sei zuvill odder zuschweer zu behalten, was ihm nodt ist zur selickeit." Luther, Werke, Vol VII (Weimar, 1897). p. 204. The work in question is entitled Ein kurcz form der zeehn gepott. D. M. L., Ein Kurcz form des Glaubens, Ein kurcz form dess Vatter unssers. ibid., pp. 204-29.

28 See St. Augustine's and St.Thomas' identical schemata, Chapter II, pp. 32 and 43.

29 "Dan drei dingk sein nott einem menschen zu wissen, das er selig werden muge: Das erst, das er wisse, was er thun und lassen soll. Zum andernn, wen er nu sicht, das er es not thun noch lassen kan auss seinen krefften, das er wisse, wo eras nehmen und suchen und finden soll, damit er dasselb thun und lassen muge. Zum dritten, das er wisse, wil er es suchen und holen soll. ...Also leren die gepott den menschen sein kranckheit erkenne, das er siet und empfindet, was er thun und nit thun, lassen und nit lassen kan, und erkennet sich einen sunder und bösen menschen. Darnach helt ihm der glaub fur und leret ihn, wo er die ertsner die gnaden, finden soll, die ihm helff frum werden das er die gepott halte. Und tseigt ihm gott und seine barmhertsickeit, in

Christo ertseigt und angepotten. Zum dritten leret ihn das Vatter unsser, wie er die selben begeren, holen und zu sich bringen soll." ibid., pp. 204-05.

30 See Gerhard Bellinger, Der Catechismus Romanus und die Reformation: die katechetische Antwort des Trienter Konzils auf die Haupt-Katechismen der Reformation (Paderborn: Bonifacius, 1970), p.40.

31 Der Kleine Catechismus für die gemeine Pfarrherr und Prediger. Werke, Vol. XXX (Weimer, 1910), pp. 239-345.

32 An impressive, although unannotated, listing of these catechisms is included in Tellechea Idigores' edition of Carranza's catechism, Vol. I, p. 86.

33 "Au commencement que je m'appliquay à éscrire ce présent livre, je ne pensaye rien moins, Sire, que d'éscrire choses qui fussent présentées à vostre Majesté. Seulement mon propos estoit d'enseigner quelques rudimens, par lesquels ceux qui seroyent touchez d'aucune bonne affection de Dieu, fussent instruits à la vraye piété." Institution de la religion chrestienne (Jean-Daniel Benoit, ed.) Tome I (Paris:Vrin, 1957), p. 27.

34 Catéchisme, c'est à dire le formulaire d'instruire les enfans en la Christienté, faict en maniere de dialogue, où le Ministre interrogue, et l'enfant respond. Geneve, 1553. Calvin's preface to this 1553 edition, entitled "Epistre au lecteur," is significant for the history of the catechism in general: "Ca este une chose que tousiours l'Eglise a sue en singuliere recommendation, d'instruire les petits enfans en la doctrine Chrestienne. Et pour ce faire, non seulement on avoit anciennement les Escoles, et commandoit-on à un chascun de bien endoctriner sa famille mais aussi l'ordre publique estoit par les temples, d'examiner les petits enfans sur les poincts qui doibuent estre communs entre tous les Chrestiens. Et à fin de procéder par ordre, on usoit d'un formulaire, qu'on nommoit Catéchisme. Depuis, le diable en dissipant l'Eglise, et faisant l'horrible ruine, dont on voit encores les enseignes en la plus part du monde, a destruit ceste saincte police; et n'a laissé que ie ne scay quelles reliques, qui ne peuvent sinon engendrer superstitions, sans aucunement édifier. C'est la Confirmation qu'on appelle, où il n'y a que singerie, sans aucun fondement. Ainsi, ce que nous mettons en avant, n'est sinon l'usage qui a de toute ancienneté este observée entre les Chrestiens, et n'a jamais esté delaissée, que quand l'Eglise a esté du tout corrumpue."

35 See Jean Dhôtel, S. J., Les origines du catéchisme moderne: d'après les premiers manuels imprimés en France (Paris : Aubier, 1967), p. 38.

36 Cited by John H. Westerhoff and O. C. Edwards, A Faithful Church: Issues in the History of Catechesis (Wilton, Connecticut: Morehouse-Barlow, 1981), p. 127.

37 The full title, in Good and Harbagh's English Edition (Chambersburg, 1849), is as follows: The Heidelberg Catechism, or Short Instruction in Christian Doctrine, as it is conducted in the churches and schools of the Palatinate and elsewhere, explained and confirmed with proofs from the Holy Scriptures; the whole adapted to the use of catechetical classes, Sabbath schools and family instruction.

38 See above, note 32, p. 105.

39 The copies I have consulted were the following: Nausea, Fredericus, Catholicus Catechismus (Cologne, 1543); and Gropper, Ioannis, Enchiridion Christianae Institutionis (Paris, 1545).

40 "...ubi mater pro peccatoribus ostendit filio pectus et ubera, et filius patri latus et vulnera. Nulla profecto poterit ibi esse repulsa, ubi tot sunt amoris insignia, maximeque huius fidei et spei firmiter habendae signa et sigilla, Christus post se reliquerit sacrosancta septem sacramenta, de quibus hoc quidem loco potissimum nobis habendum est sermo." III, 3, fol. xviii.

In the "Elenchus Capitum" at the beginning of his catechism, Nausea entitles Book III "De septem Catholicae Ecclesiae sacramentis"; whereas at the beginning of Book III in the text (fol. xvi), he has no title; while at the top of the following page (fol. xvii) occurs the title "De Spe"!

41 "Explicationi ... Symboli Apostolici, quod fidem complectitur, primus locus debebatur, quod fides ianua sit, qua ad Deum acceditur: proximum, Ecclesiae sacramenta, quae veluti quaedam Symboli pars esse videntur, atque adeo fidei nostrae certissima symbola sunt, postulabant." IV, p. 234v.

42 That, following the Creed (Part I) and the sacraments (Part II), prayer (Part III) should precede the Commandments (Part IV), and not follow them (as in Nausea's catechism), is for Gropper an important point. Twice -- at the beginning of Part III, and again at the beginning of Part IV -- he insists on the correctness of his arrangement. Both passages are worth citing:

"De ratione ac modo orandi Deum" (Part III): "Ecclesia catholica, mater nostra, in qua per baptismum renascimur Christo, eum ordinem tenet, ut Symbolum Apostolicum (quae est fidei nostrae regula) ante omnia proponat ac tradat; subinde vero posteaquam professi sumus quod credimus, orationem dominicam subiungat ac reddi iubeat, idque ordine non modo decenti, sed et necessario. Siquidem ut precemur Deum, necesse est ut fidem prius teneamus, quae utique nisi data esset, orare non possemus. Quomodo enim (uti Paulus Apostolus ait) invocabunt in quem non crediderunt? Eundem ergo ordinem nos insequentes, post Apostolici Symboli, divinorumque sacramentorum (quae veluti pars quaedam Symboli esse videntur) expositionem, ad brevem dominicae orationis dilucidationem recte properabimus." ibid, p. 196.

"De natura, distinctione, vi, ac usu legis, cum subiuncta explicatione decalogi" (Part IV): "Non temere in hac institutione doctrinae Christianae, postremum locum explicationi Decalogi dedimus, non tantum ordinem, quae res ipsa requirebat, sed et Ecclesia mentem ac praesriptum sequuti. ...Tertium vero locum dominicae orationis expositio merito tenuit, quod oratio primum ac praecipuum fidei opus et exercitium sit. Fidem enim in Deum statim sequitur invocatio. Quartum itaque ac postremum locum iure sibi Decalogus vindicat, qui regulam plane divinam praescribit, ad quam credentibus ac sperantibus in Deum, tota vita deinceps exigenda sit. Homini enim necdum fidem in Deum assequuto seu nondum renato, frustra praescripsisseris Decalogum observandum. Porro eundem ordinem Ecclesia in catechizando ac baptizando observat. Primum enim Deum precatur, ut a baptizando, quem ad fidei rudimenta vocare dignatus est, omnem caecitatem cordis (quod per fidem fit) expellat, ut omnes laquaeos Satanae, quibus is per incredulitatem fuerat colligatus, disrumpat, ut ianuam pietatis aperiat; denique, ut baptizatus sapientia Dei inbutus iniquitatum foetoribus careat, ac ad suavem odorem praeceptorum Dei laetus in Ecclesia eius ipsi deserviat. Deinde statim sub baptismum Ecclesia Symbolum et Orationem Dominicam reddi et recitari iubet." ibid., p. 234v.

43 The copies I have consulted were the following: Fredericus Streicher, S.J. (ed.), S. Petri Canisii Catechismi Latini et Germanici (Rome: Gregorian, 1933); and Friederich Josef Brand, Die Katechismen des Edmunds Augerius, S. J. (Freiburg-in-Breisgau: Herder, 1917).

44 "Non defuit qui Canisii Summum cum Sententiarum Libro compararet, nec qui Beatum Catechismi auctorem talem pro Occidente qualem S. Cyrillum Hierosolymitanum pro Orientali Ecclesia fuisse diceret." Pius XI, in his decree, Misericordiarum Deus (May 21, 1925), canonizing Peter Canisius and declaring him a Doctor of the Church, as cited by Streicher (op. cit., p.17).

45 In all the versions and editions prior to 1568 Canisius' distribution of parts is as follows: Cap. I, "De Fide et Symbolo Fidei" ; Cap. II, "De Spe et Oratione Dominica" (including "De Salutatione Angelica"); Cap. III, "De Caritate et Decalogo" (including "De Praeceptis Ecclesiae"); Cap. IV, "De Sacramentis." After 1568, Canisius rearranged the parts, to conform to the order of the Roman Catechism. I.e., while the Creed and the Decalogue remained in the first and third places respectively, the positions of the sacraments and prayer were reversed: the former moving from the fourth to the second place, and the latter from the second to the fourth. See Streicher, op. cit., p. 73.

46   The titles and sequence of the topics making up this second part of Canisius' catechism, under the general title of "De Iustitia Christiana," are as follows:
["on the capital sins" -- untitled in the Latin original]
"De peccatis alienis"
"De peccatis in Spiritum Sanctum"
"De peccatis in caelum clamantibus"
"De triplici genere bonorum operum" [viz., prayer, fasting and almsgiving]
"De virtutibus cardinalibus"
"De donis et fructibus Spiritus Sancti"
"De octo beatitudinibus"
"De consiliis evangelicis"
"De quattuor hominis novissimis"

47   "Es hangt doch alles am Glauben, Hoffnung, Lieb, Sakramenten un Gerechtigkeit, wollen wir sunst immer Gottes kinder und in Christo gerecht und selig werden. Zwar on den Glauben erkennen wir Gott nit; on die Hoffnung verzwerflen wir an Gottes gnaden; on Lieb nutzt uns weder glauden noch hoffen oder vertrawen nit, sonder wir bleiben noch in der finsternuss, ja auch im tod, wie die heyligen Aposteln schreiben. On die Sakramenten aber und ihren rechten Catholischen brauch wirt die gnad des hl. Geistes nit geschopffet noch erhalten. Wo dann nit ist die Gerechtigkeit, da ist nit Christi, sonder des Teufels Reich." ibid., p. 64.

48   Dhôtel, op. cit., pp. 50, 62-64.

49   Carranza de Miranda, Bartolome, O.P., Comentarios sobre el Catechismo Christiano. (edited by José Ignacio Tellecheria Idigoras) Madrid: BAC, 1972. 2 vols.

50   ibid., Vol. I, pp. 89-91. In his "Introducion General" Tellecheria Idigoras notes Carranza's emphasis on faith as existential and living (i.e., not as something apart from grace and charity), and on faith as equivalent to the personal confession of Christ. He quotes Carranza (without reference): "Todos los cristianos confiesan que Jesús es Cristo, pero en pocos está esta fe verdadera y perfecta. No habla aqui San Juan de la fe que tienen los malos, como la que tiene el demonio, que cree lo que nosotros; sino en la fe viva, que la acompañan las obras."

51   "La tercera parte de la doctrina cristiana contiene los sacramentos; para la inteligencia de los cuales se ha de presuponer que de dos maneras ha tratado generalmente Dios con los hombres desde el principio del mundo. La primera y la más común es por palabras. La segunda es por señales de cosas sensibiles y corporales. Hubiera de bastar y sobra para nuestra instrucción la palabra de Dios, porque no puede haber cosa más cierta ni más segura que una simple palabra de Dios, a la cual somos los hombres obligados a creer. Mas, queriendo proveer a nuestra flaqueza, añadió señales corporales a su palabra: porque con ambas cosas se confirmase en nosotros la fe y nos

asegurásemos en las promesas de Dios. Pero no siempre acompaña Dios su palabras con señales, sino en cosas grandes y de mucha importancia, en la cuales la grandeza de ellas podía hacer dificultad a la fe de su palabra" Vol. II. p. 163.

52 "En todas las diciplinas es necesario hacer éstos métodos y epítomes, que en vulgar podemos llamar atajos y sumarios: porque una de las cosas más necesarias en la doctrina es la orden. Y así la Iglesia, para dar orden en la disciplina cristiana, hizo estos sumarios que están en el Catecismo, que quiere decir, enseñamiento y doctrina cristiana. Lo primero, la Iglesia, en tiempo de los Apóstoles, recogió y sumó todas las casas de la fe que derramadamente estaban escritas en las Sagradas Escrituras, en doce artículos de que se hace el Símbolo Apóstolico. Lo segundo, Dios (como tenemos dicho) sumó todas las leyes con que habemos de ordenar nuestras vidas en los diez mandamientos, que llamamos el Decálogo. Lo tercero, todo lo que es necesario para remedio y medicina de nuestras almas recogió Dios en los siete sacramentos. Lo cuarto, todo lo que podemos y debemos demandar a Dios y tratar con el, está sumado en la oracion del Paternoster, que nos ordenó el Hijo de Dios. Todo esto se llama Catecismo Cristiano que contiene estas cuatro cosas: Los articulos de la fé, los mandamientos de Dios, los siete sacramentos, y las oraciones cristianas." Vol. I, p.440.

53 See above, note 47, p. 108.

54 Pedro Rodriguez and Raul Lanzetti, <u>El Catecismo Romano: Fuentes e Historia del Texto de la Redaccion</u> (Pamplona: Univ. of Navarra, 1982), pp. 157-59.

55 Pedro Rodriguez, "El sentido de los sacramentos según el Catecismo Romano," <u>Scripta Theologica</u>, IX (1977), p. 963.

CHAPTER FIVE

THE ROMAN CATECHISM AND THE COUNCIL OF TRENT

The thirty-four bishops who assembled in the cathedral of St. Vigilius in a small Alpine town called Trent, on December 13, 1545, knew that much was riding on the outcome of their gathering. Nearly thirty years had passed since Martin Luther had posted his theses on the church door in Wittenberg -- a challenge which the Roman Church had to answer, however reluctantly, by convoking an Ecumenical Council. There was considerable risk in making this move (which explains, in part, this tragic thirty-year delay), for Conciliarism was far from dead. Yet the risk in not calling a Council was even greater. At least as great as any crisis which occasioned any previous Council, the Protestant Reformation demanded a full deployment of the Catholic Church's resources. Her <u>Magisterium</u> of bishops in communion with the Bishop of Rome had to meet in solemn council, to assess the damage and prescribe the remedies -- to effect, in a word, an authentic Reformation. That a Council was finally convoked under the aegis of the Papacy was a significant event. That it continued in being, and slowly but steadily increased its number of participating bishops -- in the face of formidable obstacles, distractions and interruptions of all kinds -- was more significant still. That, eighteen years later, it actually completed the task it had set for itself was most significant of all. For the Council of Trent affected Catholicism in a manner and to a degree unequalled by any other Council before or since.[1]

The Council of Trent was adjourned in December, 1563; the Roman Catechism was published in October, 1566. The chronology suggests a connection -- a connection which is further and even more strikingly indicated by the fact that the Roman Catechism is commonly referred to as the "Catechism of the Council of Trent."[2] To understand the Roman Catechism, then, it is important, if not essential, to understand the Council from which the Catechism came. Justifiably termed a "classic" for its timelessness, the Roman Catechism yet bears the imprint of its origin. Accordingly, the best approach to our immediate study of the Roman Catechism -- to which, after the preceding chapters as "prologue," we finally come -- is to study its history as an integral part of the history of the Council. Our study is one of <u>context</u>: seeing the Council and the Catechism in each other's light. First, we will look at the place of the Catechism in the Council; then, at the place of the Council in the Catechism.

cf
p. vii

I

Even if there had been no Luther with his own idea of "reformation" to force the issue, the call for the Council which eventually met at Trent would have been a call for reformation. The serious trouble in which the Church found herself at the beginning of the sixteenth century stemmed from various causes: abuse of power, worldliness, even lack of faith. But grave as these were, they were not the fundamental cause. Moral defection in high places need not yet have affected the whole body of the Church, and there was still the grace of faith conferred by the sacraments. What really made the failure in morals so effective in weakening the Church -- and the faith so ineffective in protecting it -- was the wretched state of <u>religious instruction</u> in the Church at large. More than any other single factor, religious ignorance explains the Protestant Reformation -- if not its internal dynamic and enduring culture, certainly its external occasion and initial success.

There is no lack of evidence for the fact of this ignorance. It was a standard lament throughout the fifteenth century.

> With so many parents and teachers there is either no care at all for the instruction and moral training or their children, or else it is the thing last thought of.³
>
> — Gerson

This was Gerson's comment sometime before the Council of Constance. And now, a century later, Luther himself makes a formal assertion -- all

111

the more telling when we remember that it was an assertion not altogether to his advantage.

> The deplorable conditions which I recently encountered when I was a visitor constrained me to prepare this brief and simple catechism or statement of Christian teaching. Good God, what wretchedness I behold! The common people, especially those who live in the country, have no knowledge whatever of Christian teaching, and unfortunately many pastors are quite incompetent and unfitted for teaching. Although the people are supposed to be Christian, are baptized, and receive the holy sacrament, they do not know the Lord's Prayer, the Creed, or the Ten Commandments. They live as if they were pigs and irrational beasts, and now that the Gospel has been restored, they have mastered the fine art of abusing liberty.[4]

The religious ignorance recognized and addressed by Luther in 1529 was, in the minds of the bishops finally gathered at Trent in 1545, compounded by what had happened in that interval of nearly two decades. For now there was not only the inertial and negative condition of simple ignorance. There was the added confusion and demoralization caused by unauthorized instruction which, if not erroneous, was incomplete. This new and dangerous instruction was, moreover, multiplied by the untimely marriage between heresy and technology: between Lutheranism and the printing press. That wholly new literary genre of catechesis noted in the preceding chapter, the "catechism," was proving to be the most effective enemy of the faith.[5] To save the faith by dispelling ignorance and correcting error among the faithful was what the Church in council now saw as her most urgent task.

The Council had been in formal existence just over a month when, on January 22, 1546, it made a momentous decision, which affected its proceedings in general and its catechetical concerns in particular. The Fathers decided to proceed simultaneously on questions of faith and questions of reform.[6] Doctrine and discipline -- the content of the faith and its pastoral application -- would be treated by the Council, therefore, as definitely inter-related matters. Neither one nor the other in isolation was the cause of the Church's crisis; to deal with one and not the other -- even temporarily -- would not resolve it. How this would affect the Council's handling of the specific questions of catechesis is obvious: equal emphasis was to be put on both terms of the phrase, "<u>instruction</u> in the <u>faith</u>." The distinction here is not quite the same as the facile one between content and method, but it is clear enough to identify and vindicate the wisdom of Trent: the realism with which the bishops saw their responsibility for the Church, and their best means to do something about it.

The application of this premier decision to catechesis came in due course. Once the Council issued its first formal decree, "on the Symbol of the Faith,"[7] it got down to specifics. It set its agenda regarding both the doctrine of the faith to be clarified, and the disciplinary structures and procedures to implement them. While the Fathers were discussing the sources of revelation -- the obvious starting point in doctrine, especially in view of the <u>sola Scriptura</u> of the heretics -- they set up a commission to report on the state of catechetical instruction. On April 5, three days before the decree "on the sacred books and the traditions to be received in the Church," the commission made its report.

> It is an abuse that profane literature and other superfluous studies should be avidly pursued, while the study of Sacred Scripture is neglected. The Scriptures are not read in the cathedrals and churches, nor in the public schools nor in the monasteries and other religious houses; with the result that the Christian people are taught less about Christianity than anything else. And children have no chance to learn, either from their parents or their teachers, what being a Christian means.
>
> The remedy is that those whose duty it is to teach the Christian people must make their principal study the Sacred Scriptures. ...
>
> Lest those who wish to pursue this study of Scripture do so imprudently because of their unpreparedness, the Council should decree the publication of a brief but comprehensive "introduction" to this study. This "introduction" should contain, in a clear and straightforward manner, the basic headings of Christian doctrine systematically formulated. It should provide a comprehensive and coherent plan for the study of Scripture, and thus eliminate the use of other "introductions" which by their involvement in subtleties and other unnecessary details only slow down and weary the student, and keep him from approaching the springs of Sacred Scripture and tapping them for the life and nourishment of the Christian people.

> As for the instruction of children and uneducated adults, for whom milk and not solid food is in order, the Council should authorize the publication of a catechism by men noted for learning and piety, written in both Latin and the vernacular, and based on the Sacred Scriptures and the Fathers of the Church. Thus trained by their teachers, they will be in a position to remember the Christian commitment they made in baptism, and will even be ready for some further study of Sacred Scripture.[8]

The commission thus proposed two basic instruments of instruction which the Council should take in hand: first, an "introductio" providing a "methodus" for the study of Sacred Scripture in view of teaching it; and secondly, a "catechismus" providing a rudimentary but comprehensive instruction in the faith, grounded in the Scriptures and the Fathers.

Through the month of April the proposal was discussed, but despite the unanimous judgment that it was indeed an urgent problem, opinions were divided as to just what the Council should do first. Should it begin with the "methodus"? And if so, which production from the Church's store of experience -- ranging all the way from ancient Cyprian through medieval Aquinas to modern Erasmus -- should be the working model?[9] The indecision of the Council Fathers on this point seems to have inclined them to table further formal discussion on what instructional instruments they should authorize. This otherwise inexplicable disappearance of catechesis from the Council's attention, on the evidence of the Acta, is no doubt best explained by the demands increasingly made on the Fathers, as the spring of 1546 advanced, to concentrate on the momentous questions of Original Sin and Justification. The clarification of the doctrine itself -- especially the doctrine on what was the nucleus of the Protestant heresy -- apparently pre-empted the Council from pursuing what was after all, the logically subsequent clarification process called catechesis.

Late in the following year, 1547, some two months before the end of this first period of the Council, the question of the catechism resurfaced. On November 14 the presiding Cardinal De Monte noted that since some of the Fathers had frequently proposed the Conciliar publication of a catechism, a libellus catechismi "which should contain everything necessary for the celebration of the sacraments," the question should be submitted to the whole assembly for a decision. An affirmative majority was apparently reached that day;[10] and on November 18 De Monte appointed a six-man commission "ad conficiendum libellum catechismi a sancta synodo."[11] It is to be noted that what the Council was now proposing was not a "methodus" on the Scriptures but a "catechism" on the sacraments. The exclusive emphasis on the sacraments in this resolution is probably due to the fact that during the second phase of the Council's first period, i.e., during its sojourn in Bologna, the only agenda before the Fathers were the sacraments, continuing what they had begun at Trent. And that they were now giving priority (if not exclusivity) to a catechism may be due to their apprehension that the Council might not survive its vicissitudes and so prematurely end.

Because of the de facto adjournment of the Council in February, 1548, nothing immediately came of the resolution -- nor, for that matter, of any of the discussions held at Bologna. Yet, as we noted, two precisions were made which advanced the Council's thinking on catechesis beyond its original position. First, there is no longer any mention of a "methodus"; whatever the Council will eventually come up with will be a "catechismus" -- although, of course, as we intimated in the previous chapter and will have occasion to elaborate in a later one, what kind of catechism it would be had yet to be determined.[12] And secondly, whatever else this catechism would treat of, emphatic provision would be made for the sacraments.

So stood matters through the next twelve years. On September 13, 1549, the Council, already dispersed from Bologna for over a year and a half, was formally prorogued. It did not reconvene until May 1, 1551, once more at Trent. But this second period was short-lived; it was again suspended sine die on April 28, 1552. The Council's dogmatic treatment of the sacraments, begun at Trent in 1547 and continued at Bologna, was pursued, issuing in the great decrees on the Eucharist and Penance in late 1551. But the complete review of the <u>septenarium</u> was far from finished; and the simultaneous work on ecclesiastical discipline, despite the appearance of some eight reform decrees,[13] showed even less progress toward a satisfactory overall progress of reform capable of stemming -- much less, of rolling back -- the Protestant tide. Finally, in January, 1562, after two more years of delay, the Fathers gathered once more at Trent to begin the third, final and decisive period of the Council.

This narrative summary should suffice to underline the crisis still facing the Catholic Church. If anything, it had worsened since the '40's. Lutheranism was now officially recognized as the religion of nearly half the German Empire; and a second and more ominous wave of Protestantism -- in the form of Calvin's "counter church" -- was tearing France asunder, and would soon do the same to the Netherlands.[14] Outside this pivotal confrontation of Habsburg and Valois in the center, the rest of Europe saw a hardening of issues which even more gravely threatened the Church. To the North and East whole countries seemed written off to the Protestants; while to the South and West the solid bastions of Spain and Portugal were riven by the explosive questions of internal Catholic union, where king was pitted against pope, with the bishops somewhere in between. No wonder that at Trent as the Fathers reassembled, the chances for a successful completion of the Council seemed slim indeed.[15] All the greater wonder, then, that in just under two years the Council did succeed in finishing its agenda. Along with all the disputed doctrines now defined and with all the reforms in discipline now programmed, the Council in this final decisive period of its history had come back to the <u>catechism</u> which had surfaced so early and then had lain submerged for so long.

Thus, if from one point of view the many delays regarding the catechism were regrettable, from another they were a blessing in disguise. If a catechism had been produced during the first or second periods of the Council, it would have lacked the precision and enrichment of doctrine, especially regarding the sacraments, which the Council completed only later. As it happened, a kind of providential arrangement can be discerned: the two great moments of the Catechism occurred at the very beginning (1546-47) and at the very end (1562-63) of the Council — at the beginning, to assure its priority of place in the Council's <u>purpose</u>; at the end, to reserve its full share in the Council's overall <u>achievement</u>.

The history of the final and definitive involvement of the Council of Trent with the Roman Catechism can be conveniently divided into two parts, the conciliar and the post-conciliar, each of them roughly two years in duration. The first or conciliar part corresponds to the final period of the Council itself, from its resumption in early 1562 to its formal approbation by the Pope in early 1564. This part can be subdivided into two phases: the "inactive" from 1562 into early 1563, and the "active" from the rest of 1563 to the end of the Council.

Despite its "inactivity," 1562 is included here because it reminds us of the "prehistory" we have treated of earlier in this chapter, culminating in the resolution in 1547 and the consequent drafts by various theologians on this or that part of an eventual catechism.[16] Besides, the Council Fathers had a keen sense of continuity with those earlier periods of the Council, despite the "newness" of this last period.

Eventually by March, 1563, "activity" began with the appointment of two theologians to collaborate with Cardinal Seripando in getting the work once more underway.[17] Through July and into September they were joined by more theologians, who apparently were each assigned different parts to prepare on the Creed, on the sacraments, on the Commandments and on the Lord's Prayer.[18] But then, because of the unwieldiness of the group, the press of other agenda, or whatever, it was decided in October to name a new <u>deputatio</u>: a select committee of four, to rework all that had been done to date, and to submit to the Council a final draft for formal approval.[19]

Coinciding with the work of this <u>deputatio</u>, and confirming its position in the ensemble of the Council's agenda, was the great reform constitution finally passed on November 11. Its statement on the catechism now in progress was a fitting commentary on the progress it envisaged for the whole Church.

> In order that the faithful may receive the sacraments with greater reverence and devotion, the Holy Council enjoins on all the bishops that they are to explain in an appropriate manner the nature and use of the sacraments to those to whom they themselves are ministering, and that likewise they are to see to it that the same is done -- piously and prudently and, if necessary and feasible, in the vernacular -- by every parish priest. (This instruction) is to be carried out according to the form to be prescribed by the Council in the catechesis for each sacrament, which by the bishops' directives will be accurately translated into the vernacular and explained to all the faithful by their parish priests.[20]

What progress the catechism was making, or even what intention the deputatio still had to finish the work, is not clear on the record, for events were now crowding the Council to push for final adjournment within a matter of weeks.[21] And so it happened. On December 3-4, in its Twenty-fourth Session, after re-reading and re-approving all its previous decrees, and before it declared itself officially adjourned, the Council voted, among other final decrees, the following:

> The Holy Council, in its second session under Pius IV, commissioned certain Fathers to study what censures should be made regarding suspect and dangerous books, and to report to the Council their recommendations. Now that this commission has done all it could in the matter, and that for a particular and appropriate judgment the sheer number and variety of books still leaves much to be done, the Council decrees that the commission's report be referred to the Roman Pontiff, so that by his judgment and authority the matter may be concluded and published. The Council decrees that the same be done regarding the Catechism mandated by the Fathers and likewise the Missal and the Breviary.[22]

The second part of this final history is post-conciliar, and runs from January, 1564, when the Council was formally approved by Pius IV,[23] to October, 1566, when the Catechism was promulgated by Pius V. Like the first part, it too can be subdivided into two phases, corresponding to the successive roles of these two Pontiffs.

In January Pius IV appointed a new deputatio. It consisted at first of three men, only one of whom had been a member of the group named by the Council in the preceding October. This was Muzio Calini, Archbishop of Zara. He was now joined by two Dominicans, Leonardo Marini and Egidio Foscarari. Both were bishops and had participated in the Council: Marini in its third period, Foscarari in the second and third, and also as a theologian in the first. Shortly after their appointment, a fourth was added to the group, another Dominican: Francisco Foreiro. These four -- Calini, Marini, Foscarari and Foreiro -- were the real authors of the Roman Catechism.[24] However, if this final exclusive list is to be strictly complete, two more names must be added: Carlo Borromeo and Giulio Pogiani. The former was Cardinal Secretary (and eventually a canonized saint) who, as in so much else related to the pontificate of his uncle Pius IV, was the guiding spirit in the Vatican.[25] The latter was the eminent humanist called in by Borromeo to produce a stylistically single piece of work by re-casting the others' contributions. These were given to Pogiani in the summer of 1564, and in four months the re-writing was finished and ready for the press.[26]

Throughout the year 1564, then, the actual composition of the Roman Catechism as we know it took place. Although not its author in the literal sense, Cardinal Borromeo "fathered" the Catechism in a sense that was truly unique. His seeing it through that year-long process gave it a unity -- a three-fold unity -- on the reality and significance of which this entire present study is but a commentary. First, Borromeo's supervision tightly unified the overall composition of the Catechism. There were no gaps in time, and consequent possible gaps in perspective, between the writing and the re-writing of the complete text. Secondly, matching this internal unity of the Catechism was its external unity: its complete harmonization with the total corpus of the Conciliar documents, all of which was the responsibility of Cardinal Borromeo to collate and digest in view of the special Congregation of Cardinals he had persuaded his uncle to set up as a permanent authoritative appeal board for the interpretation of the Council.[27]

Forged in that same year was a third unity, the broadest and most important of all. In the mind and heart of the young cardinal now finishing his first year as a priest and bishop, and soon to be sent to take over his see of Milan, a spiritual and pastoral integration had formed. Borromeo now had, as it were, the "handbook" of his reform program on its most basic pastoral level. It was one thing for the Roman Catechism to be consistent, first with itself and then with the Council of Trent as a whole. But so far, this unity was in itself but a matter of words on paper. It was another -- and far more important -- thing for the Catechism to be consistent, from the very beginning of its existence, with the actual implementation of the Council. The Roman Catechism had the immense good fortune to be, from its beginning, a working document -- at the heart of the pastoral reform of the great church of Milan, which, thanks to St. Charles Borromeo, was destined to be the prototype of the pastoral reform of the Universal "Tridentine" Church.

Early in 1565, just one year after Pius IV's confirmation of the Council, the Catechism was sent to the printer, Paolo Manuzio in Rome.[28] The Pope, however, did not live to see it published. The honor of appointing the final commission to review the proofs and of publishing the book by formal promulgation was reserved to his successor, Pius V, elected on January 7, 1566. Appropriately, the new Pope was -- like three of the original six men who authored the Catechism -- a Dominican, and -- eventually like another one of the six -- a canonized saint. In October 1566 the "Catechism for Parish Priests by the Decree of the Most Holy Council of Trent and published by Command of Pius V, Supreme Pontiff" was ready for distribution.[29] Unlike the Breviary and the Missal, which were also authorized by the Council and promulgated by Pius V, there was no prefatory Papal statement of promulgation. The Pope must have considered that this task was already well accomplished by the Preface in the Catechism itself, so that anything added by him seemed superfluous.

II

Having seen the place of the Roman Catechism in the Council of Trent, we now come to the second part of this chapter: the place of the Council of Trent in the Roman Catechism. The very first thing to note is that the Council's name occurs in the official title: "...ex decreto Ss. Concilii Tridentini." The Catechism would not exist but for the Council; and this fact of its genesis is reflected in the fact that generally the Catechism has been known through the centuries as "the Catechism of the Council of Trent." At the same time, however, there is another relationship involved in its genesis, which likewise occurs in the official title: "...Pii V., Pont. Max. iussu editus." And this second relationship has prompted -- and justified -- a second unofficial title. "the Roman Catechism."[30] If the Catechism was conceived in Trent, it was born in Rome.

The relationship of the Catechism to the Council is, therefore, qualified. The first and most striking evidence of this qualification is the fact that the Catechism is dependent on the Council for relatively little of its overall content. The Council did not intend, of course, to be comprehensive in its doctrine; it concentrated exclusively on the doctrinal error of the Protestants. Yet, even in these controverted areas, the Catechism's formal dependence on Trent is less than what one might have expected.

Altogether, there are but four direct quotations from the Council in the text of the Catechism: one in the chapter on Baptism, one on the Eucharist, and two on Penance.[31] Indirect quotations, or paraphrases, of Conciliar pronouncements occur eighteen times. [32] Significantly, as in the case of the direct quotations, all eighteen occur in the same one part of the Catechism, viz., Part II, on the sacraments. In other words, in the three remaining Parts -- on the Creed, on the Commandments and on prayer -- there is not one textual citation from the Council. We should note, of course, a third category of reference: where the Council is not quoted nor even paraphrased, but simply referred to as a source. In this category are some eight further passages. Of these, four occur in the Part on the sacraments, while of the remaining four one is on the Creed, three on the Commandments, and none on prayer.[33]

Both the relative paucity and the uneven distribution of these occurrences of "Trent" in the Catechism are important to note. In light of them it cannot be said that the Roman Catechism is simply a summary, a condensation for popular use, of the teaching of Trent. The Catechism could hardly ignore the Council which caused its existence; and, as we shall see, its recognition and implementation of the Council were an altogether adequate acquittal of its debt to it. Yet the first point to note here -- for it is very pertinent to our study -- is that the Council of Trent is "in" the Roman Catechism only as one more (and one which happened to be, moreover, the most recent) witness to the timeless faith of the Catholic Church.[34]

Although the Council of Trent is, therefore, only one constituent among others (and a relatively minor one at that) in the total ensemble of doctrine that is the Roman Catechism, yet the Catechism illustrates the Council as perhaps no other ecclesiastical document -- including the Conciliar acta themselves -- can do. This it does in two main respects. First, more clearly than any other single source, it shows what the Council intended primarily to do, and how that primary intention was actually fulfilled. Secondly, and again with incomparable clarity, it demonstrated the "spirit" of Trent: the manner or style in which the Council's intention was pursued and achieved.

From our incidental sketch of the Council's history, it will be recalled that its general purpose, which in some sense it shared with all its predecessors, was the reform of the Church, i.e., the renewal of the Church's faith and her life flowing from that faith.[35] This two-fold purpose -- renewal in both doctrine and discipline -- was in the case of Trent put in sharp focus by the Protestant revolution, which began precisely as an unauthorized "reformation" and which thus challenged the Catholic Church to effect within her communion an authentic reform. One of the first decisions of the Council was, as we saw,[36] to address simultaneously the doctrinal and the disciplinary or pastoral aspects of the crisis. By no coincidence that decision was accompanied by a resolution to draw up a "catechism," for catechesis is precisely the point where the doctrinal and the pastoral intersect. Because of the Protestant challenge this general purpose of Trent, which it would have had in common with any truly reforming council prior to

Protestantism, was heightened by its awareness of the urgency and specificity of the situation. Nowhere is this urgency and specificity more clearly stated than in the Preface of the Roman Catechism itself.

> Now, since the preaching of the divine word must never be interrupted in the Church, it is clear that at the present time greater zeal and devotion must be applied, to instruct and encourage the faithful with sound, unchanging doctrine as with life-sustaining food. For many false prophets have gone out into the world. ... with diverse and strange doctrines to corrupt the minds of the Christian people. Their hateful campaign, fueled with satanic craft, has made such progress that there seems to be no limiting it. ... Illustrious nations which once devoutly held the true Catholic religion bequeathed them by their ancestors have now repudiated it and gone after, with loud acclaim, what was most repugnant to the faith of their fathers. No country however remote, no place however secure, no corner of Christendom can be found where this deadly infiltration is not a threat.[37]

And more specifically still:

> Those whose interest is to corrupt the minds of the faithful know that they cannot do so by immediate contact, by pouring into each one's ear their poison. They have adopted a much easier and far-reaching strategy for circulating their impious errors. There are, of course, their ponderous tomes assailing the Catholic faith, in which no great skill is required to spot the blatant heresies. No, the real danger lies in their flood of pamphlets which, under the disguise of piety, deceive the unsuspecting minds of simple souls with incredible ease.[38]

To meet this urgent and specific need, the Roman Catechism came into being. It was thus <u>the</u> work of the Council in the most concrete and comprehensive sense. Here was the "cutting edge" of the Catholic Reform in both its doctrinal and its disciplinary aspects. Just as the Roman Catechism itself contains the best description of the need to be addressed, so -- in the same Preface, immediately following the passage cited -- it provides the best description of what the Church intends to do about it.

> Accordingly, the Fathers at the Ecumenical Council of Trent, in their determination to apply the best possible remedy to this disastrous state of affairs, did not consider their task accomplished by simply defining the major points of Catholic doctrine against the heresies of our time. Rather, they saw that they had to come up with a

certain expression and pattern of instructing the Christian people in the rudiments of the faith, which would have to be followed in every local Church by those entrusted with the official duties of pastor and teacher.[39]

For all the immediacy and concreteness of these passages, however, it may be noted that the word "Protestantism" itself never occurs. The time and place are evidently the second half of the sixteenth century in western and central Europe; but neither "the present time" nor the "false prophets" nor the "illustrious nations" are formally identified. Merely a stylistic convention, perhaps. Yet something truly symbolic can be detected here -- as the history of the Tridentine Church will amply verify. The <u>catechesis</u> here set forth is no mere <u>ad hoc</u> antidote. It will be as applicable in America or Asia as it is in Europe, in the eighteenth or twentieth centuries as in the sixteenth. That is why the Roman Catechism is devoted to the <u>whole</u> of Christian doctrine, not just to what was contested by the Protestants, and why it provides for the instruction of <u>all</u> the Christian people, not just those most susceptible to heretical influence. That is why, moreover, it is not a "<u>summa</u>" in the scholastic sense, but rather a "<u>summa</u>" in the broadest <u>pastoral</u> sense.

> Although there are already many works of this kind (i.e., of general instruction in the rudiments of the faith) praiseworthy for their learning and piety, the Fathers nevertheless considered it their duty to issue by authority of the Council a book from which parish priests and any others having a teaching assignment in the Church can find and apply sure principles for the instruction of the faithful... For just as there is but one Lord and one faith, so there should be one overall determining principle for teaching the faith and forming the people in all the duties of their Christian life.[40]

The three passages here cited in sequence from the Preface of the Catechism contain the only extended reference to the Council of Trent in the entire work. There are, as we have seen, some further references but they are relatively few and unevenly distributed. So remote, indeed, is the immediate historical Trent, that it is easy to see why it probably never occurred to the authors to call their work "<u>Catechismus Tridentinus</u>." And yet the Council of Trent is there not only in its clearly declared <u>intentions</u> at once doctrinal and pastoral, but perhaps even more so in its "style" -- its "spirit": that elusive yet exact positioning of its purposes and resources within the total life that is the Church. This "spirit of Trent" which continued to enliven the Church through the next four hundred years, mainly because it was so perfectly distilled and illustrated in the Roman Catechism, can be summarized under two adjectives: "militant" and "triumphalist."

The classic description of these two components of the "spirit of Trent" occurs, once more, in the Preface, following the passages already cited. Neither term --"militant" nor "triumphant" -- is to be found there,[41] but the reality denoted by them is there, in what could well be the most important single extended passage in the entire Catechism.

> In view of the background for this book [i.e., as described in the previous three passages cited], proper order requires that, before we move on to the enumeration of the headings in which our summary of doctrine is contained, we should put down certain basic principles which the pastor must before all else have clearly in mind.
>
> In order that parish priests may know to what goal all their plans, labors and studies are directed, and how they can more surely attain that goal, they should constantly keep in mind as a first principle and summary of all Christian knowledge those words of our Savior: "This is eternal life, to know Thee the one true God, and Him whom Thou hast sent, Jesus Christ." Hence the task of anyone teaching in the name of the Church is primarily this: to make the faithful eager to know "Jesus Christ and Him Crucified." The faithful must be taught to hold with conviction and devotion the truth that "no other name has been given men whereby they are to be saved," for Christ alone is the propitiation for our sins.
>
> "By this we may be sure that we know Him, if we keep his commandments." Here is the second principle, intimately connected with the first, viz., that this life must be lived by the faithful, not in idleness as though it were somehow automatic; but with the intent to walk in the same way in which He walked. For the faithful this means, as St. Paul explained in his Pastoral Letters, that they aim at righteousness, faith, love and peace, for Christ gave Himself for us to redeem us from all iniquity, and to purify for Himself a people of His own who are zealous for good deeds.
>
> Our Lord not only preached but showed by His example the truth that the Law and the Prophets depend on love. And His Apostle reaffirmed the same truth that love is the one purpose of the Commandments and the fulfillment of the law. There can be no doubt, then, that the principal task of the teacher is to motivate the

faithful to love this immeasurable goodness of God toward us and to seek this goodness as our one ultimate and unchanging happiness, and thereby to fulfill the words of the Psalmist: "Whom have I in heaven but Thee. And there is nothing upon earth that I desire besides Thee."

This is that more excellent way of which St. Paul speaks when he subordinated all his teaching to this love which never ends. Hence, whatever may be the specific content of one's teaching -- whether it be about something to be believed, or something to be hoped for, or something to be done -- it must be presented in the light of the love of God. Thus it will be clear to anyone that whatever is done by Christian virtue comes from no other source and is directed to no other purpose than that one beginning and end which is love.[42]

The exigency of pastoral labor, mobilizing the resources of the existing clerical order and channelling them into a comprehensive, clear-cut program of religious instruction for all the faithful: this is the "militancy" that is the first component of the authentic "spirit" of Trent proclaimed by -- and embodied in -- the Roman Catechism. The second component, which complements and "quickens" the first is the expansiveness of Christocentric charity, the "triumphalism" of audacious, confident love. <u>Exigent discipline</u> and <u>expansive affection</u>: these are the two components -- the "militancy" and the "triumphalism" respectively -- of the Council of Trent and the Roman Catechism.

"Militant" and "triumphalist," then, was the Catholic Church as she emerged from the Council of Trent in 1563. Within two years thereafter the Roman Catechism had fixed in timeless language the true sense of these two terms. The dominant -- and in a sense the only -- task facing the Church in her program of reform was a <u>renewed catechesis</u>, at once "militant" in the exigency of its transmitting the faith whole and entire, and "triumphalist" in the expansiveness of its subsuming and centering all in the love of Christ.

NOTES

1   For the most comprehensive modern history of the Council of Trent, see Hubert Jedin, <u>Geschichte des Konzils von Trent</u>. Freiburg-im-Breisgau: Herder, 1949-75. 4 vols.

2   <u>"The Catechism of the Council of Trent"</u> is not its official title. Neither is <u>"The Roman Catechism."</u> What appears on the title page on the original 1566 edition is <u>"Catechismus ex decreto Ss. Concilii Tridentini ad Parochos Pii V. Pont. Max. iussu editus."</u> This title has been retained in all subsequent official editions, i.e., in those issued by the Holy See. See below, note 30, p. 133.

3   "...multorum parentum et magistrorum cura vel nulla vel ultima est de parvulorum suorum moribus, et eorum disciplinata custodia." Jean Gerson, <u>De Parvulis ad Christum trahendis</u> (Glorieux, Vol. IX, p. 673).

4   "Diesen Catechismen oder Christliche lere ein solche kleine schlechte einfeltige form zustellen, hat mich gezwungen und gedrungen die kleglich elende not, so ich newlich erfaren habe, da ich auch ein Visitator war. Hilf lieber Gott, wie manchen iamer hab ich gesehen, das der gemeine man doch so gar nichts weis von der Christlichen lere, sonderlich auff den dörffen, und leider veil Pfarher fast ungeschickt und untuchtig sind zu leren, und sollen doch alle Christen heissen, getaufft sein und der heiligen Sacrament geniessen, konnen wider Vater unser noch den Glauben odder Zehen gepot, leben dahin wie das liebe vihe und unvernunfftige sewe, und nu das Evangelion komen ist, dennoch fein gelernt haben aller freiheit meistenlich zu missgebrauchen." From the Preface to his <u>Small Catechism</u> (Weimar edition, Vol. XXX,1, pp. 264, 266).

5   The contrast between weighty theological treatises and facile catechetical pamphlets -- to the distinct advantage of the latter in terms of effectiveness -- is explicitly recognized by the Roman Catechism (Preface, 6; p. 3). See below, note 38, pp. 135-36.

6   Societas Goerresiana, <u>Concilium Tridentinum: Diariorum, Actorum, Epistolarum, Tractatum: Nova Collectio, Tomus IV: Concilii Tridentini Actorum: Prima Pars</u> (Freiburg - im- Breisgau: Herder, 1904), pp. 569-72. (This series will be hereafter referred to as "CT".)

It is noteworthy that the last speaker in this debate of January 22, Bonuccio, General of the Servite Order, had this to say: "Ex haereticorum libris facile haberi posse malos nostros mores ex mala institutione procedere idque ab ipsis haereticis comprobari." ibid., p. 572.

7   Ibid., pp. 579-81. See Conciliorum Ecumenicorum Decreta (Basel:Herder, 1962), p. 638.

8   "Abusus est, quod dum immodice vel litteris profanis vel quaestionibus quibuslibet superfluis incumbitur, negliguntur interim studia sacrarum litterarum et non est, qui eas legat neque in ecclesiis cathedralibus neque in publicis gymnasiis neque in monasteriis monarchorum neque in conventibus aliorum regularium, ita ut populus Christianus in nulla fere doctrina minus instructus sit quam in Christiana, unde et contigit, ut pueri neque a parentibus neque a magistris in re Christianae vitae, quam in baptismo professi sunt, possit erudiri.

"Remedium est, ut praecipuum studium eorum, a quibus instruendis est populus Christianus, sit in ipsis sacris litteris...

"Ne vero velut imparati in sacrosanctam Scripturam temere irrumpere videantur, qui in ea proficere cupiunt; decernat sancta Synodus, ut una quaedam brevis et compendiosa introductio habeatur, quae pure et sincere communia loca doctrinae Christianae per sententias contineat, sitque velut communis et concors omnium studiosorum methodus ad sacras litteras, ne tam prolixis diversisque et adversis introductionibus remorati et confatigati diu detineatur, quin ipsos sacrae Scripturae fontes adire possit et ex eis haurire, quae aliquando in populum Christianum effundant.

"Pro pueris autem et adultis indoctis erudiendis, quibus lacte opus est et non solido cibo, curet sancta Synodus a viris doctis et piis in lingua latina et vulgari edi catechismum ex ipsa sacra Scriptura et patribus orthodoxis excerptum, ut illius paedagogia instituti a magistris suis et memores sint Christianae professionis, quam fecerunt in baptismo, et praeparentur ad studia sacrarum litterarum. ..." CT, V, pp. 72-73.

9   "De methodo: Plurimi probant factam a Magistro sententiarum, demptis delendis. Aliqui illam Cypriani, aliqui Enchiridion Erasmi, aliqui divi Thomae. Aliqui quod nova fiat, in qua tantum articuli fidei, sacramenta et similia comprehendantur. Non fiat tamen methodi mentio in decreto, antequam edatur. Aliqui censent, esse faciendam nunc mentionem, ut synodus saltem ex verecundia eam facere compellatur. Et si est facienda, quidam cuperet committendam universitati Parisiensi, quidam ex synodo deligendis. Aliqui verentur, si fieret nova methodus, ne detrahatur iis qui alias fecerunt, quasi illae reprobentur.

"De catechismo: Quod fiat, et ea tantum, quae ad fidei fundamenta spectant, (in eo) ponantur, fiatque a synodo. Aliqui tamen cupiunt, non fidei mentionem illius, antequam edatur. (Aliqui quod nunc fiat mentio.)" from the "Censurae" of the General Congregation held on April 15, 1546 (CT, V, p. 120). The reference to "Cyprian" is explained by the mistaken medieval attribution of a late fourth-century work on the Creed by Rufinus of Aquilea.

This entire discussion on the catechism had been under the rubric, "Decretum de lectoribus et praedicatoribus Sacrae Scripturae propositum," which reflects the influence of the dogmatic decree in the previous Session IV, and the need now to follow it up with a disciplinary decree remedying the abuses of Scripture teaching. Jedin (op. cit., Vol. II, p. 108, note 1) calls the first draft of this decree "Form I" (see CT, V, pp. 105-08). "Form II" (CT,V, pp. 125-27) omits all mention of "catechism" or even "method." The same is true of the third draft, or "Form III" (CT, V, pp. 226-28), and the final decree as approved in Session V, June 17 (CT, V, pp. 241-43). See Conciliorum ... decreta, pp. 641-43.

10   CT, VI, p. 589.

11   Ibid., p. 602.

12   Thus, for instance, in the discussion on November 14, 1547, one bishop reminded the assembly that a proposed "liber sacerdotalis" -- a kind of manual for administering the sacraments, was already on the agenda (see notes on August 30, 1547, in CT, VI, p. 416); another bishop spoke of the need of this libellus "tum pro instruendis baptizandis tum episcopis et sacerdotibus" (ibid., p. 589). And some others, including the Master General of the Dominicans, did not want the libellus to be called a "catechism" at all (ibid.).

13   Faithful to its initial policy, the Council deliberated on disciplinary reform along with its deliberations on doctrine. There were three reform decrees issued in the first period of the Council (in Sessions V, VI and VII, in 1546-47), two more in the second period (Sessions XIII and XIV, in 1551), and three more in the third period (Sessions XXI, XXII and XXIII, in 1562-63), up to the "great" reform decree of November 11, which we will consider later (see text, pp.117-18, and note 20, p. 131).

14   The "second generation" of the Protestant movement was dominated by John Calvin, whose ecclesiology (reflecting his theology) formalized the rupture of Christendom into a situation that the "first generation" under Luther only dimly imagined and scarcely provided for. This is mentioned here only as a reminder of the considerable difference between the first and the last periods of Trent, in terms of the "existential" order of things -- both religious and secular -- which the Council had to face.

15   An additional problem, which implied far more than a procedural nicety, was the question: was the Council in 1562 a

resumption of the one suspended in 1552, or was it a new Council? Pius IV and his legates warily skirted the question until, with the evident success of the 1562 sessions, the problem receded.

16   The members of this first commission dating from November, 1547, were the following bishops: Benedetto de Nobili ("Aciensis"), Robert Cenan ("Abricensis"), Alviso Lipomano (coadjutor bishop of Verona), Gian Pietro Farretto ("Mylensis"), Egidio Falcetta ("Caprulanus"), Cornelio Musso ("Bituninus") who later resigned and was replaced by Balthasar Limpo de Musa ("Portuensis"). All were Italian, except Cenan who was French, and Limpo who was Portugese. No trace of their work remains. (See above, note 11, p. 129.)

17   The two theologians were Cristobal Santo-Tis, an Augustinian, and Miguel Medina, a Franciscan, both Spaniards. Besides whatever revisions in general they may have made, they were said to have worked specifically on the Creed: Medina on the Fourth Article (on the Redemption), and Santo-Tis on the Ninth (on the Church). See Pio Paschini, Il Catechismo Romano del Concilio di Trento (Rome: Lateran, 1923), p. 43. As for Seripando, he died that same month (March 17, 1563); but his involvement with the idea of a catechism, as a veteran of the Council from its very beginning, had earned for him the title, "Father of the Catechism." See Bellinger, op.cit., p. 29.

The origin of this unofficial title is hard to trace. It may have come from his friend Muzio Calini, who said at his funeral: "As for myself I would prefer such a death to the dignity of the papacy, for around his deathbed the angels were waiting to carry this good and holy man to paradise" (quoted by Jedin, Papal Legate to the Council of Trent; St. Louis: Herder, 1947; p. 701). Seripando clearly deserves special recognition for his role in this history. But perhaps the title "Grandfather of the Catechism" may be more appropriate. For his contribution was more indirect, clarifying the basic premise of "reform" as the essential background of the eventual book. Genuine reform could come, he asserted, only with "inner reform: the awakening of a spirit of religion based on firm dogmatic ground" (ibid., p. 263). And this meant recourse to the sources of faith, not to philosophy. "The preacher should proclaim simply the positive contents of the Scriptures and not indulge in speculations, and he should impart to the children Christian doctrine, not in the form of an excerpt from philosophy but under the guidance of Holy Writ" (ibid., p. 286). See CT, I, p. 505; V, p. 26.

If Seripando, by our nomination, is better named "Grandfather of the Catechism," the title "Father of the Catechism" goes -- by Seripando's own implicit nomination -- to St. Charles Borromeo. See below, note 25, p. 132.

18 These were: Pedro Fuentiduena (on the Seventh Article: the Last Judgment), three unnamed French theologians (on Baptism, Confirmation and Eucharist), Niccolo Ormaneto (on Penance), Benedetto Arias Montano (on Extreme Unction), Damiano Hortulano (on Holy Orders), Pedro Fernandez (on Matrimony), four unnamed French theologians (on the first four Commandments), Juan de Ludena, a Spanish Dominican (on the Fifth Commandment), Benedetto Herba, an Italian Dominican (on the Sixth Commandment), Eliseo Capys, an Italian Dominican (on the Seventh Commandment), Alfonso de Contreras, a Spanish Franciscan (on the Eighth Commandment), Juan de Fonseca (on the Ninth and Tenth Commandments), and several unnamed French and Flemish theologians (on prayer). See Bellinger, op. cit., p. 30.

19 The members of this new four-man commission were:Muzio Calini (Archbishop of Zara), Giancarlo Bovio (bishop of Astuni), Antonio Sebastiano Mintorno (bishop of Ugento), and Pedro de Fuentiduena. CT, II, p. 706.

20 "Ut fidelis populus ad suscipienda sacramenta maiori cum reverentia, atque animi devotione accedat, praecipit sancta Synodus episcopis omnibus, ut non solum, cum haec per se ipsos erunt populo administranda, prius illorum vim et usum pro suscipientium captu explicent, sed etiam idem a singulis parochis pie prudenterque, etiam lingua vernacula, si opus sit, et commode fieri poterit, servari studeant, iuxta formam a sancta Synodo in catechesi singulis sacramentis praescribendam; quam episcopi in vulgarem linguam fideliter verti, atque a parochis omnibus populo exponi curabunt; necnon ut inter Missarum solemnia aut divinarum celebrationum, sacra eloquia et salutis monita eadem vernacula lingua singulis diebus festivis vel solemnibus explanant; eademque in omnium cordibus, postpositis inutilibus quaestionibus, inserere atque eos in lege Domini erudire studeant." Decretum de Reformatione, cap.7 (Sess. XXIV, Nov. 11,1563). Canones et Decreta Sac. Oecum. Conc. Tridentini (Turin: Marietti, 1913), pp. 187-88. Conciliorum ... Decreta. p. 740.

As already noted (see above, note 13, p. 129), the Council issued many "reform decrees" in its earlier sessions; and in fact it would issue one more such decree at its final session (XXV). However, this decree of November 11, 1563, is frequently referred to as the reform decree of Trent, because of its content (twenty-one wide-ranging and detailed capita) and its impact as being in effect the Council's "last word" on reform.

21 Besides the natural desire to get back to their dioceses after two intensive years of work, and before another winter set in, the bishops had an additional motive for urgency. Pius IV fell gravely ill, and the possibility of his death, and the complications posed by both the interim sede vacante and the election of a new pope

convinced the Council Fathers of the expendibility of much of their remaining agenda.

22 "Sacrosancta Synodus in secunda sessione sub sanctissimo domino nostro Pio IV celebrata delectis quibusdam patribus commisit, ut de variis censuris ac libris, vel suspectis vel perniciosis, quid facto opus esset, considerarent atque ad ipsam sanctam Synodum referrent; audiens nunc, huic operi ab eis extremam manum impositam esse, nec tamen ob librorum varietatem et multitudinem distincte et commode possit a sancta Synodo diiudicari: praecipit, ut, quidquid ab illis praestitum est, sanctissimo Romano Pontifici exhibeatur, ut eius iudicio atque auctoritate terminetur et evulgetur. Idemque de catechismo a patribus, quibus illud mandatum fuerat, et de missali et breviario fieri mandat." ibid., p. 773. This is the entire decree. Entitled "Super indici librorum, catechismo, breviario et missali," it was issued along with six other equally brief "decreta publica die secunda sessionis," December 3-4, 1563.

23 In the bull Benedictus Deus, January 26, 1564.

24 "Von allen Katechismusbearbeitern haben die vier von Pius IV, ernannten die Hauptarbeit geleistet, so dass man mit Recht sagen kann, dass diese die eigentlichen Verfasser des Romischen Katechismus waren." Bellinger, op. cit., p. 35. The "curricula vitae" of all four men are given, in varying lengths, by Bellinger (pp. 35-37), Paschini (pp. 17-23), Rodriguez-Lanzetti (pp.91-106), and John Baptist de Toth, De auctoritate theologica Catechismi Romani (Budapest, 1941), pp.13-15.

25 "A man of fruits, not of flowers, of actions and not words" was Cardinal Seripando's description of Borromeo (Jedin, op. cit., p. 507). This justifies our conjecture that Seripando would gladly have transferred the title "Father of the Catechism" to the young Cardinal of Milan, forty-two years his junior, whom in some remarkable ways he himself had "fathered." (See above, note 17, p. 130). Borromeo's close personal friendship with Forscarari and Foreiro was probably as important, regarding his influence on the course of the work on the catechism, as his relationship with his uncle the Pope. One indication of the importance of his role is the fact that after his departure from Rome for Milan, in September 1564, the progress of the Catechism slowed down notably. (See Paschini, op. cit., p. 25.) By all accounts, the personal charm of the saint was a truly providential factor in this history.

26 If and to what extent Pogiani contributed anything to the Catechism beyond the reworking of the others' contribution is uncertain. It has been suggested that he may have written some portions of Part IV.

Besides Borromeo's absence in 1565, Rodriguez-Lanzetti suggest another possible reason for the delay in getting the Catechism to press: viz., the trouble Carranza was still having with the Inquisition. (op. cit., pp. 118-19)

27 The Sacred Congregation of the Council (S. Cardinalium Concilii Tridentini Interpretum) was established by Pius IV in August, 1564, and continued to exist under that title until 1967, when Paul VI renamed it the Sacred Congregation for the Clergy. Catechetics is still one of the areas reserved to this Congregation.

28 To see the work through the press, i.e., to proof-read the galleys and make any final revisions, a third deputatio (following the first in October, 1563, and the second in January,1564) was named by Pius IV in April, 1566. This committee, headed by Cardinal Gulielmo Sirleto, comprised Leonardo Marini and Tomas Manriquez, with others as consultors, including Eustachio Locatelli and Mariano Vittori. Marini, the sole "survivor" of the previous deputatio, was called back to Rome by Sirleto. (Calini and Foreiros had left Rome before the end of 1564, and in December, 1563, Foscarari had died.) Manriquez was a Dominican and Master of the Sacred Palace, a close associate of Pius V. Sirleto's role in this final phase of the Catechism's composition was very active. For his "dictamina," especially on Part IV of the Catechism, see Rodriguez-Lanzetti, op. cit., pp. 117-20 and 349-79.

Son of the famous Venetian printer, Aldo Manuzio, Paolo came to Rome in 1561 at the invitation of Seripando. The first book from his press "ad aedes populi Romani" was Pole's de Concilio. Because of conflicts with some officials under Pius V, he left Rome before the expiration of his twelve-year contract. The "Vatican Press" was not established until 1587 under Sixtus V. See Jedin, op. cit., pp. 557-61.

29 Pius V was not wholly pleased with the final product. For some reason Manuzio's edition had no divisions in the text, e.g., into parts and chapters. Writing to Cardinal Hosius about getting out a Polish edition, the Pope told him to put some divisions into the text, but otherwise to make no changes. See Rodriguez-Lanzetti, p. 213; Ludwig von Pastor, The History of the Popes from the close of the Middle Ages, Vol.XVI (St Louis: Herder, 1928), p.193.

30 The title "Roman Catechism" first occurred in the (Latin) edition printed one year later in Germany (Dillingen, 1567). Cardinal Von Truchsess of Augsburg, who got permission for this first edition north of the Alps, on the condition that Canisius supervised the job, wrote in his preface this explanation of the new title: "We gladly hear and approve that this book should be called the Roman Catechism, not only because it was written, approved and published in Rome, but because it provides such rich and ample evidence of the faith and teaching of Rome, i.e., that authentically pure faith and sound teaching which the Apostle Peter first gave to the Romans." See Rodriguez-Lanzetti, pp. 224-25.

31   The four passages in the Roman Catechism, with their respective direct quotations from the Council, are the following:
   1) II, 2, 42 (p. 112): on the effects of Baptism (Sess. V, cap. 5; DS 1515).
   2) II, 4, 38 (p.144): on transubstantiation (Sess. XIII, can. 2; DS 1652).
   3) II, 5, 23 (p.167): on contrition (Sess. XIV, cap. 4; DS 1676).
   4) II, 5, 66 (p.184): on satisfaction (Sess. XIV, cap. 8; DS 1690).

32   The eighteen passages in the Roman Catechism, with their respective indirect quotations from the Council, are the following:
   1) II, 2, 24 (pp. 105-106): on the validity of Baptism by non-Catholics (Sess. VII, can. 4 on Baptism; DS 1617).
   2) II, 2, 43 (p.112): on concupiscence remaining after Baptism (Sess. V, can. 5; DS 1515).
   3) II, 2, 50 (p. 115): on justification as not only removal of sin but infusion of grace, i.e., internal renovation (Sess. VI, cap. 7; DS 1528).
   4) II, 4, 42 (p. 146): on the word "transubstantiation" (Sess. XIII, can. 2; DS 1652).
   5) II, 4, 55 (p.150): on the three kinds of communicants (Sess. XIII, cap. 8; DS 1648).
   6) II, 4, 57 (p. 152): on receiving Holy Communion when in mortal sin (Sess. XIII, can. 11; DS 1661).
   7) II, 4, 65 (p.154): on the two species not for all communicants (Sess. XXI, cap. 1; DS 1727).
   8) II, 4, 67 (p. 155): on the laity receiving from priests, and priests communicating themselves (Sess. XIII, cap. 8, DS 1648).
   9) II, 4, 68 (p. 156): on explaining the Mass to the people (Sess. XX, cap. 8; DS 1749).
   10) II, 4, 72 (p. 157): on the reality of the sacrifice of the Mass (Sess. XX, can. 1; DS 1751).
   11) II, 4, 74 (p. 157): on the ordination of the Apostles as priests (Sess. XX, cap. 2; DS 1752).
   12) II, 4, 78 (p. 158): on the propitiatory character of the Mass (Sess. XX, can. 3; DS 1753).
   13) II, 5, 1 (p. 159): on the distinction between Baptism and Penance (Sess. XIV, cap. 1 and can. 2; DS 1568, 1701-02).
   14) II, 5, 13 (p. 164): on the three parts of Penance (Sess. XIV, cap. 3; DS 1673).
   15) II, 5, 41 (p. 174): on the need for integral confession because of the judicial character of the sacrament (Sess. XIV, cap. 5; DS 1679).
   16) II, 5, 65 (p. 183): on punishment left over after remission of guilt (Sess.XIV, cap. 12; DS 1712).
   17) II, 6, 3 (p. 190): on the reality of the remission of sin in Extreme Unction (Sess. XIV, can. 2; DS 1717).
   18) II, 6, 5 (p. 190): on the matter of Extreme Unction: oil blessed by the bishop (Sess. XIV, can. 1; DS 1695).

33   The eight passages in the Roman Catechism, with their respective references to the Council in general, are the following:

1) I, 3, 2 (p. 18): on the results of original sin.
2) II, 2, 30 (p. 108): on baptismal sponsors.
3) II, 3, 5 (p. 123): on the distinction between Baptism and Confirmation.
4) II, 4, 10 (p. 133): on the number of the sacraments.
5) II, 4, 30 (p. 142): on the Real Presence.
6) III, 2, 11 (p. 228): on the veneration of images.
7) III, 7, 5 (p. 266): on canonical penalties for certain sins of lust.
8) III, 7, 11 (p. 269): on pastoral counselling for purity.

To these should be added the references to the Council made in the Preface (5-8; pp. 2-3), regarding which see pp. 123-24.

34 This central theme of our entire study is clearly enunciated in the one part of the Catechism where the Council is given prominence, viz., in the Preface (especially, 5-10; pp. 2-5). That is why the rest of this chapter is almost exclusively a commentary on those passages.

35 "Reform" was the dominant theme in all the medieval Councils of the Latin Church. For the full import of this term, see Gerhart B. Ladner, <u>The Idea of Reform: its Impact on Christian Thought and Action in the Age of the Fathers</u> (Cambridge: Harvard University Press, 1959).

36 See above, pp. 112-13.

37 "At vero, cum haec divini praedicatio nunquam intermitti in Ecclesia debeat, tum certe hoc tempore maiori studio et pietate elaborandum est, ut sana et incorrupta doctrina, tanquam pabulo vitae, fideles nutriantur et confirmentur. Exierunt enim falsi prophetae in mundum ... ut variis doctrinis et peregrinis Christianorum animos depravarent. Quae in re illorum impietas, omnibus Satanae artibus instructa, tam longe progressa est, ut nullis fere certis finibus contineri posse videatur. ... Nam, omittamus nobilissimas provincias, quae olim veram et catholicam religionem, quam a maioribus acceperant, pie et sancte retinebant, nunc autem, derelinquentes viam rectam, erraverunt, atque in eo se maxime pietatem colere palam profitentur, quod a patrum suorum doctrina quam longissime recesserunt; nulla tam remota regio, at tam munitus locus, nullus Christianae Reipublicae angulus inveniri potest, quo haec pestis occulte irrepere non tentarit." Praef., 5; p. 2.

38 "Qui enim fidelium mentes corrumpere sibi proposuerunt, cum fieri nullo modo posse intelligerent, ut cum omnibus coram colloquerentur, et in eorum aures venenatas voces infunderent, idem alia ratione aggressi, multo facilius ac latius impietatis errores disseminarunt. Nam praeter illa ingentia volumina, quibus Catholicam fidem evertere conati sunt (a quibus tamen cavere, cum apertam haeresim continerent, non magni fortasse laboris ac diligentiae fuit), infinitos etiam libellos conscripserunt, qui cum pietatis speciem praeseferrent, incredibile est, quam facile incautos simplicium animos deceperint." <u>ibid</u>., 6; pp. 2-3.

39 "Quamobrem Patres Oecumenicae Tridentinae Synodi, cum tanto et tam pernicioso huic malo salutarem aliquam medicinam adhibere maxime cuperent, non satis esse putarunt, graviora Catholicae doctrinae capita contra nostri temporis haereses decernere; sed illud praeterea sibi faciendum censuerunt, ut certam aliquam formulam et rationem Christiani populi ab ipsis fidei rudimentis instituendi traderent, quam in omnibus Ecclesiis illi sequerentur, quibus legitimi pastoris et doctoris munus obeundum esset. " ibid., 7; p. 3.

40 "Multi quidem adhuc in hoc scriptionis genere cum magna pietatis et doctrinae laude versati sunt; sed tamen Patribus visum est maxime referre, si liber Sanctae Synodi auctoritate ederetur, ex quo parochi, vel omnes alii, quibus docendi munus impositum est, certa praecepta petere atque depromere ad fidelium aedificationem possent; ut, quemadmodum 'unus est Dominus, una fides,' ita etiam una sit tradendae fidei, ad omniaque pietatis officia populum Christianum erudiendi communis regula atque praescriptio." ibid., 8; p. 3.

41 Interestingly, the two terms are found, and in conjunction, in the Catechism's description of the Church in the Ninth Article of the Creed (I, 10, 5; p. 59). There the Church is seen as consisting of two parts: the "triumphant" in heaven , and the "militant" on earth. And in the following section (I, 10, 6; ibid.) the Catechism insists that these two realities are not "two churches" but "two parts of one Church." See below, Chapter VII, p. 182.

42 "Quae cum ita sint, antequam ad ea singillatim tractanda accedamus, quibus huius doctrinae summa continetur; institutae rei ordo postulat, ut pauca quaedam exponantur, quae pastores considerare sibique ante oculos proponere in primis debent." Praef., 9; p. 3.

"Igitur, ut sciant, quoniam, veluti ad finem, omnia eorum consilia, labores et studia referenda sint, quove pacto id, quod volunt, facilius consequi et efficere possint; illud primum videtur esse, ut semper meminerint, omnem Christiani hominis scientiam hoc capite comprehendi: vel potius, quemadmodum Salvator noster ait, 'haec est vita aeterna ut cognoscant te solum verum Deium et quem misisti Jesum Christum.' Quamobrem in eo praecipue ecclesiastici doctoris opera versabitur, ut fideles scire ex animo cupiant, Iesum Christum et hunc crucifixum; sibique certo persuadeant, atque intima cordis pietate et religione credant, aliud nomen non esse datum hominibus sub coelo, in quo oporteat nos salvos fieri; siquidem ipse propitiatio est pro peccatis nostris.

"At vero, quia 'in hoc scimus quoniam cognovimus eum, si mandata eius observemus', proximum est, et cum eo quod diximus maxime coniunctum, ut simul etiam ostendat, vitam a fidelibus non in otio et desidia degendum esse, verum oportere ut, 'quemadmodum ipse ambulavit, ita et nos ambulemus,' sectemurque omni studio iustitiam, pietatem, fidem, caritatem, mansuetudinem; dedit enim semetipsum pro nobis, ut nos redimeret ab omni iniquitate, et mundaret sibi populum acceptabilem sectatorem bonorum operum quae Apostolus Pastoribus praecipit, ut loquantur et exhortentur.

"Cum, autem Dominus et Salvator noster non solum dixerit, sed etiam exemplo suo demonstrarit, Legem et Prophetas ex dilectione pendere; Apostolus deinde confirmarit caritatem esse finem praecepti, ac legis plenitudinem; dubitare nemo postest, hoc, tanquam praecipuum munus, omni diligentia curandum esse, ut fidelis populus ad immensam Dei erga nos bonitatem amandam excitetur, ac divino quodam ardore incensus, ad summum illud et perfectissimum bonum rapiatur, cui adhaerere, solidam et veram felicitatem esse is plane sentiet, qui illud Prophetae dicere poterit: Quid enim mihi est in coelo, et a te quid volui super terram?

"Haec nimirum est via illa excellentior, quam idem Apostolus demonstravit, cum omnem doctrinae et institutionis suae rationem ad caritatem, quae nunquam excidit, dirigeret. Sive enim credendum, sive sperandum, sive agendum aliquid proponatur, ita in eo semper caritas Domini nostri commendari debet, ut quivis perspiciat, omnia perfectae Christianae virtutis opera non aliunde, quam e dilectione ortum habere, neque ad alium finem, quam ad dilectionem, referenda esse." ibid., 10; pp. 3-4.

CHAPTER SIX

THE DIMENSIONS OF THE ROMAN CATECHISM

In the preceding two chapters we have examined the immediate context of the Roman Catechism: in Chapter IV the catechisms of the fifteenth and sixteenth centuries, in Chapter V the Council of Trent and, following it, the action of St. Pius V. We are now in a position to address the text itself. In this present chapter we will discuss what I call the "dimensions" of the Roman Catechism: first, the text as such; secondly, the elements which comprise the text -- their provenance and their distribution; and finally, a schematic summary of the Catechism's contents taken as a whole.

I

The Roman Catechism -- or, more properly, the "Catechism for Parish Priests, as decreed by the Council of Trent and published by order of the Supreme Pontiff, Pius V"[1] -- began its career as something utterly unique. Not only was it the one official manual of Catholic doctrine issued by the highest authority in the Universal Church; it was also the first such thing ever issued. Nothing went before it as a precedent, just as nothing stood beside it as a peer.

Although, as we have seen, it had a definite historical context, it is somehow a fitting testimony to its uniqueness that no lists of agenda, no outlines, no preliminary drafts of the Roman Catechism as a whole are known to exist.[2] Indeed, until just five years ago (1984) the original manuscript itself had been lost.[3] Accompanying this most important discovery, which will now make possible a definitive critical edition, there have been other discoveries -- various "dictamina", emendations made by the final commission under Cardinal Sirleto.[4] If similar discoveries are eventually made of documents dating from the earlier stages of the Catechism's composition, much of great value will be added to our knowledge of the final redaction. Pending that, however, we must turn to the printed book, the famous first edition in-folio, "ex aedibus Romanis" of Paolo Manuzio, 1566.[5]

This first edition was elegantly done. The solid blocks of type-face, the wide margins intermittently annotated, the finely wrought index, the relatively few "corrigenda," provide an appropriate setting for a work which in its unassuming straightforwardness and "gravity" was eminently Roman. Regretable, however -- and this defect was immediately noted and deplored by Pius V [6] -- was the absence of any <u>divisions</u> in the text, beyond the titles (unenumerated) of three of the four main parts: "De Sacramentis," "De Dei Praeceptis in Decalogo Contentis," and "De Oratione."[7] The twelve articles of the Creed are set off in capital letters, as are the names of the seven sacraments, the text (from Exodus) of the Ten Commandments, eight subdivisions of the preliminary treatise on prayer, and the seven petitions of the Our Father. In addition to these headings, there are occasional terms set in capital letters and beginning a paragraph -- e.g., "Pater" under the first article, "Sanctorum Communio" under the ninth article "Quotidianum" under the fourth petition of the Our Father, etc.

Thus there is <u>some</u> indication that the text is logically divided on three distinct levels which we can call respectively "parts" (i.e., the four main parts of the complete text), "chapters" (corresponding to the articles of the Creed, the individual sacraments, the Commandments and the petitions in the Our Father), and "sections" corresponding to a subdivision, in a phrase or an individual word, of an article, sacrament, etc.). But this indication is neither consistent nor enumerated. When, moreover, this minimal division and subdivision of the text is accompanied by a minimal use of paragraphing and no use at all of the top of the page to indicate any division of contents, an easy orderly reading of the text, whether for private study or for public exposition, is definitely hampered.[8]

Any authoritative step to remedy this deficiency was, most unfortunately, not taken before Pius V's death in 1572. The result has been a succession of editions in which one of the two values -- fidelity to the original text, or adaptation to practical needs -- has been opted for, at the expense of the other.⁹ As early as 1588, however, one editorial feature was introduced which stabilized a certain balance in this regard, and which has prevailed through so many subsequent editions that it has become the "textus receptus." In that year there appeared from the press of Guillermo Rovillio of Lyons a new edition of the Catechism, in which for the first time <u>numbered sections</u> subdivided the text, i.e., within each chapter and part respectively.¹⁰ These "Rovillian numbers" constitute the form of textual citation for the Roman Catechism which has become standard.¹¹

A very modest quantitative description of the Roman Catechism, based on the pagination of the original <u>Manutian text</u> in-folio, and on the section numbers of the <u>Rovillian text,</u> ¹² provides an adequate basis for our analysis of its content. Out of the total of 359 pages, the Preface comprises six pages, Part I (on the Creed) 77 pages, Part II (on the sacraments) 136 pages, Part III (on the Decalogue) 72 pages, and Part IV (on prayer) 68 pages.¹³ In terms of proportion, the Preface is 2% of the total, Part I is 21%, Part II 38%, Part III 20%, and Part IV 19%. The four Parts are divided into chapters as follows: Part I has thirteen chapters (i.e., an introduction, and each of the twelve Articles of the Creed); Part II, eight chapters (i.e., the sacraments in general, and each of the seven in turn); Part III, ten chapters (i.e., an introduction, and each of the Commandments -- with the ninth and tenth combined); and Part IV, seventeen chapters (i.e., eight introductory chapters on prayer in general, an introduction to the Our Father, each of the seven petitions, and a final chapter on "Amen").¹⁴

As the chapters divide the Parts, so the sections divide the chapters. Of the total of 1013 sections, thirteen (1%) are in the Preface, 175 (17%) are in Part I, 378 (37%) in Part II, 237 (23%) in Part III, and 210 (21%) in Part IV. The sections run a little longer in the Preface and Part I, and shorter in Parts III and IV; but the overall proportions on this level are fairly constant. On the chapter level, however, there is a glaring disproportion. In Part I the average number of sections <u>per chapter</u> are

13.5; in Part II, 47; in Part III, 23.5; in Part IV, 12.3. This last set of comparisons has relevance if the chapters as such are taken as instructional units. In that case one would have to be very careful to maintain the true proportion of content, especially regarding the sacraments, as intended by the Roman Catechism.[15]

II

From even the most cursory reading of the text comes the immediate impression that the source far outdistancing all others combined is <u>Holy Scripture</u>. And more careful reading will only confirm this sense of the ubiquity and depth of the Scriptural presence. First, on the purely editorial level once more, the original Manutian text is quite deficient by contemporary standards, not only because it uses no quotation marks, but because its marginal references are, for accuracy and consistency, what can only be called capricious.[16] Because of this situation, it is extremely difficult to get an exact count of the Scriptural verses <u>actually quoted</u> in the text.

But there is a second reason which makes the difficulties resulting from the first not really worth the effort to resolve. It is the practical impossibility to distinguish between a direct quotation and a paraphrase, and -- on the next level down -- between a paraphrase and an allusion.[17] On all three levels the abundance is such that the Roman Catechism can almost be called a Scriptural mosaic. Here are four examples, taken from the four Parts respectively:

> In the New Testament [as compared with the Old Testament] God is much more frequently and meaningfully called "Father." For Christians have not received the spirit of slavery to fall back into fear, but have received the spirit of adoption as sons of God, whereby they cry "Abba! Father!" For the Father has given us that love that we should be called children of God, and so we are. And if children, then we are heirs -- heirs of God and fellow heirs with Christ, Who is the first-born among many brethren, and Who is not ashamed to call them brethren.[18]

> Such was the Deluge, that vast purgation of the world's evils by water, as St. Peter noted in his first Epistle. The passage through the

Red Sea, according to St. Paul in his first Epistle to the Corinthians, was another figure of this same reality. We need only mention the cleansing of Naaman the Syrian or the marvelous power of the pool of Bethesda as further examples of this same symbolism and mystery.[19]

It [the Decalogue] should be his [the pastor's] study night and day. Not simply that he should order his own life by its norms, but that he should instruct in it the people committed in his care. The lips of a priest should guard knowledge, and men should seek instruction from his mouth, for he is the messenger of the Lord of hosts. This injunction is even more applicable to the priests of the New Law; for they are yet nearer to God, and are meant to be changed into His likeness from one degree of glory to another, for this comes from the Lord Who is the Spirit. Our Lord Himself called them the light of the world. They must therefore be a light to those in darkness, a corrector of the foolish, a teacher of children. And if one is overtaken in any trespass, they as spiritual men should restore him in a spirit of gentleness.[20]

We do not ask that we be in no way tempted, for temptation is the life of man on earth. It is useful and profitable to us, for only by temptation do we come to know ourselves in our weakness. Thus we humble ourselves under the mighty hand of God, and we manfully strive as we look forward to the unfading crown of glory. For he who competes is not crowned unless he competes according to the rules. And, as St. James says, blessed is the man who endures trials, for when he has stood the test he will receive the crown of life, which God has promised to those who love Him. And if at times we are depressed by the enemy's temptations, we should be lifted up by the thought that we have a high priest able to sympathize with our weaknesses, for in every respect He too was tempted. ...[21]

Although a strict quantitative analysis of the Scriptural presence is practically impossible because of its very richness, yet some statistical sketch of the provenance and frequency of Scriptural citations in the text of the Roman Catechism is appropriate and helpful. Of the individual books cited (at least indirectly), all but seventeen in the Old Testament and four in the New Testament are present. The missing books are all -- it is safe to say -- peripheral; i.e., they are either very short (e.g., Haggai, Philemon), or repetitious (e.g., 2 Ezra, 3 John), or less immediately illustrative of the Catechism's topics (e.g., Judges, Jude). As for the books used, their frequency has a considerable spread. In the Old Testament the Psalter is by far the most frequently cited: 143 times, or nearly half the total. Then follows a rather even mix of "Law,"

"Prophets" and "Writings"; Isaiah (39), Genesis (27), Deuteronomy (25), and Proverbs (22) account for almost half of the remaining half. In the New Testament (whose total is well over half again as many as in the Old Testament) the spread is somewhat more even. Despite St. Matthew's clear dominance (124 citations), the Gospels are balanced by the Epistles: 1 Corinthians (77), St. John (76), Romans (63), and St. Luke (61); and not too distant are the Acts of the Apostles (27) and the Apocalypse (25). All in all, then, we find a density and a distribution of Biblical citations which justifies our description of the Roman Catechism as a "Scriptural mosaic."[22]

More important than the mere presence of the "pagina sacra" is the purpose of that presence. Citations from Scripture are meant to establish the truth of the doctrine of the faith, but they do that in the Roman Catechism not as isolated "proof texts," as was to become a characteristic of the average "Counter-Reformation" catechism.[23] Rather, they "prove" the truth almost incidentally, as it were, by putting us into the truth of the faith as revealed in those very words. As the Roman Catechism itself puts it (in connection with the abundance of texts establishing the truth of Christ's second coming, which it could cite but does not):

> This (second) coming is called in Sacred Scripture "the day of the Lord." St. Paul refers to this when he speaks of the day of the Lord as coming like a thief in the night. And Our Lord Himself says that of that day and hour no one knows. Regarding the fact of the Last Judgment the authority of the Apostle suffices: we must all appear before the judgment seat of Christ, so that each may receive good or evil, according to what he has done in the body. The witness of Sacred Scripture on this matter is ample; the pastor will find it more than enough, not just to prove its truth, but to place its reality vividly before our very eyes...[24]

Yet more vivid is the Roman Catechism's description of Sacred Scripture as a well from which the faithful can draw the inexhaustible truths of God:

> Priests charged with the care of souls will draw from the boundless flow of the Sacred Scriptures those riches which will move them on to a desire and zeal for the kingdom of heaven.[25]

And again:

> Our treatment of this matter, both in the first phrase of this petition ("forgive us our trespasses ") and in the article of the Creed on the forgiveness of sins, has been sufficiently detailed for the pastors' instructional purpose. Of course, they can always delve deeper by drawing yet more from that sacred source that is Scripture.[26]

This approach to Sacred Scripture, so characteristic of the Roman Catechism and setting it so clearly apart from what has been called the "Counter-Reformation," derives from that same deep instinct which prompted St. Thomas Aquinas to consider "sacred doctrine" and "Sacred Scripture" as synonymous.[27] This does not mean, of course, that the authors of the Roman Catechism were still living in the thirteenth century, blissfully unaware of the horrendous rupture of the doctrine of the faith being wrought in the name of Sacred Scripture. The grave danger was already noted in the Preface -- it was the very reason for the Catechism's existence in the first place. And in the body of the text itself the crucial distinctions necessary for the proper understanding and use of Sacred Scripture are clearly spelt out. Two passages summarize the point with great clarity and economy of words. The first passage occurs in the discussion of the Real Presence as established by Sacred Scripture:

> These Scriptural passages should be explained by the pastor, and any obscurity or uncertainty should be removed, especially as they have been interpreted by the sacred authority of God's Church.[28]

The organic unity of Scripture with the living Church is the cardinal principle of all hermeneutic, as derived from the very nature of the Scriptures as being the <u>Church's</u> gift from God, and from the experience of the Church in her use of that gift from the beginning. Denying or even obscuring that principle is a serious threat to the faith -- and a serious abuse of Sacred Scripture. The second passage from the Roman Catechism puts it bluntly:

> This Word of God is gravely insulted whenever anyone turns the true meaning of the Sacred Scriptures to serve the purposes of

heresy and impiety. St. Peter has a warning on this sin: "There are some things in them hard to understand, which the ignorant and unstable twist to their own destruction, as they do the other scriptures." This irreverence toward Sacred Scripture can be manifested in various ways, all of which are profanities and therefore sins against the holiness of God. Examples would be citing Scriptural passages for amusement, self-serving, flattery, fortune-telling, mockery, etc. The Council of Trent has alerted us very specifically on such perversions of Sacred Scripture.[29]

What we are warned against in these passages is fundamentally the same danger that we saw in a certain "fundamentalism" respecting the literal sense of Scripture. The two passages cited seem to anticipate respectively the two "fundamentalist" extremes: the extreme of "objectivization" which seeks to vindicate the "truth" of Scripture on no other terms but its own, and the extreme of "subjectivization" which seeks to vindicate the "sufficiency" of Scripture on reductively the same terms, viz., one's self. Both extremes thus come eventually to the same result: the destruction of the faith and -- exactly as the Roman Catechism warns -- the betrayal of the Sacred Scriptures themselves. That is why, positively, the Roman Catechism speaks of Scripture so often in conjunction with the "other source" of the Church's faith: the Sacred Tradition.

This conjunction of "Scripture and Tradition" comes early on in the Roman Catechism. In the Preface we read:

> The entire sense of sacred doctrine, which must be handed on to the faithful, is contained in the word of God, which in turn is transmitted in Sacred Scripture and Sacred Tradition.[30]

The Latin text has "traditiones" -- the same term that is used in the corresponding canon in the Council of Trent.[31] The famous "et..." of that decree, replacing the "partim...partim" of the original draft, has occasioned a long-standing controversy as to its precise meaning. The controversy has involved the Roman Catechism, as it would almost have had to in any case, because of the Catechism's connection with the Council and because of its preeminent position in the Ordinary Magisterium of the Church. The Catechism's own phrase, which was not taken from the Council, "distributum est," has been construed as endorsing the "<u>partim... partim</u>" interpretation of the Tridentine decree, i.e., that only part of divine revelation is contained in Scripture, the other part being contained in the non-written "traditions."[32] Such a construction of the "<u>distributum est</u>" is not justified. For what the Roman Catechism states here is simply a repetition in similar words of the Council's final statement on the matter: its "<u>Scripturam traditionesque</u>" simply echoes the Council's "<u>et...</u>" The argument for the "two sources" is therefore not advanced by invoking the Roman Catechism.

Whether the Council changed its mind in this matter -- as it changed its words (i.e., from the preliminary draft to the final decree) -- is a valid question. Perhaps the best response to it is that what really changed was not a new officially <u>closed</u> position replacing a previous unofficially closed one (viz., "<u>partim ...partim</u>"), but rather a new officially <u>open</u> position where there had been no official position -- open or closed -- before. If the best argument seems to be that what the Council really intended in its decree was simply to define that there were "two sources" but not to define how the two were inter-related, then <u>a fortiori</u> that was also the intent of the Roman Catechism. <u>A fortiori</u> because the Catechism was not about to "define" what the Council had deliberately left undefined.

Moreover, from many passages elsewhere in the Catechism it is evident that what the authors intended was precisely what the Council intended, viz., to maintain the divine authority of the "traditions" for whatever doctrines and practices were sanctioned by the Church but were not clearly "proved" by Scripture,[33] and at the same time maintain the <u>unity</u> of that divine authority as revealing itself to us in the Scriptures "and" in tradition.[34] We can perhaps best summarize the Roman Catechism's position on "Scripture and Tradition" by saying that, just as it faithfully registered and applied the mind of Trent (which was one of non-definition), so too it remarkably anticipated the mind of Vatican II (which was also one of non-definition).[35] And the Roman Catechism did this, not in some timid and static manner, but in the calm assurance of its dynamic continuity with the <u>one</u> "source" behind all

Scripture and all "the traditions," viz., the <u>Apostolic Tradition</u> itself. The Catechism describes the term "Apostolic," which was not actually in the Apostles' Creed, as follows:

> Also from her origin, which derives by the grace of revelation from the Apostles, the true Church can be recognized. Her teaching is not some localized recent truth, not something heard only or for the first time by us. No, it came originally from the Apostles, and it has subsequently spread across the entire earth. Hence, as no one can possibly doubt, the impious opinions of heretics are far removed from the faith of the one true Church; for they are opposed to that teaching which in the Church has been preached from the days of the Apostles right down to our own. That all may know, therefore, which church is the true Catholic Church, our fathers in the faith added in the Nicene Creed the word "Apostolic." For the Holy Spirit, Who governs the Church, does so by no other ministers than by those who are Apostolic by succession. That same Holy Spirit Who was first given to the Apostles is He Who, in the supreme goodness of God, abides with her forever.[36]

The reference to the "fathers" just cited reminds us of the second great textual source of the Roman Catechism. Its Patristic derivative is second only to what it derives from the Sacred Scriptures themselves. Not that the Fathers of the Church comprised a kind of "second canon"; they are themselves not so much a "source" as they are <u>witnesses</u> to the source: the Apostolic Tradition, as pre-eminently given us in the Scriptures. This primary role of the Fathers, viz., as witnesses to the truth of that Tradition, is beautifully summarized by our authors:

> To ascertain the Church's understanding ..., there are two lines of inquiry. The first is to consult the Fathers of the Church, those eminent witnesses of her teaching from the earliest times and in each successive age.[37]

This intimate connection of the Fathers with the Sacred Tradition is the prevalent -- almost the unique -- aspect of their presence in the pages of the Roman Catechism. That is why there is practically no "historical" (chronological, geographical, philological, etc.) sense in it: no concern to trace continuities, to appreciate perspectives, to speculate on contingencies.[38] It is hard to say whether our authors were aware of certain historical problems, or -- being aware of them -- dismissed them as irrelevant to the purpose of the Catechism.

In any case, what they have assembled is an impressive array of Patristic texts, many of which are imbedded in their paragraphs as integrally as are the Scriptural texts previously noted.[39] And again, for the same reasons previously noted, it is as difficult to come up with an exact count on them as it was for Scripture.[40] However, a few quantitative data are important for our basic understanding of the ingredients of the Roman Catechism. There are altogether some two hundred citations, direct or indirect, in the text, from some twenty Fathers. The distribution is very uneven: about half of the total comes from St. Augustine alone, who thus ranks with the Psalmist and St. Matthew -- and in terms of proportion far outranks them. The very distant runners-up are St. Ambrose (some twenty citations), St. John Chrysostom, St. Jerome and Denis the Areopagite (each in the 10's), trailed by St. Gregory the Great, St. Basil the Great, and St. John Damascene (more than five apiece). As for the four Parts of the Catechism, over half of the Patristic citations are found in Part II (on the sacraments); Parts I and III are about even with approximately 40% of the remainder, with the final 20% of the remainder in Part IV.[41]

Following the Scriptures and the Fathers comes the third and final category of textual sources for the Roman Catechism. The best rubric for this last group is probably "Magisterium," although that term occurs but rarely in the text itself.[42] What the Catechism does mention -- altogether about fifty times -- are the names (and, more rarely, the direct statements) of several Councils. Trent, naturally, has preeminence here; it is cited thirty times.[43] The other Ecumenical Councils referred to are Florence (five times), Lateran IV (four times), Constantinople I (four times), Nicea II (two times) and Nicea I (once). Some non-ecumenical councils are also mentioned: Carthage, Vercelli, Milevum, Rome. There are, finally, a few statements from individual Popes (other than Sts. Leo the Great and Gregory the Great, whom we classified as "Fathers"), all from the early Church: from Anacletus to Innocent I.[44]

It is highly significant that no author later than St. Bernard ("the last of the Fathers") is quoted or even mentioned, except in a few very generic references. "Theologians" and "scholastics" both occur, but on those rare occurrences no identification is offered.[45] This reserve on the part of our authors is not contrived, i.e., they are not avoiding names which, by virtue of the matter being treated, really should be present. "Theologians" are, quite simply, out of place in the Catechism! The last thing, in the Council's judgment -- and in the concurring judgment of Pius V and Borromeo -- that the Catholic faithful needed or were looking for in this work was "theology" in the scholastic sense -- or rather, in the "scholastic" sense as the Erasmians would define it. In this respect the Erasmian influence in the Council, and through the Council on the Catechism, was a positive good.

Yet, such was the true greatness of our authors (and, it may be conjectured, of their Roman mentors as well), that the Roman Catechism is a veritable monument to "theology" in its purest and fullest sense. To the discerning reader the unspoken presence of the great medieval masters -- and especially St. Thomas Aquinas -- is abundantly evident. And equally evident is the authors' discretion in limiting their "theologians" to what was held in common in the schools. Speculation could with caution be included in the Catechism. What had to be rigorously excluded was factional speculation. The Roman Catechism has been called a "Thomist" document. That appellation is correct if by "Thomist" we mean adherence, not to a particular school in the Church, but to the teachings common to all the schools as taught by the "Common Doctor" of the Church: St. Thomas Aquinas.[46]

III

In the original Manutian edition the body of the text, beginning "Ea est humanae mentis et intelligentiae ratio...," follows immediately after the title of the book. There is no indication of a "Preface"-- much less of a table of contents; and so the most important part of the entire work was left by the authors to be discovered for itself. It is clearly the most important part, for here in these first seven paragraphs we have the <u>Sitz in Leben</u>, the purpose, the <u>genre</u> and the structure of the Catechism. Important for a specialized study such as this present work (as evidenced by its constant citation in these pages), it is even more important for the general reader. Without it he will have but the faintest understanding of the Catechism <u>as a whole</u>; he will have missed the forest for the trees. For, with the exception of but one later passage,[47] which at that only intimates the order of the antecedent and subsequent parts, there is no indication anywhere of the book's structure and flow.

Yet, as it stands in that first edition, the Preface has the advantage of being so wholly absorbed into the <u>body</u> itself of the book, that the general reader cannot even be tempted to omit it -- as is often the case when he is confronted with a formal "preface." In fact, the Manutian "Preface" is longer than the Rovillian one. It seems to extend into what the later editions marked off as the beginning of "Part I."[48] This curious over-lap is not without its significance. The Preface, however it may be explicitly subdivided and captioned, is -- to say the least -- <u>integral</u> to the Roman Catechism. And for the reasons given elsewhere in our study, it is not too much to say that, passage for passage, it is the most important part of the entire work.

After a brief introduction on "Faith and the Creed" (which the "textus receptus" calls "Chapter I," but which, as already mentioned, seems to be the last part of the Preface), Part I proceeds immediately to the First Article of the Creed. This "Chapter 2" is the second longest chapter in this Part I (only Chapter 10, on the Church, is longer); it treats of God as He is in Himself -- One and Three, and of His first work -- Creation and Governance. It is a practical summary of the "Prima Pars" of the <u>Summa Theologiae</u>, admirably condensed and discreetly concluded with the great Thomist thesis of prevenient providence: "eius occultissima vis ad singula."[49]

Chapters 3 through 8 treat of the six articles of the Creed devoted to the Second Person of the Trinity and to the work of Incarnation and Redemption. The Incarnation itself is introduced (in Chapter 3) as redemptive: the Fall of Man immediately leads (via a resume of the Old Testament) to the contemplation of Jesus Christ. "Contemplation" is not inappropriate here; the truly prayerful approach to the mysteries of the life, death and resurrection of Our Lord is most beautiful. It is at the same time analytical, structured to answer the questions "who," "what," "how" and "why." Together, the contemplation and the analysis are catechetically most effective.

With Chapter 9 the Third Person of the Trinity and the work of sanctification -- the last five articles of the Creed -- are introduced. Chapter 10 is most distinctive of the Roman Catechism: its ecclesiology strikes the note which, as we shall see later in this study, is the keynote of the entire work.[50] The Church is here portrayed as primarily neither a "government" nor a "people," but a "<u>communion</u>,"-- a communion caused by the Holy Spirit, unifying and vivifying us through the instrumentality of "holy things": the sacraments. The note struck here pervades the remaining chapters on the remission of sins and the final resurrection and eternal life. And it forms the nexus -- however implicitly stated -- with the remaining three parts of the Catechism, the three other constituents, following the Creed and faith, of the classic catechesis.

> Not only will the pastor urge the faithful on to this blessed consummation; he will also frequently remind them that the only sure way to attain it lies in their persevering use of prayer and the sacraments, as with faith and charity they fulfill the commandments of brotherly love.[51]

Then begins Part II, which, as we have already noted, is by far the largest part of the book. Well over one-third and so much more than the logical one-fourth of the total, this Part emphatically reflects the dominant centrality of the sacraments in the overall structure of the Roman Catechism. It begins with a long chapter on the sacraments in general, and then treats of the individual seven sacraments, arranged in the order canonized by the Council of Florence.⁵² As for the order of instruction regarding each sacrament within its respective chapter, there is a somewhat consistent pattern (modeled on that of the Summa Theologiae?), viz., its name, its parts (matter and form), its institution (or sacramentality), its minister and recipient, its dispositions and effects, its ceremonies.⁵³ However, this general order is never allowed to interfere with the particular instructional exigencies of each sacrament. There is nothing cut and dried in the Roman Catechism's procedure. Rather, the special characteristics of each sacrament are given full play for discussion. This is perhaps most evident in the altogether felicitous manner in which the various names given to several of the sacraments (especially baptism and the Eucharist) are treated as indicating the various aspects of its reality as "sign." This particular feature not only preserves the Roman Catechism from a deadening "manuality"; it also reminds us of the enlivening -- and essential -- contribution to theology deriving from liturgy and pious custom.

A similar prevalent feature of this Part II is the emphasis so frequently made on the moral and pastoral aspects of the sacraments. The sacraments, in the words and things ("matter" and "form") essential to their signification, are -- evidently by divine institution -- an exquisitely apt and efficacious school in Christian living. And this divine intent is just as evidently seconded by the Church's desire to instruct her children by means of the attendant ceremonies she has devised over the course of centuries. What is explicitly stated as the conclusion to its discussion of baptism is equally applicable to all the other sacraments:

In all of this there was but one principal purpose, which the pastor must never overlook or diminish. This instruction must always be essentially pastoral in its orientation. That is to say, it must be equivalently an exhortation, urging and encouraging the faithful to persevere in the fulfillment of their baptismal promises, and so live as to be worthy of the name of Christian.[54]

In summary, Part II admirably fulfills its role as "centerpiece" of the Roman Catechism. Its judicious blending of the purely dogmatic with the pastoral, of the analytical with the contemplative, of categoric definition with customary practice, of Sacred Scripture with hagiographic traditions, of grand synthesis with picturesque detail, make it a true masterpiece of catechesis. Even the curious fact that by far the largest number of changes which have had to be made in the text because of the formulary and disciplinary changes coming from Vatican II occur in this Part II in no way really diminishes its perennial value. Rather, it only accentuates the vitality of a text which can absorb such modifications without losing its basic distinctiveness, the "classicalness" of which is thus once more confirmed.

The treatment of the Commandments in Part III parallels those of the preceding two Parts with the Creed and the sacraments respectively. That is, it deals with each Commandment in successive chapters, following an introductory chapter on the topic as a whole. This first chapter is brief but superbly executed. Its one point is that the Decalogue is not to be equated with Moses; rather, it over-arches Sinai, originally springing from the natural law itself and finally merging integrally into the law of the Gospel. This perspective, so important at the outset, is maintained throughout. The historic role of the Old Testament as such, as a kind of intermediary between the unwritten law of conscience at the begining and the perfect law of love that came finally with Christ, is touched on, of course. But it seems not to have been a part of this Chapter I in the mind of the authors. Conversely to the case of Part I -- where the "textus receptus" added several paragraphs to the first Article at the expense of the Introduction -- here the "textus receptus" transferred an approximately equal amount (having to do, precisely, with the Old Testament) from the First Commandment back to the Introduction.[55] This particular editorial detail does not significantly affect the overall picture, except to point up the premise undoubtedly important to the authors, viz., the truly comprehensive and perennial aspect of the Decalogue.

As with the sacraments, there is no rigidly uniform pattern for the treatment of the individual Commandments. In fact, a certain variety seems to be purposely stressed; each Commandment seems to have a uniqueness, a "personality," all its own, e.g., the intrinsic primacy of the First Commandment, the "mediational" role of the Fourth, the vibrant reticence of the Sixth. On the other hand, the Ninth and Tenth Commandments are discussed jointly (just as Exodus is given precedence over Deuteronomy as the captioned text), and so the difference between the "Catholic" and the "Protestant" numerations of the Decalogue is minimized. The only methodological device common to most (but not all) of the Commandments is the division into "positive" and "negative" in their contents: what the Commandments enjoin is at least as prominent as what they forbid.

Perhaps the most vivid instance of the "positive" occurs under the Fifth Commandment. Here what is in effect the Great Commandment of Love is introduced as a kind of corollary to a rather routine description of the particular sins forbidden by this one Commandment. The surprise -- and possible regret -- at this arrangement seems to be more than compensated for by this trenchant reminder that the Great Commandment is not some starry abstraction (as might be the case if it were put in some "improved" context of the Beatitudes), but rather a very concrete and downright "homely" reality. Thus, in general and in constantly recurring detail the moral instruction found in the Roman Catechism is solid, balanced, complete and totally <u>Christian</u>.

The last part of the Catechism, on prayer in general and on the Our Father in particular, is the shortest of the four. Yet in number of chapters it has the most. This is because, instead of having one introductory chapter (as each of the preceding three parts has), its introduction is divided into eight chapters, treating successively the necessity, the benefits, the parts and degrees, the objects, the persons for whom and to whom to pray, the preparation, and finally the manner of prayer. Richly condensed and always eminently pastoral, this "mini-course" in prayer provides a perfect transition from the imperatives of the moral life summarized in the Decalogue to the aspirations of the life wholly committed to the union with God exemplified and taught us by Our Lord Himself.

The seven petitions of the Our Father are then perused; and for sheer wealth of Christian wisdom in both depth and range there is nothing in the preceding Parts to surpass or even equal this final and culminating part of the Catechism. The harmonization, for instance, of zeal and resignation, of solitude and community, of sorrow for sin and exultation in grace, of the rhythms of time ("our daily bread") and the finality of eternity, are all exquisitely portrayed -- with a force of conviction and a delicacy of feeling such as one finds only in the greatest classics of spiritual literature. Truly, it is a <u>Catholic</u> commentary as worthy of the Prayer as can be achieved this side of the Scriptures themselves -- where what is done on earth is indeed what is done in heaven.

With the final "Amen" of the Our Father, and with the whole vast synthesis which this one little word connotes, the Roman Catechism ends. And so ends this cursory summary of its "dimensions."[56] This leads us to that study toward which it -- and all the antecedent data of the catechetical tradition -- have hopefully prepared us: the synthesis of these dimensions in the <u>structure</u> of the Roman Catechism.

NOTES

1   See above, Chapter V, note 30, p. 133.

2   The best history of the Roman Catechism is Pedro Rodriguez-Raul Lanzetti. <u>El Catecismo Romano: Fuentes e Historia del Texto y de la Redaccion: Bases Criticas para el Estudio Teologico del Catecismo del Concilio de Trento</u> (Pamplona: Universidad de Navarra, 1982).

3   See Rodriguez-Lanzetti's follow-up volume, <u>El Manuscrito Original del Catecismo Romano: Description del Material y los Trabajos al Servicio de la Edicion Critica del Catecismo del Concilio de Trento</u> (Pamplona: Universidad de Navarra, 1985), occasioned by this discovery, which the authors themselves made.

4   <u>Ibid.</u>, "Capitulo III: Los Dictamenes sobre el manuscrito del Catecismo Romano," pp. 107-53.

5   Catechismus // Ex Decreto Concilii Tridentini // ad Parochos // Pii Quinti Pont. Max. // Iussu Editus // Romae // In aedibus Populi Romani // apud Paulum Manutium // MDLXVI // cum privilegio Pii V. Pont. Max.

Preceding the text is a two-page (unnumbered) "Motu Proprio" of Pius V granting Manuzio exclusive rights to publish the Catechism in Latin or in the vernacular for a five-year period. The first sentence gives an interesting summary of the final phase of the redaction of the Catechism: "Motu proprio, etc. Pastorali officio cupientes quam diligentissime possumus divina adiuvante gratia fungi, et ea, quae Sacro Tridentino Concilio statuta, et decreta fuerunt, exequi curavimus, ut a delectis aliquot theologicis in hac alma Urbe componeretur Catechismus: quo Christi fideles de eis rebus, quas eos nosse, profiteri et servare oporteret, Parochorum suorum diligentia edocerentur. Qui liber cum Deo iuvante perfectus, in lucem edendus sit: providendum duximus, ut quam diligentissime et fidelissime imprimatur."

There was a second printing of the Roman Catechism by Manuzio: in octavo, officially dated the following year, 1567. For a comparison of these two editions, see Rodriguez-Lanzetti, <u>El Catecismo Romano,</u> pp. 209-16.

6   <u>Ibid.</u>, p. 213. In note 12, an excerpt from Piux V's letter to Cardinal Hosius (n.d.) is quoted: "Illud admonemus, ut librum cures in totidem <u>partes</u>, quot sunt res, quae eius initio explicandae ponuntur, dividendum, et unamquamque earum partium suis <u>capitibus</u> apte distinguendam; quod in prima eius editione, quorumdam incuria, parum diligenter factum esse, moleste tulimus."

7   The first Part, which normally would have been entitled "De Symbolo" or "De Articulis Fidei," seems to have been inadvertently omitted. The only indication of it in the MS was "Credo in Deum," which apparently the printer assumed was the title of the first Article.

8   To convey a more visual impression of the book, it may be noteworthy to state that out of the 358 pages of text, some 200 pages have no paragraph breaks nor any other kind of break. As for the headings at the top of the pages, they read the same throughout, viz., "Catechismus" on the left-hand side (verso) and "Ad Parochos" on the right-hand side (recto).

9   The two extremes in this tug of war were probably the following two editions: 1) on the side of adaptability: the "Fabrician" edition of Antwerp, 1572, which recast the complete Catechism into a question-and-answer format (see Rodriguez-Lanzetti, op. cit., pp. 241-42); and 2) on the side of fidelity: the "Clementine" edition of Rome, 1761, which returned to the original Manutian text, i.e., it deleted all Part, Chapter and Section headings (although, inexplicably, it altered the text in some respects). (ibid., pp. 303-05)

10 Catechismus ex decreto Sacrosancti Concilii Tridentini, iussu Pii V. Pont. Max. Nunc primum in capita, sectionesque distinctus, variisque Patrum sententiis, et auctoribus munitus. Lugduni, apud Guliel. Rovillium, sub scuto Veneto, M. D. LXXXVIII. (Ibid., p. 261)

11 The "Rovillian numbers" designate the part, the chapter and the section respectively. E. g., "I, 5, 3" refers to Part I (on the Creed), Chapter 5 (on the Fourth Article), Section 3. It should be noted that in Parts I, II and III there is one introductory "Chapter 1," and consequently each Article (in Part I), sacrament (in Part II) and Commandment (in Part III) is designated by its proper number plus one. E.g., the Fifth Commandment is in Chapter 6.

12 There have been some minor fluctuations in the total of the Rovillian numbers, because a few sections were subsequently combined. Thus, in the original Rovillian edition the numbers were: 13 sections in the Preface, 175 in Part I, 379 in Part II, 239 in Part III, 211 in Part IV; for a total of 1017 sections. (ibid., p. 263) In the edition I have followed (Padua, 1930), the numbers are: 13 in the Preface, 175 in Part I, 378 in Part II, 237 in Part III, 210 in Part IV; for a total of 1013.

13 These numbers were rounded off to the nearest approximation of a full page. In the Manutian edition no "chapters"--not even the "parts"-- began on a new page, except accidentally.

14 The number of pages in each chapter is as follows:
Preface: 6 pp.

I, 1:	1.5 pp.	II, 1:	13.5 pp.	III, 1:	4 pp.	IV, 1:	1.5 pp.
I, 2:	8.5 pp.	II, 2:	23.5 pp.	III, 2:	10 pp.	IV, 2:	3 pp.
I, 3:	6.5 pp.	II, 3:	8.5 pp.	III, 3:	9 pp.	IV, 3:	2 pp.
I, 4:	5.5 pp.	II, 4:	30 pp.	III, 4:	7.5 pp.	IV, 4:	1 p.
I, 5:	7.5 pp.	II, 5:	30.5 pp.	III, 5:	7.5 pp.	IV, 5:	2 pp.
I, 6:	7 pp.	II, 6:	6 pp.	III, 6:	6.5 pp.	IV, 6:	1 p.
I, 7:	4 pp.	II, 7:	13 pp.	III, 7:	5 pp.	IV, 7:	1.5 pp.
I, 8:	4.5 pp.	II, 8:	11 pp.	III, 8:	8 pp.	IV, 8:	2.5 pp.
I, 9:	5 pp.			III, 9:	8.5 pp.	IV, 9:	7 pp.
I,10:	10 pp.			III,10:	6.5 pp.	IV, 10:	3 pp.
I,11:	4.5 pp.					IV, 11:	6 pp
I,12:	7 pp.					IV, 12:	7 pp.
I,13:	5.5 pp.					IV, 13:	7 pp.
						IV,14:	8.5 pp.
						IV, 15:	8 pp.
						IV, 16:	5 pp.
						IV, 17:	2 pp.

15   This is but one more instance where an essentially mechanical device intended to facilitate study and comprehension (viz., by breaking up a block of material into pedagogical units) can militate against that purpose if not properly used.

16   E.g., in a random perusal of three pages (pp. 150-52), thirteen Scriptural citations are indicated, twelve are not. Again, in pages 188-90, five texts are cited, seven are not.

17   E.g., consider the following passage:
"Quamvis ...ex Apostoli sententia, natura et divina lex iubeat, ut qui altari servit ex altari vivat; tamen quaestus et lucri causa ad altare accedere maximum sacrilegium est. ...Hi vero sunt quos Salvator noster mercenarios appellat; et quos Ezechiel dicebat seipsos et non oves pascere; quorum turpitudo et improbitas non solum sacerdotali ordini magnas tenebras offundit, ita ut iam nihil fere a fideli populo haberi possit contemptius et abiectius, verum etiam efficit, ut ipsi nihil amplius ex sacerdotio consequantur, quam Judas ex Apostolatus munere, quod ille semptiternum exitium attulit." (II, 7, 4; p. 197) Question: how many Scriptural quotations are in this passage? how many paraphrases? how many allusions?

Incidentally, this literary genre involving Scripture should be quite familiar to us, especially after its frequent usage in the documents of the Second Vatican Council.

18   "Deus Pater Christianorum dicitur, qui non acceperunt spiritum servitutis in timore, sed acceperunt spiritum adoptionis filiorum Dei, in quo clamant, Abba Pater; eam enim caritatem dedit nobis Pater, ut filii Dei nominemur et simus; quod si filii et haeredes, haeredes quidem Dei, cohaeredes autem Christi, qui est primogenitus in multis fratribus." (I, 2, 9; p. 12) See Rom 8:15, 17, 29; Heb 2:11; 1 Jn 3:1.

19 "Diluvium ... quo mundus purgatus est, quod multa malitia hominum esset in terra, et cuncta cogitatio cordis intenta esset ad malum, huius aquae figuram et similitudinen gessisse, Apostolorum Princeps in priori Epistola ostendit. Et maris rubri transitum eiusdem aquae significationem habuisse, D. Paulus ad Corinthios scribens exposuit; ut interim omittamus tum Naaman Syri ablutionem, tum probaticae piscinae admirabilem vim, et alia id genus multa, in quibus huius mysterii symbolum inesse facile apparet." (II, 2, 9; p.100) See Gen 6:17; Exod 14:21; 2 Kgs 5:14; Jn 5:2; 1 Cor 10:1; 1 Pet 3:21.

20 "... cum sit totius legis summa, pastores oportet in eius contemplatione die noctuque versari, non ut vitam suam modo ad hanc normam componant, sed etiam ut populum sibi creditum in lege Domini erudiant. Nam labia sacerdotis custodient scientiam, et legem requirent ex ore eius, quia angelus Domini exercituum est; quod ad pastores novae legis maxime pertinet, qui Deo propiores a claritate in claritatem transformari debent, tanquam a Domini spiritu. Et cum eos lucis nomine nuncuparit Christus Dominus, propriae sunt illorum partes, ut sint lumen eorum qui in tenebris sunt, eruditores insipientium, magistri infantium; et si quis praeoccupatus fuerit in aliquo delicto, ipsi, qui spiritales sunt, huiusmodi instruant." (III, 1, 2; p. 220) See Ps 1:2; Mal 2:7; Mt 5:14; Rom 2:20; 2 Cor 3:18; Gal 6:1.

21 "Nec vero petimus ne omnino tentemus; est enim tentatio vita hominis super terram. Est autem ea res utilis et fructuosa hominum generi; nam in tentationibus nos ipsos, id est vires nostras cognoscimus. Quamobrem etiam humiliamur sub potenti manu Dei, viriliterque decertantes expectemus immarcescibilem coronam gloriae. Nam et qui in agone contendit, non coronatur nisi legitime certaverit, et, ut inquit sanctus Iacobus: Beatus vir, qui suffert tentationem; quoniam, cum probatus fuerit accipiet coronam vitae, quam repromisit Deus diligentibus se. Quod si urgemur nonnunquam hostium tentationibus, magnae nobis erit levationi illa cogitatio habere nos adiutorem Pontificem, qui possit compati infirmitatibus nostris, tentatum et ipsum per omnia." (IV, 15, 14; p. 349) See Job 1:12 and 7:1; 2 Tim 2:5; Heb 4:15; Js 1:12; 1 Pet 5:4 and 5:6.

22 Illustrating the point made earlier (see above, note 17, p. 158, the following list of different countings must suffice as a statistical resume of Scriptural citations in the Roman Catechism:

a) actual citations (direct and indirect) b) marginalia

	my count	Bellinger's count	Manutian ed.	Paduan ed.
Old Test:	398	300	468	612
New Test:	676	500	1100	866
	1074	800	1568	1478

23   Bellinger, op. cit., p. 78.

24   "Hic adventus in sacris litteris Dies Domini apellatur, de quo ait Apostolus: Dies Domini, sicut fur in nocte, ita veniet; et Salvator ipse: De die autem illa et hora nemo scit. Ac de summo iudicio satis sit illa auctoritas Apostoli: Omnes nos manisfestari oportet ante tribunal Christi, ut referat unusquisque propria corporis, prout gessit, sive bonum sive malum. Plena enim est sacra Scriptura testimoniorum, quae passim parochis occurrent, ad rem non solum comprobandam, set etiam fidelium oculis subiciendam..." (I, 8, 2; p. 48)

25   "...haurient animarum curatores sacerdotes ex uberrimis divinarum litterarum fontibus ea, quae fidelibus desiderium studiumque commoveant regni coelorum..." (IV, 11, 4; p. 317)

26   "Quam sententiam quoniam persecuti sumus, quantum res ferebat, in proemio huius precationis, et in ea Symboli parte quae est de remissione peccatorum; inde assument parochi, quae ad hunc locum instruendum pertinere videbuntur; reliqua haurient ex divinarum litterarum fontibus." (IV, 14, 11; p. 340)

27   See above, Chapter III, note 1, p.73.

28   "Haec ... Scripturae loca a pastoribus explicanda erunt; atque in primis docendum nihil in iis dubii, aut incerti relictum esse; praesertim cum haec Ecclesiae Dei sacrosancta auctoritas interpretata sit." (II, 4, 28; p. 140)

29   "Dei autem verbum summa iniuria afficit, quicumque sacram Scripturam a recta et germana eius sententia ad impiorum dogmata et haereses flectit; cuius sceleris admonet nos Princeps Apostolorum his verbis: Sunt quaedam difficilia intellectu, quae indocti et instabiles depravant, sicut et ceteras Scripturas ad suam ipsorum perditionem. Praeterea foedis et inhonestis maculis sacra Scriptura contaminatur, cum eius verba et sententias, quae omni veneratione colenda sunt, ad profana quaeque nefarii homines torquent ac scurrilia scilicet fabulosa, vana, assentationes, detractiones, sortes, libellos famosos, et si quae alia sunt id genus, in quod peccatum sacra Tridentina Synodus animadverti iubet." (III, 3, 27; pp. 241-42)

Another pertinent text, equally blunt, is the following:

"Ut autem illud est certum propinquae mortis signum, cum non possunt homines vel cibum sumere vel sumptum retinere; sic magnum est desperatae salutis argumentum, cum vel non quaerunt verbum Dei, vel si adsit, non sustinent, et eam impietatis vocem in Deum effundunt: Recede a nobis, scientiam viarum tuarum nolumus. In hoc furore animi et mentis caecitate versantur illi, qui, neglectis iis, qui legitime eis praesunt, Catholicis et episcopis et sacerdotibus, a sancta Romana Ecclesia

30 "Omnis autem doctrinae ratio, quae fidelibus tradenda sit, verbo Dei continetur, quod in Scripturam Traditionesque distributum est." (Praef., 12; p. 5)

31 Decretum de libris sacris et de traditionibus recipiendis (Session IV, April 8, 1546), DS 1501.

For two complementary views on this decree, see: Edmond Ortigues, "Ecriture et Traditions apostoliques au Concile de Trente," "Revue des sciences religieuses, 36 (1949), pp. 271-99; and Charles Boyer, "Le Concile de Trente et l'insuffisance de l'Ecriture," Doctor Communis, 16 (1963), pp. 5-17.

32 See Heribert Schauf, Die Lehre der Kirche uber Schrift und Tradition in den Katechismen (Essen, 1963), p. 174. However, in a subsequent article Schauf makes the following admission: "... de iis (catechismis) qui schema vetus expositionis Symboli Apostolorum, mandatorum, orationis Dominicae, etc. vel Catechismum Romanum ita sequuuntur, ut nostram quaestionem non tangant." "De traditione constitutiva ad mentem catechismorum, " Seminarium, 4 (1964), p. 271.

33 As examples of "proof" from Tradition apart from Scripture, the following passages are typical:
"...idque ab Apostolica traditione Ecclesiam accepisse, communis Patrum sententia et auctoritas confirmat." (II, 2, 32; p. 108): on infant baptism.
"...hoc enim Apostolica traditio nos docuit, et Ecclesiae Catholicae auctoritas firmavit." (II, 4, 13: p. 134): on unleavened bread in the Eucharist.
"...ex eadem Christi Domini doctrina ab Apostolis tradita accepimus." (II, 5, 14; p. 164): on the form of the sacrament of Penance.
"Quod quidem ex Apostolorum traditione acceptum esse docuit Ecclesia." (II, 7, 14; p. 200); on clerical tonsure.

For other examples, see:
II, 1, 24; p. 94 (on the use of special ministers for the sacraments).
II, 3, 7; p. 124 (on the matter of Confirmation).
III, 2, 20; p. 231 (on sacred images)
IV, 5, 3; p. 299 (on praying for enemies).
etc.

34 As examples of "proof" from Tradition and Scripture, the following passages are typical:
"Ac de huius quidem doctrinae veritate , quam et Scripturarum testimoniis et Apostolica traditione confirmatam esse sancta concilia declarant ..." (I, 6, 3; p. 38): on Purgatory.

"Ex quibus verbis plura quidem a sacris Scripturis colliguntur, quaedam vero in Ecclesia ex Apostolica traditione conservata sunt." (II, 4, 21; p. 137): on the form of consecration of the chalice.

"Ad quorum rationem, quod caput est, consuetudo accedit ab Apostolis accepta, et in Ecclesia Dei perpetuo retenta et conservata. Cuius rei quis firmius aut clarius requirat argumentum divinae Scripturae testimonio, quae sanctorum laudes celebrat admirabiliter?" (III, 2, 12; p. 228); on the invocation of the saints.

"...in sacris litteris et apud sanctos Patres facile erit parocho multa colligere et fideli populo tradere." (III, 10, 21; p. 290): on evangelical poverty.

For other examples, see:
I, 9, 6; p. 56 (on the procession of the Holy Spirit).
II, 1, 19; p. 92 (on the number of the sacraments).
II, 7, 29; p. 206 (on the ordination of a bishop by three bishops).
III, 3, 19; p. 240 (on the taking of oaths).
etc.

35 "Sacra Traditio... et Sacra Scriptura arcte inter se connectuntur atque communicant. Nam ambae, ex eadem divina scaturigine promanantes, in unum quodammodo coelescunt et in eundem finem tendunt. ...quo fit ut Ecclesia certitudinem suam de omnibus revelatis non per solam Scripturam hauriat. Quapropter utraque pari pietatis affectu ac reverentia suscipienda et veneranda est." Dei Verbum, 9 (AAS, 58:821).

36 "Sed ex origine etiam, quam revelata gratia ab Apostolis ducit, Ecclesiae veritatem agnoscimus. Siquidem eius doctrina veritas est, non recens, neque nunc primum orta, sed ab Apostolis iam olim tradita, et in omnem orbem terrarum disseminata. Ex quo fit, ut nemo dubitate possit, impias haereticorum voces longe a verae Ecclesiae fide abesse, cum doctrinae Ecclesiae, quae ab Apostolis ad hanc diem praedicata est, adversantur. Quare ut omnes intelligerent, quaenam esset Ecclesia Catholica, Patres in Symbolo illud divinitus addiderunt Apostolicam. Etenim Spiritus Sanctus, qui Ecclesiae praesidet, eam, non per aliud genus ministrorum, quam per Apostolicum gubernat. Qui Spiritus primum quidem Apostolis tributus est, deinde vero summa Dei bonitate semper in Ecclesia mansit." (I, 10, 17; p. 64)

37 "Ad cuius sententiae cognitionem duplici via et ratione possumus pervenire. Prima est, cum Patres, qui ab initio Ecclesiae atque omni deinceps aetate floruerunt, et Ecclesiasticae doctrinae optimi testes sunt, consulimus." (II, 4, 29; p. 140)

38 A random example or two can be found in the various ascriptions to ancient Popes of certain ecclesiastical practices of obviously later origins; e.g., St. Peter and the institution of tonsure (II, 7, 14; p.200), and St. Melchiades and the fully developed rite of Confirmation (II, 3, 4: p. 122). Of course, the facile identity of "Dionysius Areopagita, Athenarum Episcopus" (ibid) -- with all

the inevitable anachronisms it entails -- confirms the legitimacy of expecting from the Roman Catechism no more (nor less) of historical accuracy and consciousness than any other work of its time.

39 See above, notes 18-21, pp. 158-59.

40 See above, note 17, p. 158.

41 The total number of Patristic citations, by my count, is 215. This total is somewhat greater than Bellinger's 198 (op.cit., p. 83) and the 185 in the marginalia of the Manutian edition.

42 See, e.g., II, 3, 12; p. 125.

43 For these thirty citations, identified and categorized, see Chapter V, notes 31, 32 and 33, pp. 134-35.

44 Viz., Anacletus, Alexander I, Hyginus, Urban I, Fabian, Melchiades, Damasus I, and Innocent I.

45 "Theologians" (theologi) occurs four times:
I, 3, 9; p. 22: on the "mental word" as analogous to the mystery of the Trinity.
I, 8, 9; p. 51: on the "pain of loss" in hell.
I, 8, 10; p. 52: on the "pain of sense" in hell.
II, 8, 3; p. 209: on the definition of Matrimony.

"Scholastics" (scholastici) occurs three times:
I, 12, 13; p. 77: on the condition of glorified bodies.
II, 1, 4; p. 85; on the definition of "sacrament".
IV, 12, 11; p. 325: on the distinctions in the "divine will."

Two other terms occur: "writers" (scriptores) four times (II, 4, 8; p. 132. II, 4, 17; p. 135. IV, 1, 1; p. 292. IV, 2, 1; p. 293), and "philosophers" (philosophi) once (IV, 10, 7; p. 315).

46 Antoine Regnault, ("Reginaldus"), O.P., in his vigorous De Catechismi Romani auctoritate dissertatio (Naples, 1765), quotes the following (anonymous) objection: "...nemo non videt, eos Patres, qui Catechismum composuerunt, excessisse formam finesque mandati; cum multa in hoc Catechismo docuerint quae nunquam Concilium docuit, imo quae ipsi sanctae Synodo sunt opposita. Quare dicendum est ... multa in Catechismo tres illos Patres, utpote Thomistas et ex Ordine Dominicanorum, scripsisse magis partium quam veritatis studio, eodemque spiritu Pium V ex eodem etiam Ordine illa quae isti scripserant approbasse." (pp. 168-69) In his lengthy reply, Regnault does not deny that the Roman Catechism teaches "praemotio physica" (I, 2, 22; p. 17, and IV, 10, 7; p. 315); he simply says that that teaching is true. In contrast, Francis Suarez, S.J., in his De divina gratia (Lyons, 1651), tactfully asserts that the authors of the Roman Catechism had no intention to teach metaphysics: "Incredible profecto est, auctores illius libri eum sensum intendisse, quia valde alienum

erat a fine et utilitate Catechismi quaestionem valde metaphysicam et incertam definire, et parochos proponere, ut iuxta eam populum instruerent ac docerent, cum neque communis populus eam intelligere neque ipsi parochi eam percipere ordinarie valeant aut explicare." (p. 178; note 2630)

Perhaps the best statement on the matter is the comment of H. Lennerz, S.J., quoted by Toth, op. cit., p. 86, note 255: "Seine Geschichte zeigt nicht nur, dass es keine der in den katholischen Schulen strittigen Fragen entscheiden wollte, sondern gerade auch, dass es seinen Dekreten eine Fassung gab, die nur das ausdrucken sollte, worin die verschiedenen Schulen ubereinstimmen: die traditionelle katholische Lehre. ...Soll damit nur gesagt sein, die Lehre des Konzils von Trient sei 'thomistisch,' insofern die Lehre des hl. Thomas und seiner Schule mit der in den andern katholischen Schulen vertretenen Ansicht ubereinstimmt, so liesse sich mit ganz dem gleichen Recht sagen: die Lehre des Triente Konzils ist 'skotistisch,' 'augustinisch,' usw. Das hat eben nur den Sinn: die Lehre des Konzils ist 'katholisch.'" Or, more succinctly and most happily put, the comment of St. Robert Bellarmine (also quoted by Toth, ibid., p. 90) is our own conclusion: "... notitia dogmatum ecclesiasticorum, in quo genere tutissima est doctrina S. Thomae et Catechismi Tridentini."

47 viz., I, 13, 13; p. 84. See below, note 51.

48 The first three sections in the present Chapter 1 of Part I ("De Fide et Symbolo Fidei") follow immediately on the Preface without any break indicated. Section 4 (which is the last section in this Chapter 1) begins in the Manutian edition with the subheading: "Credo in Deum." See above, note 7, p. 157.

49 I, 2, 22; p. 17. See above, note 46.

50 See below, Chapter VII, pp. 176-78.

51 "...non solum ad eam beatitudinem fideles excitabunt, verum etiam eius consequendae certam rationem hanc esse frequenter monebunt, ut fide et caritate instructi et in oratione et sacramentorum salutari usu perseverantes, ad omnia benignitatis officia in proximos se exerceant." (I, 13, 13; p. 84) See above, note 47.

52 Decretum pro Armeniis, November 22, 1439 (DS 1310).

53 In the case of Baptism there is an explicit resume by headings (II, 2, 76; p. 121).

54 "Quae omnia ob eam praecipue causam docenda esse pastores meminerint, ut fideles in hac cura et cogitatione perpetuo versentur, ut in iis quae adeo sancte et religiose spoponderunt

cum Baptismo initiati sunt, fidem servent, atque eam vitam instituant, quae sanctissimae Christiani nominis professioni respondeat." (II, 2, 76; p. 121) This passage follows immediately after the one referred to in the preceding note.

55 The last four sections (11-14) in the present Chapter 1 of Part III seem to have been intended as the beginning of the treatment of the First Commandment (i.e., the present Chapter 2). Inserted at this point in the Manutian edition is the text of the First Commandment: "Ego sum Dominus Deus tuus, qui eduxi te de terra Aegypti, etc."

56 For a more detailed analysis of the contents, see Appendix.

CHAPTER SEVEN

THE STRUCTURE OF THE ROMAN CATECHISM

In the preceding chapter we examined the dimensions of the Roman Catechism: its actual text and the texts which it encompasses, i.e., its statement of "the rudiments of the faith," and the statements from the antecedent tradition -- Scriptural, Patristic, Magisterial -- which it uses, either by quotation or by allusion. With these dimensions in mind, we are now in a position to examine that which is the main object of our study: the structure of the Roman Catechism, i.e., the order it gives to these statements so as to achieve a "formula et ratio" in the teaching of the faith.¹ The "rudimenta fidei," in themselves multiple and diverse, are so arranged by our authors as to form a unity, comprehensive and coherent, for the teaching of the faith which, for all the diversity of its parts, is one -- "unus est Dominus, una fides."² If the purpose, then, of the preceding chapter was to see the parts (the "dimensions") of our Catechism, it was only to enable us now to see the structure which makes of these parts a single whole.

I

Although the Preface (from which we have taken the several terms cited in the preceding paragraph) is rich -- indeed invaluable -- as the interpretative guide to the Roman Catechism, it does not tell us, in a single lapidary sentence, what that structural principle is by which the parts of the Catechism are ordered into a single organic whole. Nevertheless, it does so equivalently, in a passage which we must now quote in extenso, for it is the key text of our entire study.

> Because the truths divinely given us are so many and varied, they are not easy to comprehend or retain, to insure that when they come to be taught they can be promptly and adequately explained. That is why our fathers in the faith so wisely apportioned the entire thrust and meaning of the doctrine of salvation within the framework of four parts, viz., the Apostles'

Creed, the sacraments, the Decalogue, and the Lord's Prayer. For whatever must be held by Christian faith -- whether about God in Himself and His creation and providence, or about man's redemption and the rewards for the just and the punishments for the wicked -- all is contained in the doctrine of the Creed. As for the signs and instruments whereby divine grace is ours, that comes in the doctrine of the seven sacraments. Whatever laws we are under, leading us to love, are given us in the Ten Commandments. And finally, whatever can be the object of human hope, leading us to pray for salvation, is contained in the Lord's Prayer. Thus it follows that with the explanation of these four parts, as the four comprehensive categories of Sacred Scripture, nothing is left out which a Christian must know.[3]

These four -- the Creed, the sacraments, the Decalogue and the Our Father -- are identified by the Roman Catechism not as its "comprehensive categories" ("communia loca") nor even as the "comprehensive categories" of the Tradition in general, but explicitly as those of Sacred Scripture. "What is written," the "sacra pagina": here is where the Holy Spirit has reserved and secured that body of doctrine which, through the teaching function of the living Church -- especially in that most characteristic form of its ordinary teaching called catechesis -- becomes the "doctrine of salvation."

Where are these "communia loca" found in the Scriptures? They are not individual passages of Scripture, however important or extended they may be; for such passages are not sufficiently comprehensive ("communia"). Nor are they the major divisions or parts of Scripture as they have been usually classified, such as "the Law, the Prophets and the Writings" (with the corresponding parts in the New Testament), for such divisions are not "categories" ("loca") of the Scriptures in as radical a sense as can and must be understood in order to fit into the present context. No, the adequate meaning of "comprehensive categories" ("communia loca") as used in our text can only be the meaning itself -- or, rather, the meanings themselves (in the plural) -- of Sacred Scripture.[4]

That the meaning of Scripture is multiple is a truth we have already examined at length.[5] Both its truth and its relevance to catechesis is something we need not repeat in detail. Since, however, we must proceed to a more profound examination of them, as constituting the fundamental structure of the Roman Catechism, a brief resume of the main points of our earlier inquiry is clearly in order here.

A millennial tradition saw in the Sacred Scriptures a <u>four-fold meaning</u>. There was, primarily and necessarily, the <u>literal</u> sense, i.e., the historical meaning intended and expressed in <u>words</u> by the human author inspired by the Holy Spirit. Then there was a <u>spiritual</u> sense, i.e., the "real" meaning intended by the principal author, the Holy Spirit, and expressed in <u>things</u> (<u>res</u>). This spiritual meaning is founded first in the reality of the New Testament, in such wise that this New Testament is, literally and really, identified with the Incarnate Word, Jesus Christ. Because of the relationship of type and anti-type between the two Testaments, the first spiritual sense of Scripture was called the <u>typical</u> (or allegorical) sense. But this reality expressed in the spiritual sense was not only the individual Person of Christ; it was also the whole Mystical Body of that same Christ, whose members live by the grace of His Holy Spirit. Hence there was another spiritual sense called the <u>tropological</u> (or moral) sense, which concerns the life of the members of Christ. Moreover, this same life must be finally fulfilled in the members' participation in the glorious resurrection of Christ. This third spiritual sense of Scripture, appropriately called the <u>anagogical</u> (or eschatological) sense, expresses this ultimate and eternal reality of beatitude.

As we have seen in some detail, this <u>four-fold sense</u> of Sacred Scripture can be aligned with the <u>four-fold content</u> of the catechetical tradition.[6] It is true, no one explicitly made that alignment, not even St. Thomas Aquinas. He came the closest, however, to doing so, for it was he who gave us the definitive formulation of the four-fold sense of Scripture; and in a sense he did the same for the four-fold content of catechesis -- in the sense, that is, that he added the sacraments to the triad of Creed (faith), prayer (hope) and Commandments (charity), not as something appended to them from outside but as something binding them together from within.[7] The sacraments are <u>inside</u> the Creed, not only as so many further objects of our assent, but as the efficacious signs of the faith itself. Likewise, they are inside the Commandments, not merely as so many added remedies and aids toward their observance, but as specifying in terms of grace the moral activity called for by the Decalogue. And the same can be said for that highest moral activity called prayer; it too is implicitly (i.e., at least in voto) sacramental.

This contribution by St. Thomas was decisive, for the authors of the Roman Catechism, whether consciously or not, followed his construction in their arrangement of the four-fold content. Changing every arrangement of this same content made by their contemporaries,[8] they came up with one which -- if it is not to be dismissed as wholly arbitrary -- can only be explained as a "ratio doctrinae" rooted in and stemming from the millennially traditional way of reading and teaching the Sacred Scriptures. For what they did in effect was align -- at long last! -- the four-fold content of catechesis with the four-fold meaning of Scripture. They did not say this in so many words, but they did say that, in presenting their Catechism as being a "communis regula atque praescriptio" of Christian doctrine in four consecutive parts, they were giving us the "communia loca" of Sacred Scripture.

The hypothesis just now proposed has, admittedly, no documentary evidence (beyond those phrases quoted from the Preface), at least in the present state of our knowledge of the sources of the Roman Catechism. The only evidence, therefore, is internal, i.e., in the very substance and structure of the work. It is that evidence which we must now examine.

II

The most immediate and impressive datum, already amply documented in the preceding chapter, is the pre-eminence of the sacraments in the total ensemble of the Catechism's contents. Not only is Part II the Catechism's center of gravity, holding together the other parts by its own preponderant mass and density; it is also the center of energy for the other parts as well, enlivening them by its own limitless -- its almost extravagant -- radiation. This solar image is not an extravagant analogy! The plain fact is that "sacrament(s)" as used in the Roman Catechism is implicitly most comprehensive. It covers -- or, better, it penetrates -- the workings of grace, both in the individual Christian and in the Church as a whole, whereby the three theological virtues become operative and move the soul (and the Church) toward her ultimate fulfillment. Since this life of faith, hope and charity is the Christian life, and since the elementary comprehensive instruction in the Christian life is catechesis, we can say that, in a certain profound sense, the entire content of catechesis is "sacramental."[9] (Or, at the very least, we can say that without the sacraments, nothing really intelligible and efficacious can be taught.) The catechesis of faith teaches us the Creed -- and the sacraments. The catechesis of hope teaches us the Our Father -- and the sacraments. The catechesis of charity teaches us the Commandments and the Our Father -- and the sacraments.

The sacraments occupy this comprehensive and integrating position in catechesis because that is the position they occupy in Sacred Scripture. They are the things which constitute the "real" meaning of Scripture, viz., the New Testament realization of the Old Testament types; and thus they fulfill (however differently) the literal meaning of the Scriptures in both Testaments. And from within the sacraments, as from the first "real" or spiritual meaning of Scripture, come the other two spiritual realities or meanings referring respectively to the life of personal morality on earth and the life of beatitude in heaven.

It should be obvious, of course, that wherever "sacrament(s)" occurs in the preceding paragraph, "Christ" can -- and must -- be understood. Without Christ, i.e., without the mysteria carnis suae, the seven sacraments would be essentially no different from the sacraments of the Old Testament. That is to say, they would be nothing in themselves but signs pointing to Christ. To make of them nothing more than mere external props to our faith in Christ would be to reduce Christianity to the regime of the Old Law.[10] The reality of Christianity is, on the contrary, the active presence of Christ. And that active presence is realized, according to the normal economy, by the seven sacraments: the actual presence of His Person in the case of the Holy Eucharist, and the presence of His actions in the case of all seven. The septenarium is, therefore, in the actual and enduring state of the Economy called the "New Testament" the essential, the indispensable link between us and Christ. Christ is no more accessible outside of the sacraments (at least implicitly) than God is accessible outside of Christ. The consequent analogy is exact: the seven sacraments are "the sacraments of Christ" (or, equivalently, the Church is "the sacrament of Christ") as Christ is "the sacrament of God."

All that we have said here about the sacraments being the "comprehensive category" (and, by virtue of their inter-action with the three theological virtues, constituting with them the four "comprehensive categories" of Scripture -- and therefore catechesis) is not found explicitly so stated in the Roman Catechism. However, there is a passage which gives us what is essentially the equivalent of this truth. The passage occurs in Part II, Chapter I, on "the sacraments in general," and must be quoted here in its entirety:

> These mysterious, divinely instituted signs called sacraments properly signify, by the same divine ordinance, more than just one reality. Besides the reality already mentioned, viz., the divine grace and our sanctification, there are in each of the sacraments two other realities, both of which are most intimately connected with that grace and sanctification. These other realities are, first, the Passion of our Lord, and, secondly, the life of the blessed in heaven. They are related to our sanctification as its source and as its culmination respectively. Thus each sacrament of its very nature, as the Doctors of the Church have taught us, has a threefold signification: it recalls something from the past, it indicates something in the present, and it anticipates something in the future.
>
> This teaching is more than a mere opinion for it is solidly based on the authority of Sacred Scripture. When St. Paul says, "All of us who have been baptized into Christ Jesus were baptized into his death"(Rom 6:3), he shows that baptism is a sign in that it reminds us of the Passion and the Death of our Lord. When he goes on to say, "We were buried therefore with him by baptism into death, so that as Christ was raised from the dead by the glory of the Father, we too might walk in newness of life" (Rom

6:4), he also shows that baptism signifies the infusion of divine grace into the soul, by which we are enabled to renew our lives and fulfill what is expected of us. Finally, when he says, "If we have been united with him in a death like his, we shall certainly be united with him in a resurrection like his" (Rom 6:5), he shows that baptism also signifies the eternal life itself -- the life which through baptism we shall one day attain.[11]

This exceedingly rich text calls for some analysis.

The first signification of the sacraments, i.e., as "sign" related to "signed," is relationally in the direction of the past. This signification is genetically first because it indicates the origin of the sacraments. Their origin is historical: they spring from the events of Christ's earthly life, i.e., from Christ's "institution," as solemnly defined by the Church.[12] Those events -- and especially His Passion, Death and Resurrection -- constitute the substance of the Gospel, the "Good News," which in turn fulfilled "all that was written," viz., the Scriptures of the Old Testament. The data of both Testaments thus form the content of the Creed, viz., the summary of the Apostolic teaching.

There is, then, an analogy between the first signification of the sacraments (viz., the signification of events in salvation history) and the historical (or literal) meaning of Sacred Scripture. And since faith finds its object in these same events of salvation history, it is not without reason that in the classic catechesis this object has always been treated (i.e., taught and learned) in chronological order. From Creation to Redemption to Sanctification, the truth of the faith is the truth of salvation history. And it is this truth of salvation history that is given us in the literal sense of Sacred Scripture in the Old and New Testaments, and in the Creed -- and in the sacraments. The fact that the sacraments are not nominatim in the Apostles' Creed is therefore not some regrettable oversight, but rather a profound intuition on the part of the ancient Church. For to say that "the sacraments are in the Creed" is less true than to say that "the Creed is in the sacraments." Indeed, for the classic catechesis -- as, specifically, for St. Augustine and St. Thomas -- the sacraments and the Creed are radically but one reality: "one faith ...one baptism."[13]

Coming now to the second signification of the sacraments precisely as signs, viz., as "signing" the present reality of grace in the Christian, we see a similar analogy involving the sense of Scripture and the theological virtues. Just as the first sacramental signification regarding the past involved the historical sense of Scripture and the virtue of faith, so this second signification regarding the present involves the spiritual sense of Scripture and the virtue of charity. This second analogy corresponding to the second signification is, however, even more intimate and binding than the first. For now we are comparing no longer two senses of Scripture (the historical and the spiritual) but two aspects of a fundamentally single sense (the spiritual sense, subdivided into the typical and the tropological), and no longer two virtues (faith and charity) but two aspects of a fundamentally single virtue (the virtue of charity, subdivided into the charity of Christ as Head and the charity of Christians as members).[14] That is why this signification, although genetically second, is ontologically and logically first. The sacraments are primarily the sign of grace here and now present, and only secondarily the sign of its cause (Christ's Passion in the past) and of its fulfillment (heavenly glory in the future).

In this present and primary sacramental signification, the only real distinction on which our analogy is based is the distinction between members and Head. This distinction within the Mystical Body of Christ is indeed real. Without its reality, the true relationship between the individual Christian (or any number of individual Christians) and Christ is lost. Both the dependence and the cooperation of the member(s) regarding the Head are secured only by the reality of this distinction. The member(s) can do nothing without Christ, but neither can Christ do what He wills to do without the member(s) as subject of His action. The distinction, therefore, only highlights the connection: the sacramental order, which is Christ's action here and now, calls for the moral order, which concerns human action here and now -- and vice versa. As a result of this connection, we can speak (as the Roman Catechism clearly implies) of a practical identity between the sacramental life and the moral life of the Christian. The sacraments of faith are in vain if they are not also the "sacraments of charity," i.e., of the charity enjoined by the Commandments. And, reciprocally, this life of true charity can no more exist apart from the sacraments (at least in voto) than faith can. That this reciprocity between the sacraments and charity is indeed closer, in a practical sense, than what obtains even between the sacraments and faith is reflected in the fact that whereas in Part I of the Roman Catechism (on the Creed) the "sacraments" -- or even "sacrament" -- are seldom mentioned (apart from Chapter 10, for a very significant reason which we will discuss later), in Part III (on the Decalogue) they are frequently and emphatically mentioned.[15]

Because of its supreme importance, both speculatively and practically, as affecting our proper understanding of the supreme virtue (charity), we must make one further comment on this second (in our consideration, but in reality the first) signification of the sacraments. The criticism has been made that the Roman Catechism, along with practically the entire "pre-Vatican II" catechesis, made a serious mistake in keeping the Decalogue as the matrix of its moral doctrine.[16] What was lost thereby, we are told, was a truly Christian morality; for it was displaced by a crude revival of Old Testament morality, anachronistically sophisticated by a humanist natural-law morality.[17] This criticism, which would remedy the situation by substituting the Beatitudes for the Commandments, is gravely misleading.

To address this criticism, three brief but important points will suffice. First, as a matter of history, the Roman Catechism's choice of the Decalogue was in perfect continuity with an unbroken tradition which antedated Augustine, deriving as it does directly from the Didache and indeed from the New Testament itself.[18] Secondly, as a matter of textual content, Part III of the Roman Catechism is saturated with "charity." Not only are the two commandments to love, which summarize the Decalogue, given explicit and ample treatment in Chapter 2, on the First Commandment of the Decalogue, and Chapter 6, on the Fifth Commandment, respectively; their own inter-relationship is explained in Chapter 5 (on the Fourth Commandment) and the over-all context of "commandments" as such is more than adequately handled in Chapter 1 (Introduction).[19] The fact that the <u>word</u> "love" is not mentioned in the Decalogue is no more relevant to a Christian reading of the Decalogue (i.e, as Christ and His Apostles read it) than the fact that the same word "love" is likewise missing from the Our Father -- and the Beatitudes! This suggests a third and final point. Not only is this would-be renewal of an "authentic" Christian moral catechesis contrary to the undeviating tradition, and not only is it an ironic re-introduction of a "fundamentalist" fetish for <u>words</u>; it is also -- and most dangerously -- a re-introduction of a subtle Gnosticism which is scandalized by the Old Testament and by natural law itself, and which would purify Catholic morality in the name of a new and truly "spiritual" Christianity. The Commandments as they are treated in the Roman Catechism are quite adequately "Christianized"; that is, they are given their <u>real</u>, i.e., <u>New</u> Testament, sense. And the best guarantee of that -- beyond all mere words -- is the authors' recurring reminder that the sacramental life and the moral life must be one integral life: the one integral Christian life, in which the law of Christ and the love of Christ are one reality.

The third and last direction of the sacraments as "signs" is toward the future, where the "signed" is the life of the blessed in heaven. This reality corresponds to the fourth and final sense of Sacred Scripture, viz., the anagogical sense; and the theological virtue operative here is hope -- and, through hope, charity.[20] In its function, hope is obviously subordinate to charity. Just as the role of faith in "realizing" the first sense of Scripture is essential (for, without faith, charity has no object -- more than hidden in the "letter," it does not exist at all!), so too the role of hope in "realizing" this last sense of Scripture is essential to charity. The "good-in-itself," which is the object of charity, must first be the "good-for-myself." The reference to <u>self</u>, which hope implies and which charity transcends, is <u>not</u> a defect in our prayer. Christ not only provides for it ("give <u>us</u> this day ...forgive <u>us</u>..."); He positively encourages it with His constant references to "reward."[21] "Self" is the "scandal" of the fourth sense, just as "law" is the "scandal" of the third sense, and "fact" is the "scandal" of the first. But all three (which, by no coincidence, are usually always together) are eminently Christian, because all three are organically related to the greatest "scandal" of all: that of the second sense, which is the "scandal" of Christ Himself who emptied Himself and willed to be present in the sacramental sign here and now.

The co-existence, therefore, of charity and hope in the direction of the future is at least as important as the co-existence of charity and faith in the direction of the past. For only thus is secured the co-existence of charity with the entire spectrum of the Economy -- from the beginning of the historical in Genesis to the end of the eschatological in the Apocalypse -- and pre-eminently with its term and culmination: the eternal life. Indeed, the three terms "love," "grace" and "glory" refer ontologically to the same reality. As uncreated, they are the Triune God Himself. As created, they are intrinsic to the Sacred Humanity of Christ, which is thus, from the beginning to the end of the Economy, the one "Sacrament."

The text from the Roman Catechism which we have analyzed occurs fairly early in the chapter on "the sacraments in general." From it the general tenor of the term "grace," as it occurs throughout the entire Catechism, can be gauged. Applying the later post-Tridentine terminology, we can say that for the Roman Catechism grace is always "sanctifying grace." That it is also, by analogy, "actual grace" is something the authors scarcely note.[22] Now, if grace is always sanctifying grace, it is also always sacramental grace.

This intrinsic connection between grace and the sacraments is so fundamental to the Catechism that the authors did not wait until Part II to affirm it. Already in Part I, in Chapter 10, dealing with the Ninth Article, "...the holy Catholic Church, the communion of saints," three consecutive points are made which constitute the essential "vis et ratio doctrinae" of the Roman Catechism. The three points are these: 1) the entire doctrine on the Church stems directly, exactly as in the wording of the Creed, from the doctrine on the Holy Spirit; 2) the Church is essentially holy because, in the Holy Spirit, she is indissolubly united to

God; and 3) the total holiness of the Church is founded on and mediated by the sacraments. Or, in other words, the communion -- with God and man -- which the Church is essentially, is a "communion of holy things."

These three points occur in Sections 1, 15 and 24 respectively. Their capital importance demands their repetition in the words of the text itself.

1) The Church and the Holy Spirit:

> This article stems from the preceding one "I believe in the Holy Spirit" for, as it was then made clear, the Holy Spirit is the source and giver of all holiness. We now go on to profess our faith in a church endowed with holiness by that same Holy Spirit.[23]

2) The Church and indissoluble union with God:

> The Church is called holy because she is consecrated, given over completely to God. Similar to this was the holiness of certain things in the Old Testament, even inanimate things such as vessels, vestments and altars, or again the first-born. Because they were set aside for God's use in worship, they were called holy.
>
> It should not surprise us that the Church is called holy even when she counts many sinners among her children. The faithful are called holy because they are in fact the People of God, truly consecrated to Christ by faith and baptism . And this holds even when they offend God in many ways and fail to live up to what they promised. Just as an artist who is deficient in his art is still called an artist. That is also why St. Paul called his Corinthians "saints" even while he was upbraiding some of them for their obviously grave offenses.
>
> A further reason why the Church is called holy is the fact of her union as a body with Christ as her head, for Christ is the source of all holiness, from whom flow all the gifts of the Holy Spirit and all the riches of God's goodness...
>
> A yet further reason for her being called holy is the fact that she has the exclusive custody of the true sacrificial worship and the use of the sacraments, those efficacious instruments of grace whereby God makes us truly holy ...[24]

3) The Church and "the communion of holy things":

> ...The unity of the Spirit, by whom she is directed, brings it about that whatever she possesses from Him is held in common. The benefits from all the sacraments belong to all the faithful. For by these sacraments, as by sacred bonds, they are brought together and joined to Christ. This is especially true of Baptism, which is as it were the door leading into the Church. The "communion of saints" should be understood as a "communion of sacraments," i.e., of "holy things." For in the Nicene Creed, the statement corresponding to the "communion of saints" is "I confess one Baptism." And after Baptism there comes, first, the Holy Eucharist, then the other sacraments. All the sacraments are indeed in this "communion," for all of them unite us to God and make us sharers in His grace. But it belongs properly and pre-eminently to the Eucharist to be the cause of this "holy communion."[25]

In the very expression "communio sanctorum," in the sense of "holy things" (i.e., rather than "saints" or "holy persons"), two truths are identified and combined, which, we now see, are fundamentally one, viz., 1) the truth of the sacraments as being "res et sacramentum" (i.e., the reality of certain outward signs, and the sign in turn of sanctifying grace), and 2) the truth of the primary spiritual (the "typical") sense of Scripture as being the "Novum Testamentum" (i.e., the reality of the Old Testament, and the sign in turn of the life of charity and the glory of heaven).[26] Or, in other words, the reason why the sacraments occupy the center (and from the center cover all the parts) of the Roman Catechism is that they are the sign and the reality of Christ Who, by virtue of the primary spiritual meaning of Scripture, is the center (and from the center covers all the parts) of the divine revelation "that comes to us from the Apostles."[27]

What we have said throughout this chapter about the sacraments (in the plural) must, of course, be said pre-eminently (as the Roman Catechism just did in the last passage quoted) of the Holy Eucharist.[28] For this one sacrament is Christ, not only in His action but in His Person as well. To it all the other sacraments are directed, and from it they flow. This final identification of the Holy Eucharist with the "central meaning" of Sacred Scripture is, I submit, the simplest (and most sublime) synthesis of the "classic catechesis" -- and of its most perfect expression to date: the Roman Catechism.

III

We cannot finish this chapter, however, without a more explicit presentation of that which was its purpose to convey, viz., the "overall determining principle" ("communis regula atque praescriptio") of the structure of the Roman Catechism. As we have now seen at some length, this principle was presented by the authors of the Catechism -- following the tradition of the "classic catechesis" in its millennial development -- as consisting essentially of the "comprehensive categories" ("communia loca") of Sacred Scripture: its four senses aligned with the four components of catechesis. What remains to do is simply repeat what the authors themselves have given us as their briefest resume of this principle which is the ultimate determinant of this alignment, and which is therefore the ultimate determinant of not only the structure but the very spirit of the Roman Catechism.

As already frequently noted in this chapter, all the synthetic principles of the Roman Catechism are found, in one way or another, in the Preface. There are to be found the several phrases or expressions --"vis et ratio doctrinae," "communis regula atque praescriptio," "formula et ratio," "communia Sacrae Scripturae loca"-- in which we have discovered the "ratio" of the Catechism itself.[29] Is there one more such expression which in one word identifies this ultimate determinant? Unfortunately perhaps, the answer is no. This, however, should not surprise or disappoint us. Our authors were not given to putting "labels" on things; they preferred to let their principles speak for themselves. And in this final instance their point, spoken mostly (and characteristically) in the words of Scripture, is unmistakably clear. The "overall determining principle" of the Roman Catechism is Christocentrism. In the Preface we read the following:

In order that parish priests may know to what goal all their plans, labors and studies are directed, and how they can more surely attain that goal, they should constantly keep in mind as a first principle and summary of all Christian knowledge those words of our Savior: "This is eternal life, to know Thee the one true God, and Him whom Thou has sent, Jesus Christ." Hence the task of anyone teaching in the name of the Church is primarily this: to make the faithful eager to know "Jesus Christ and Him crucified." The faithful must be taught to hold with conviction and devotion the truth that "no other name has been given men whereby they are to be saved," for Christ alone is the propitiation for our sins.

"By this we may be sure that we know Him, if we keep his commandments." Here is the second principle intimately connected with the first, viz., that this life must be lived by the faithful, not in idleness as though it were somehow automatic; but with the intent to walk in the same way in which He walked. For the faithful this means, as St. Paul explained in his pastoral letters, that they aim at righteousness, faith, love and peace, for Christ gave Himself for us to redeem us from all iniquity, and to purify for himself a people of His own who are zealous for good deeds.

Our Lord not only preached but showed by His example the truth that the Law and the Prophets depend on love. And His Apostle reaffirmed that same truth that love is the one purpose of the commandments and the fulfillment of the law. There can be no doubt, then, that the principal task of the teacher is to motivate the faithful to love this immeasurable goodness of God toward us and to seek this goodness as our one ultimate and unchanging happiness, and thereby to fulfill the words of the Psalmist: "Whom have I in heaven but thee? And there is nothing upon earth that I desire besides Thee."

This is that more excellent way of which St. Paul speaks when he subordinated all his teaching to this love which never ends. Hence, whatever may be the specific content of one's teaching -- whether it be about something to be believed, or something to be hoped for, or something to be done -- it must be presented in the light of the love of God. Thus it will be clear to anyone that whatever is done by Christian virtue comes from no other source and is directed to no other purpose than that one beginning and end which is love.[30]

Christocentrism is, therefore, that principle which identifies Jesus Christ as the unique and total supernatural reality. Christ is indeed "the first and the last, the alpha and the omega" -- and everything in between. He is the source and finisher of faith, the one hope, the supreme and total love. As Christ is the <u>Center</u>, so all else <u>centers</u> on

Him. And since all else is <u>there</u> only because of His creating and redeeming <u>love</u>, this "centering" on Christ must, first and last, consist in our <u>loving Him</u> in return.

This "centering on Christ" as a <u>Person to be loved</u> is echoed throughout the Catechism. Two instances are particularly striking, as a sober presentation of doctrine gets "carried away" by love. The first occurs at the end of the Second Article of the Creed, and is occasioned by a reflection on what the term "Our Lord" really means.

> To conclude his instruction on this article, the pastor will exhort his people to keep in mind what they can never really forget: that they as Christians have received so much from Christ in terms of knowledge and love, that to Him they are bound by a consecration that is forever. ...
>
> What heart can remain impervious to the advances of such a Lord Who, though He holds us totally in bondage to His redeeming power, yet calls us not His slaves but His friends and brothers? Here certainly is reason enough for us forever to acknowledge and adore and love Him Whom in this article we call "Our Lord."[31]

The second comes in Part IV, at the end of the Second Petition of the Our Father:

> Let us, finally, beg God's Holy Spirit to command us to do His holy will, and to destroy that power of Satan, from which we may stand free on the final day. May Christ conquer and reign! May His laws be obeyed, and may there be no slackers or traitors in the ranks. May we be such now that when we are summoned into His kingly presence, we may hasten to Him and take possession of that which He promised: to be with Christ in His kingdom forever.[32]

The Christ of the Roman Catechism is infinitely more than a word, an idea, a "force," a "principle." He is a <u>Person</u>. And because this is so (and <u>only</u> because this is so), the <u>Church</u> also, in the Roman Catechism, is pre-eminently -- exclusively -- "personal." This is already clear in the first formal presentation on the Church: the great Chapter 10 of Part I, where (as we have seen) the emphasis is almost exclusively on "grace" and "communion."[33]

The Church, therefore, is neither a juridical machine nor a sociological abstraction (which seem to be the only two choices in the opinion of all too many people, including Catholics). Rather, she is the "Spouse of Christ" and "our Mother." A perfect jewel of a text summarizes the Roman Catechism's ecclesiology, and it is all the more brilliant for its unexpectedness -- for who usually sees the First Petition of the Our Father in this light?

> The main object of this first petition is Holy Church: that we see and love her for what she truly is -- the Spouse of Christ and our Mother. For she alone is that overflowing and inexhaustible fount of grace that forgives all sins. As dew distilled from heavenly water-spouts, all the sacraments are gathered up in her, and from her they flow as streams of salvation and holiness. To her alone, and to her children clasped to her breast, belongs this prayer: this invocation of the Name, than which there is no other name under heaven by which we are to be saved.[34]

This personality of the Church as Spouse of the New Adam and Mother of all the Living evokes the radiant image and reality of the Blessed Virgin Mary. Witnessing to a most ancient tradition, and anticipating its development in most recent times,[35] the Roman Catechism, in its explanation of the Second Article of the Creed, tells us that we are no longer children of wrath "<u>propter Evam</u>," but children of grace "<u>a Maria</u>."[36]

Unspoken but implicit in this reference to Our Lady in terms of grace is the point which the Catechism will insist on in its explanation of the Ninth Article of the Creed, viz., the essential unity of the Church Militant and the Church Triumphant in the <u>one</u> only Church.

> From these two parts we are not to infer that there are two churches. Rather, they are but the two parts of the one same Church. One part precedes: it is now at home in heaven. The other part follows: it moves forward with each day, joined to Christ, until that eternal day when it too will happily rest.[37]

The perfection of the Church in heaven -- and by that very perfection holding fast her communion of grace and charity with her still imperfect and struggling children on earth -- finds its perfect prototype in the person of Blessed Mary. And just as the Triumphant Church reinforces her unity with the Church on earth by Mary's mediation of grace, so too the Church Militant reinforces her unity with the Church in heaven by her prayer to Our Lady. Like a matching jewel to the text we quoted earlier on the flow of grace downward from Mother Church to us, there is text in which the authors allude to the flow of prayer upward from the children of the Church to their Mother in heaven. The Hail Mary is first a prayer of praise and thanksgiving: we thank God for Our Lady, and we offer her our praise. Only then comes the "Holy Mary": we ask her to help us.

> By this prayer we offer to God our highest praise and gratitude for the heavenly gifts He has lavished on this most holy Virgin. And turning to her, we congratulate her on her singular blessedness. Rightly does holy Church join in this prayer of thanksgiving her prayer of petition to the glorious Mother of God. To her we run, poor sinners, for refuge, and through her from God we receive all that we need for eternal life.[38]

Yet again -- so rich is its truth and so important its role in our lives as Christians -- this same personality of the Church as "Mother" evokes another image and reality, this time on earth and imbedded in history, viz., that of the Roman Church, "The Mother and Teacher of all the Churches."[39] As itself a "Roman" document, the Catechism speaks of the Roman Primacy with great sobriety. It speaks with logic:"...a visible Church requires a visible head."[40] But, much more, it speaks with faith:"...God has made the visible head the one who holds the Holy See of Rome as the legitimate successor of Peter, the Prince of the Apostles."[41] After citing the testimony of the Fathers, the Catechism leaves it at that: the One Holy Catholic and Apostolic Church is Roman, and the Roman Church is our Mother.

This double reference to the Church as "Mother"-- implicitly to the Blessed Virgin Mary and explicitly to the Roman Church -- illustrates most vividly the truth enunciated in the Catechism that the Church is indeed simultaneously Triumphant and Militant, in heaven and on earth.[42] For the personality of the Church is no more divisible than is the personality of Christ her Spouse.

And indeed, in some profound sense, this indivisibility of her person includes its indivisibility from His Person. For by virtue of Him alone is this mystery of the Church realized and made known to us.[43] Realized pre-eminently in the role of Our Lady, and made known pre-eminently in the role of Blessed Peter and his successors, the Church shares with Christ in perfect spousal community all that is His and all that is hers. To be totally "Christian" is to be totally "Catholic." For the Roman Catechism, "thinking with the Church" ("sentire cum Ecclesia") and "Christocentrism" are the same one thing.

NOTES

1 "...Patres Oecumenicae Tridentinae Synodi...censuerunt, ut certam aliquam formulam et rationem Christiani populi ab ipsis fidei rudimentis instituendi traderent..." (Praef., 7; p. 3)

2 Ibid., 8; p. 3.

3 "...quoniam quae divinitus tradita fuerunt multa sunt et varia, ut nec ita facile aut animo comprehendi, aut etiam mente comprehensa memoria teneri possint, ut, cum se obtulerit docendi occasio, eorum parata sit et prompta explicatio; sapientissime maiores nostri totam hanc vim et rationem salutaris doctrinae in quattuor haec capita redactam distribuerunt: Apostolorum Symbolum, Sacramenta, Decalogum, Dominicam Orationem. Nam omnia, quae Christianae fidei disciplina tenenda sunt, sive ad Dei cognitionem, sive ad mundi creationem et gubernationem, sive ad humani generis redemptionem spectent, sive ad bonorum praemia et malorum poenas pertineant, Symboli doctrina continentur. Quae autem signa sunt, et tanquam instrumenta ad divinam gratiam consequendam, haec septem Sacramentorum doctrina complectitur. Iam vero quae ad leges referuntur, quorum finis est caritas, Decalogo descripta sunt. Quidquid denique ab hominibus optari, sperari ac salutariter peti possit, Dominica Precatione comprehenditur. Quare sequitur, ut explanatis quattuor his, quasi communibus Sacrae Scripturae locis, nihil fere ad eorum intelligentiam, quae Christiano homini discenda sunt, desiderari possit." (ibid., 12; pp. 5-6)

4 The tie-in between these four "capita" of catechesis and these four "loca" of Scripture is given further "vim" by what the Preface goes on to say in the next (and concluding) section:
"Itaque visum est monere parochos ut, quoties usuvenerit, ut aliquem interpretentur Evangelii, vel quemvis alium divinae Scripturae locum, intelligant eius loci, quicumque is fuerit, sententiam cadere sub unum aliquod quattuor illorum capitum, quae diximus; quo, tanquam ad eius doctrinae fontem, quod explicandum sit, confugient." (ibid., 13; p. 6)

5 See above, Chapter III.

6 See above, ibid., pp. 65 and 70.

7 "Nunc restat considerandum de Ecclesiae sacramentis; quae tamen omnia comprehenduntur sub uno articulo [viz., Art. IX], quia ad effectum gratiae pertinent..." Opuscl. IV, In Articulos

Fidei et Sacramenta Ecclesiae Expositio (Parma edition, Vol. 16, p. 119). See above, Chapter II, note 50, p. 54.

8   See above, Chapter IV, pp. 95-100. For a superb analysis, in greater detail, of the particular inter-relationship between Gropper and Carranza and the consequent significance of the different arrangement made by the authors of the Roman Catechism, see Pedro Rodriguez, "El sentido de los sacramentos segun el Catecismo Romano," Scripta Theologica, 9 (1977), pp. 951-84.

9   This conclusion makes only the more striking the contrast with the Lutheran (and, a fortiori, the Calvinist) doctrine on the sacraments, and the consequent placing of the doctrine as an "appendix" in the Protestant catechisms. See above, Chapter IV, pp. 92-93.

10 This reduction was indeed effected by John Calvin, who expressly denied any essential difference between the sacraments of the New Testament and those of the Old. They are all mere signs of Christ, God's attestations to our faith in Him; they are in no sense "causes" of grace. L'Institution chrétienne, IV, 14, 23-26 (Genève: Labor et Fides, 1958; Tom. IV, pp. 288-93).

This distinctively Calvinist equation of the sacraments of the two Testaments is clear from the nineteenth-century American edition of the Heidelberg Catechism cited earlier (see above, Chapter IV, note 37, p. 106). The Catechism's meaning of the sacraments as "signs" is explained as follows: "...as signs, they more fully declare to us the promise of the Gospel, that we may the better understand it. That is, heavenly benefits promised us in the gospel are here imaged to us in earthly signs, and set before our eyes. For example: Circumcision is a representation of the removal of sin. Washing in baptism is a representation of the washing away of sins. The killing of the Paschal Lamb is a representation of the offering of Christ on the cross. The broken bread and the consecrated wine is a representation of the crucified body, and the shed blood of Christ." (op. cit., p. 154)

11 "Iam vero hisce mysticis signis, quae a Deo instituta sunt, illud etiam praecipue convenit, ut ex Domini institutione non unam aliquam rem, sed plures simul significent. Quod in singulis sacramentis licet cognoscere, quae non solum sanctitatem et iustitiam nostram, sed praeterea duo alia cum ipsa sanctitate maxime coniuncta declarant: Christi scilicet redemptoris passionem, quae sanctitatis causa est, et vitam aeternam coelestemque beatitudinem, ad quam sanctitas nostra, tanquam ad finem referri debet. Quod quidem cum in omnibus sacramentis perspici possit, merito sacri doctores unicuique sacramentorum triplicem significandi vim inesse tradiderunt: tum quia alicuius rei praeteritae memoriam afferat; tum quia aliam praesentem indicet ac demonstret; tum quia aliam futuram praenunciet.

"Neque vero existimandum est, hoc ita ab illis doceri, ut etiam sanctarum Scripturarum testimonio non probetur. Nam cum Apostolus ait: 'quicumque baptizati sumus in Christo Iesu, in morte ipsius baptizati sumus'; plane ostendit, idcirco baptismum signum dicendum esse, quod Dominicae passionis et mortis nos admoneat. Deinde cum inquit: 'Consepulti enim sumus cum illo per baptismum in mortem, ut quomodo Christus surrexit a mortuis per gloriam Patris, ita et nos in novitate vitae ambulemus'; ex iis verbis perspicuum est, baptismum signum esse, quo coelestis gratia in nos infusa declaratur, cuius munere nobis datum est, ut novam vitam instituentes, omnia verae pietatis officia facile et libenti animo exequamur. Postremo cum addit: 'Si enim complantati facti sumus similitudini mortis eius, simul et resurrectionis erimus'; apparet baptismum vitae etiam aeternae, quam per illum consecuturi sumus, non obscuram significationem dare." (II, 1, 12; p. 88)

12 Council of Trent, Session VII (March 3, 1547), <u>Decretum de sacramentis</u>, can. 1 (DS 1601).

13 For St. Augustine: see <u>De Symbolo ad catechumenos</u>, I, 1; VII, 15; VIII, 16 (cited in Chapter II, notes 15, 16 and 17 respectively, pp. 48-49).
For St. Thomas: see above, note 7, pp. 185-86.

14 See above, Chapter III, p. 71.

15 The references to the sacraments in Part III (on the Decalogue) are the following:
III, 4, 25; p. 249 (on frequent Confession and Sunday attendance at Mass).
III, 4, 27; p. 250 (on adoration of the Blessed Sacrament).
III, 5, 9; p. 253 (on parents' introduction of their children to the sacraments).
III, 5, 11; p. 254 (on children's provision of the last sacraments for their parents).
III, 5, 12; p. 255 (on children's remembrance of their deceased parents at Mass).
III, 7, 1; p. 265 (on matrimony as the efficacious protector of the Sixth Commandment).
III, 7, 6; p. 266 (on the Sixth Commandment to be observed in matrimony).
III, 7, 8; p. 267 (on the gravity of adultery as a violation of a sacrament).
III, 7, 12; p. 269 (on Confession and Holy Communion as the most efficacious means to purity).
III, 10, 19; p. 290 (on the Ninth Commandment as a protector of matrimony).
III, 10, 20; p. 290 (on marital status as affecting the object of the Ninth Commandment).
It is, of course, obvious that these references are of unequal value when it comes to substantiating the assertion made in the text.

16 See, e.g., an anonymous pamphlet, entitled Pour la formation chrétienne des enfants (n.p., 1976), in which the author (aliunde identified as a P. Lallement) severely criticizes the Roman Catechism for a) its failure to emphasize grace and charity, and b) its basing of Christian morality on the Decalogue. The author's evident orthodoxy in general makes his critique only the more gratuitous and groundless. See below, note 17, and note 22, p. 189.

17 Answering his own question, "Comment expliquer que, malgré ces défauts [viz., its identifying Christian morality with the Decalogue (and thus cutting it off from "the faith" in Part I), and, more specifically, its relegating love of God to the First Commandment and love of neighbor ("bizarrement") to the Fifth Commandment], ce catéchisme ait si longtemps retenu la faveur de la hierarchie," P. Lallement gives this explanation: "Les défenseurs de la foi étaient déjà préoccupés de rejoindre les humanistes sur leur propre terrain; à ce moment, c'était celui de l'exaltation de la nature humaine. Les theologiens voulaient donc surtout montrer ce qu'exigeait la religion naturelle, la morale naturelle, estimant que c'était le mieux pour défendre le christianisme." (ibid., p. 7) After admitting that the Old Testament was God's pedagogy leading from the imperfect to the perfect, he makes ("bizarrement"?) the following conclusion: "on peut ainsi comprendre qu' à l'inverse il se soit trouvé des chrétiens fervents qui ont vu toute la loi, même avec sa perfection évangélique, dans les mots du décalogue." (ibid., p.8)

18 See Guy Bourgeault, S.J., Decalogue et morale chrétienne: enquête patristique sur l'utilisation et l'interprétation chrétiennes du decalogue de c. 60 à c. 220 (Montréal: Bellarmin, 1971), pp.146-149; 312-14.

19 A few excerpts from the chapters cited in the text should suffice to establish the Roman Catechism's "saturation" of its Decalogue in "love":

"...docendum est, Deum, qui amorem requisivit, amoris vim inserere cordibus per Spiritum Sanctum suum. Hic autem Spiritus bonus petentibus a Patre coelesti datur. ...Quia igitur Dei auxilium praesto nobis est, ...non est quod quisquam rei difficultate deterreatur. Nihil enim est amanti difficile." (III, 1, 7; p. 222)

"At si bonitatis et dilectionis ipsius effusas in nos divitias contempletur, illum poteritne non amare? Hinc est illud prooemium, hinc illa conclusio, qua in praecipiendo mandandoque in Scriptura utitur Deus, 'Ego Dominus.'" (III, 2, 4, p. 226)

"At vero zelum hunc Dei suavissimum ac dulcissimum experimur, cum summa eius atque incredibilis in nos voluntas zelo ipso demonstratur. Nec enim aut amor ardentior inter homines, aut maior arctiorque coniunctio quam eorum, qui coniugio copulati sunt, reperitur. Igitur, quam nos valde diligit, ostendit Deus, cum crebro se vel sponso vel marito comparans, zelotem vocat." (III, 2, 29; p. 233)

"Nam illa [viz., the first three Commandments] finem, qui Deus est, continuo spectant; haec [viz., the last seven Commandments] nos ad proximi caritatem erudiunt; etsi longius progressa, ad Deum, idest illud extremum, cuius gratia proximum ipsum diligimus, perducunt. Quamobrem Christus Dominus praecepta illa duo de diligendo Dec et proximo similia inter se esse dixit." (III, 5, 1; pp. 250-51)

"Cumque hac lege de caritate et amore praeceptum sit, tum omnium etiam illorum officiorum atque actionum, quae caritatem ipsam consequi solent, praecepta traduntur. 'Caritas patiens est,' inquit divus Paulus; patientia igitur nobis praecipitur, in qua nos animas nostras possessuros Salvator docet. Beneficentia deinde caritatis comes est et socia; quoniam 'caritas benigna est.' Benignitas autem atque beneficentiae virtus late patet, eiusque officium in iis rebus maxime versatur, ut pauperibus suppeditemus res necessarias, cibum esurientibus, sitientibus potum demus, nudos vestiamus, et quo quisque opis notrae magis indiget, eo in illum plus liberalitatis conferamus." (III, 6, 17; p. 262)

20 See above, Chapter III, p. 71. See S.T., II-II, 17, 8.

21 See Mt. 5:12, 46; 6:1, 2, 5, 16; 10:41, 42; Mk 9:41; Lk 6:23, 35; etc.

22 It is interesting to note that in the little treatise on contrition as an integral part of the sacrament of Penance (II, 5, 22-35; pp. 167-73), the word "gratia" occurs only twice, and both times it clearly means sanctifying grace. In section 25 (p. 168) we read:"...doloris proprium est nomen quo ex amissa Dei gratia atque innocentia afficimur." Actual grace is obviously present, but its effect is to make us notice that "grace" is absent! Again, in section 35 (p. 172):"...in primisque divinae gratiae praesidio se adiuvari petat, ne in posterum eadem illa peccata admittat." Yes, "grace" is "adiuvans," but only after one has regained "grace"!

In the little treatise on temptation, which is the Sixth Petition of the Our Father (IV, 15; pp. 344-52), "gratia" occurs three times: twice as the object which "Jerusalem" is "tempted" to lose (IV, 15, 12; p. 349), and once as the object we are to pray for as a force to restore us when our own forces fail (IV, 15, 11; p. 348). This latter could be actual grace; but in a similar context earlier in the chapter (IV, 15, 3; p. 345) what is clearly actual grace is called, rather, "dexterae coelestis auxilium."

This should adequately meet P. Lallement's objection about the minimization of "grace" in the Roman Catechism. See above, note 17, p. 188.

23 "Pendet autem hic articulus a superiori; quia, cum iam demonstratum sit, Spiritum Sanctum omnis sanctitatis fontem et largitorem esse, nunc ab eodem Ecclesiam sanctitate donatam confitemur." (I, 10, 1; p. 58)

24 "Apellatur autem sancta, quod Deo consecrata dedicataque sit; sic enim caetera huiuscemodi, quamquam corporea sint, sancta vocari consueverunt, cum divino cultui addicta et dedicata sunt; cuius generis sunt in lege veteri vasa, vestes et altaria; in qua primogeniti quoque, qui Deo altissimo dedicabantur, sancti sunt appellati.

"Nec mirum cuiquam videri debet, Ecclesiam dici sanctam, tametsi multos peccatores continet. Sancti enim vocantur fideles, qui populus Dei effecti sunt, quive se, fide et baptismate suscepto, Christo consecrarunt; quamquam in multis offendunt, et quae polliciti sunt, non praestant; quemadmodum etiam qui artem aliquam profitentur, etsi artis praecepta non servent, nomen tamen artificum retinent. Quare D. Paulus Corinthios sanctificatos et sanctos appellat, in quibus nonnullos fuisse prespicuum est, quos ut carnales et gravioribus etiam nominibus acriter obiurgat.

"Sancta etiam dicenda est, quod veluti corpus cum sancto capite Christo Domino totius sanctitatis fonte coniungitur, a quo Spiritus Sancti charismata et divinae bonitatis divitiae diffunduntur. ...

"Accedit etiam, quod sola Ecclesia legitimum sacrificii cultum, et salutarem habet sacramentorum usum, per quae, tanquam efficacia divinae gratiae instrumenta, Deus veram sanctitatem efficit. ...." (I, 10, 15; p. 63.)

25 "Unitas enim Spiritus, a quo illa (Ecclesia) regitur, efficit, ut quidquid in eam collatum est, commune sit. Omnium enim sacramentorum fructus ad universos fideles pertinet; quibus sacramentis, veluti sacris vinculis, Christo connectuntur et copulantur; et maxime omnium baptismo, quo, tanquam ianua, in Ecclesiam ingrediuntur.

"Hac autem Sanctorum communione sacramentorum communionem intelligi debere, Patres in Symbolo significant illis verbis, "Confiteor unum baptisma'; baptismum vero in primis Eucharistia, et deinceps caetera sacramenta consequuntur. Nam etsi hoc nomen omnibus sacramentis convenit, cum Deo nos coniungant, illiusque participes, cuius gratiam recipimus, efficiant; magis tamen proprium est Eucharistiae, quae hanc efficit communionem." (I, 10, 24; p. 66)

26 This equation of the sacraments with the primary spiritual sense of Scripture does not necessarily demand the absolute verification of the principle of "res et sacramentum" in all seven sacraments. It is sufficient that this principle is verified in at least

four sacraments, viz., the Holy Eucharist (where the "res et sacramentum" is the <u>Real Presence</u>), and Baptism, Confirmation and Holy Orders (where the "res et sacramentum" is the <u>character</u> -- itself an analogous "real presence"). However, in the remaining three sacraments a very good case can be made for an equally analogous presence of an intermediate reality, i.e., mediating the external rite (the matter and the form) and the internal grace, viz., the <u>reconciliation with the Church</u> (in the case of Penance and the Anointing of the sick) and the <u>marriage bond</u> (in the case of Matrimony). If this hypothesis regarding all seven sacraments is granted, our conclusion here is immensely enhanced. But in any case, the general validity of the principle is amply verified--to the considerable illumination, reciprocally, of both sacrament and Scripture. See above, Chapter III, note 39, p. 81.

27 Roman Missal, the First Eucharistic Prayer.

28 Regarding the unique position of the Holy Eucharist in the "<u>septenarium</u>," it is most significant that the authors in effect <u>repeat</u> the passage on the "triple-sign" of the sacraments-in-general (II,1,12; p. 88), already quoted in this chapter (see above, note 11, pp. 186-87), and apply it <u>specifically</u> to the Holy Eucharist:

"Tria vero sunt, quae nobis hoc Sacramentum indicantur. Primum est Christi Domini passio, quae iam praeteriit; ipse enim docuit: 'Hoc facite in meam commemorationem,' et Apostolus testatus est: 'Quotiescumque manducabitis panem hunc et calicem bibetis, mortem Domini annuntiabitis, donec veniat.' Alterum est divina et coelestis gratia, quae praesens ad animam alendam et conservandam hoc Sacramento tribuitur. Quemadmodum enim Baptismo in novam vitam gignimur, Confirmatione roboramur, ut Satane repugnare et palam Christi nomen profiteri possimus, ita Eucharistiae Sacramento alimur ac sustentamur. Tertium est, quod futurum praenuntiat, aeternae iucunditatis et gloriae fructus, quos in coelesti patria ex Dei promissione capiemus. Haec igitur tria, quae instantis, praeteriti, et consequentis temporis varietati distingui perspicuum est, sacris mysteriis ita significantur, ut totum Sacramentum, quamvis ex diversis speciebus constet, ad singula horum declaranda, tanquam ad unius rei significationem referatur." (II, 4, 11; p. 133)

29 For the "ratio" of the Preface itself, see above, Chapter VI, p. 150.

30 For the Latin text of this passage, see above, Chapter V, note 42, pp. 136-37.

31 "Quod igitur reliquum est, parochus fidelem populum ad eam rationem cohortabitur, ut sciat, aequissimum esse prae caeteris homnibus, nos, qui ab eo nomen invenimus, Chritianique vocamur, et quanta ille in nos beneficia contulerit, ignorare non possumus, ob id maxime quod eius munere haec omnia fide intelligimus, aequum esse, inquam, nos ipsos, non secus ac

mancipia, redemptori nostro Domino in perpetuum addicere et consecrare. ...Sed cuius animum amoris facibus non incendat tanti Domini tam benigna et propensa in nos voluntas, qui, tametsi nos in potestate sua et dominatu veluti servos sanguine suo redemptos habeat, ea tamen caritate complectitur, ut non servos vocet sed amicos, sed fratres? Haec profecto iustissima causa est, atque haud scio an omnium sit maxima, cur eum perpetuo debeamus Domunum nostrum agnoscere, venerari et colere." (I, 3,12; p. 24)

32 "...ad extremum petemus a Dei Spiritu...ut vincat et triumphat Christus; ut vigeant eius leges toto orbe terrarum; ut decreta serventur; nullus ut proditor et desertor eius sit, sed tales se praebeant omnes ut in regis Dei conspectum non dubitanter veniant, et constitutam illis ex omni aeternitate possessionem adeant regni coelorum, ubi beati cum Christo sempiterno aevo fruantur." (IV, 11,19; p. 322)

33 See above, notes 23, 24, 25 , p. 190.

34 "Quod autem maxime rem continet in hac petitione illud est, ut omnes agnoscant ac venerentur sanctissimam Iesu Christi Sponsam, et parentem nostram Ecclesiam; in qua una est fons ille amplissimus atque perpetuus ad eluendas et expiandas omnes peccatorum sordes, unde hauriantur universa salutis et sanctificationis sacramenta; quibus quasi coelestibus quibusdam fistulis in nos a Deo ille sanctitatiss ros et liquor effunditur; ad quam solam et ad eos, quos suo sinu et gremio complexa est, pertinet divini illius imploratio Nominis, quod unum sub coelo datum est hominibus, in quo oporteat nos salvos fieri." (IV, 10, 8; pp. 315-16)

35 See St. Justin, Dial. cum Tryphone, 100 (PG 6:709); St. Irenaeus, Adv. Haereses, 3, 22, 4 (PG 7:959); Tertullian, De carne Christi, 17 (PL 2:782); Vatican II, Lumen Gentium, 56 (AAS 57:60-61).

36 "Propter Evam nascimur filii irae; a Maria Iesum Christum accepimus, per quem filii gratiae regeneramur." (I, 4, 9; p. 28) Note that the parallel between Eve and Our Lady is nor pursued to the repetition of "propter." For an equally incisive distinction between the unique mediation of Christ and that of the saints in general, see III, 2, 14; p. 229.

37 "Neque idcirco tamen duas esse Ecclesias consendum est; sed eiusdem Ecclesiae, ut antea diximus, partes duae sunt: quarum una antecessit et coelesti patria potitur; altera in dies sequitur, donec aliquando cum Salvatore nostro coniuncta, in sempiterna felicitate conquiescit." (I, 10, 6; p. 59) See above, Chapter V, note 41, p. 136.

38 "...Deum summis et habendis laudibus et gratiis agendis celebramus, quod sanctissimam Virginem omni coelestium donorum munere cumulavit; ipsique Virgini singularem illam gratulamur felicitatem.

"Iure autem sancta Dei Ecclesia huic gratiarum actioni preces etiam et implorationem sanctissimae Dei Matris adiunxit; qua pie atque suppliciter ad eam confugeremus, ut nobis peccatoribus sua intercessione conciliaret Deum, bonaque tum ad hanc tum ad aeternam vitam necessaria impetraret." (IV.5, 8; p. 300)

39 "Verum hoc [viz., the form of the sacrament of Extreme Unction] ad nos fideli Patrum traditione permanavit, ita ut omnes Ecclesiae eam formae rationem retineant, qua omnium mater et magistra sancta Ecclesia Romana utitur." (II, 6, 6; p.191) The very casualness of this statement, coming rather "unsystematically" in the middle of the treatise on the sacraments, makes it the more impressive.

40 "...sic Ecclesiae, quam ipse (Christus) intimo spiritu regit, hominem suae potestatis vicarium et ministrum praefecit. Nam cum visibilis Ecclesia visibili egeat, ita Salvator noster Petrum universi fidelium generis caput et pastorem constituit..." (I, 10, 13; p. 62)

41 "Unus est etiam eius rector ac gubernator: invisibilis quidem Christus, quem aeternus Pater dedit caput super omnem Ecclesiam, quae est corpus ipsius; visibilis autem is, qui Romanam cathedram Petri Apostolorum principis legitimus successor tenet." (I, 10, 11; p. 61) The immediate juxtaposition of the "invisible" and the "visible" in this passage -- as, equivalently, in the preceding one -- is significant.

42 "Ecclesiae autem duae potissimum sunt partes, quarum altera triumphans, altera militans vocatur. Triumphans est coetus ille clarissimus et felicissimus beatorum spirituum, et eorum qui de mundo, de carne, de iniquissimo daemone triumpharunt, et ab huius vitae molestiis liberi ac tuti aeterna beatitudine fruuntur. Militans vero Ecclesia est coetus omnium fidelium, qui adhuc in terris vivunt; quae ideo militans vocatur, quod illi cum immanissimis hostibus mundo, carne, Satane perpetuum sit bellum." (I, 10, 5; p. 59) See above, Chapter V, note 41, p. 136.

43 "This mystery of the Church realized and made known to us" is indeed grounded in the mystery of the Incarnation: the visible and the invisible, the earthly and the heavenly, the human and the divine united indivisibly in one Person. This mystery of the Church surely confirms -- and epitomizes -- what we saw earlier regarding the <u>unity</u> of the senses of Scripture: both literal and spiritual, and, within the spiritual, both in the present and in the future. There is a passage in the chapter on the Holy Eucharist which restates this mystery of both the Church and the Scriptures, and thus provides a fitting conclusion to this central point in our study.
"Sed nihil est profecto, quod ad piorum iucunditatem et fructum addi possit, cum huius altissimi sacramenti dignitatem contemplantur. Primum enim intelligunt, quanta sit evangelicae legis perfectio, cui datum est, id reipsa habere, quod signis tantum et figuris Mosaicae legis tempore adumbratum fuerat.

Quare divinitus dictum est a Dionysio Ecclesiam nostram mediam esse inter Synagogam et supremam Ierusalem, ac propterea utriusque participem. Ac profecto satis mirari fideles nunquam poterunt sanctae Ecclesiae perfectionem eiusque gloriae altitudinem, cum inter eam et coelestem beatitudinem unus tantum gradus interessee videatur. Hoc enim nobis cum coelitibus commune est, ut utrique Christum Deum et hominem praesentem habeamus; sed, quo uno gradu ab iis distamus, illi praesentes beata visione perfruuntur, nos praesentem et tamen ab oculorum sensu remotum, sacrorum mysteriorum admirabili integumento se occultantem firma et constanti fide veneramur. Praeterea fideles hoc sacramento Christi Salvatoris nostri perfectissimam caritatem experiuntur. Eius enim bonitatem maxime decuit, naturam, quam a nobis sumpserat, a nobis nunquam subtrahere, sed quantum fieri posset, esse, versarique nobiscum velle, ut illud omni tempore vere et proprie dictum videretur: 'Deliciae meae esse cum filiis hominum.'" (II, 4, 32; p. 142)

CONCLUSION

In our seventh and final chapter we reached at last the thesis of this study: we presented the structure of the Roman Catechism as consisting essentially of an alignment of the four components of the classic catechesis with the four senses of Sacred Scripture. Or, to use the words of the Catechism itself, we have shown that its "overall determining principle" (<u>communis regula atque praescriptio</u>) consists of the "expression and pattern" (<u>formula et ratio</u>) of the "comprehensive categories of Sacred Scripture" (<u>communia Sacrae Scripturae loca</u>).[1]

Now, by way of conclusion, let us offer a few observations on what we noted at the outset as a topic strictly extraneous to our thesis, yet obviously related to it as extending down to our own time and into the future, viz., that "timelessness" that accrues to a classic catechesis, of which the Roman Catechism is so preeminently an instance.[2]

The first thing to note about the Roman Catechism in respect to its subsequent history is that it must be judged always and only in the light of its authors' <u>intent</u>. What they intended was clearly stated in the Preface.

> Although there are already many works of this kind (i.e., of general instruction in the rudiments of the faith) praiseworthy for their learning and piety, the Fathers nevertheless considered it their duty to issue by authority of the Council a book from which parish priests and any others having a teaching assignment in the Church can find and apply sure principles for the instruction of the faithful. For just as there is but one Lord and one faith, so there should be one overall determining principle for teaching the faith and forming the people in all the duties of their Christian life.
>
> Since so much pertains to the full understanding and living of the Christian religion, it cannot be supposed that the Council intended to produce in one book something similar in range and detail to the work of professional theologians. Such a project, besides demanding far more time and labor than was available, would not have fulfilled the Council's precise intent.

> What the Council intended was the instruction of parish priests and others having the care of souls in that which is proper to their pastoral office, and proportioned to the capacities of the faithful. It wished to provide them with a means of basic pastoral instruction, especially if they had had no training in advanced theological studies.³

What was intended, then, was a book (<u>liber</u>) for parish priests (<u>parochi</u>), to give them sure principles (<u>certa praecepta</u>) for the instruction (<u>aedificatio</u>) of the faithful.

This intent is more clearly seen when we contrast it with what was evidently <u>excluded</u> by the authors. What they did not intend was either of the two kinds of thing originally discussed at the Council when the topic of religious instruction first came up! On the one hand, they excluded a "catechism" in the (by then) conventional sense, viz., a <u>booklet</u> for children and uneducated adults; on the other hand, a "methodus," viz., a <u>tome</u> on the basic contents and techniques of professional theology.⁴ Although called a "catechism," what they intended and produced was a book which today we would call a "directory," i.e., a guide for parish priests (and other ministers of the word) in that most concentrated and immediate exercise of their ministry: "feeding" the faith, hope and charity infused into the souls of their people at their Baptism.⁵

The most characteristic feature of the Roman Catechism is undoubtedly the tone pervading the entire work stemming from this <u>pastoral</u> intent. It blends the "<u>exhortatio</u>" with the "<u>explanatio</u>" in a manner totally Patristic.⁶ It thus exemplifies to perfection that organic unity of the <u>pastoral</u> and the <u>doctrinal</u> which is at the very heart of all authentic catechesis.⁷

Reinforcing this apect of the pastoral was the unusual procedure adopted by the Holy See in its very act of issuing the Roman Catechism. Unlike the Missal and the Breviary, which were promulgated at the same time by the same Conciliar and Papal authority, the Catechism had no accompanying Bull mandating its immediate and exclusive use.⁸ It was as though Pius V relied on the <u>intrinsic</u> authority of the Roman

Catechism to make effective its reception throughout the Church in space and time. That the Roman Catechism was thus never imposed, neither at the outset nor subsequently, bespeaks a profound confidence in its intrinsic authority on the part of the Holy See.[9]

What is this intrinsic authority of the Roman Catechism? It consists primarily in the fact that, as the only catechism by the whole Church for the whole Church,[10] it is an official statement of the faith issued by the "ordinary and universal Magisterium."[11] Twice in the Preface is this authority alluded to. First, in the passage already cited, the authority of the Council is invoked as grounding the Catechism's authority: "...the Fathers ... considered it their duty to issue, by authority of the Council, a book."[12] But earlier in the Preface, several paragraphs before any of the passages so far cited in this entire study, occurs what was undoubtedly meant to be the first premise of the Church's -- and therefore the Council's, and therefore the Catechism's -- authority.

> Lest anyone should take the words of God spoken by the ministers of the Church as mere human words, and not as the words of Christ Himself as they really are, Our Lord gave to this teaching office such authority that -- as He put it -- "Whoever hears you hears me, and whoever rejects you rejects me" (Lk 10:16). He willed this to be understood not only of those to whom He was directly speaking, but of all those who by rightful succession would assume that same teaching office, for He promised that He would be with them until the end of the world (Mt 28:30).[13]

Now, besides the primary intrinsic authority of the text itself, as based on its unbroken linkage with that of Christ the one Teacher, can we not perceive here an intrinsic authority on a secondary level, viz., on that of the Catechism's structure, as based on its linkage with the classic catechesis? This perception was enunciated in an epochal conference given in 1983 by the Prefect of the Sacred Congregation for the Doctrine of the Faith, Joseph Cardinal Ratzinger.

> The intrinsic consistency between the word and the organism which bears it lies at the source of catechesis. Its structure shows through all the major moments of the Church's life, and corresponds with the essential dimensions of Christian existence. Thus, from the very beginning, a catechetical structure was born, its origins coeval with the origins of the Church herself. Luther used this structure as

> naturally as the authors of the Catechism of the Council of Trent did. This was because it had to do, not with some artificial system, but simply with a synthesis of memorizable material indispensable to the faith, which at the same time reflects the elements indispensable to the Church: the Apostles' Creed, the sacraments, the Decalogue, the Lord's Prayer. These four classic components and headings of catechesis have across the centuries served as matrix and resume to the Bible and to the Church's life. We said that they correspond with the dimensions of Christian existence. This is what the Roman Catechism affirms when it says that in these components the Christian finds what he is to believe (the Creed), what he is to hope for (the Our Father), what he is to do (the Decalogue), and in what vital milieu he will find all three possible (the sacraments and the Church). At the same time this structure manifestly aligns with the four ways of reading Scripture which were worked out in the Middle Ages, and which can also be seen as a response to questions posed by the four stages of human existence.[14]

Authoritative as it surely is by its structure, the Roman Catechism is, however, first and last authoritative by its <u>faith</u>. And if the faith is by definition timeless, the question of the future of that book once called "the <u>Religionsbuch</u> of the Catholic Church"[15] is in substance resolved.

> This knowledge [of the supernatural beatitude destined for us which is beyond cour powers to attain and which therefore must be received from God] is properly called <u>faith</u>. By virtue of it we give our assent to what the authority of Holy Church has affirmed as something given us by God. For any uncertainty among those who believe is impossible concerning that of which the author is God, Who is truth itself.[16]

God is not the author of the Roman Catechism; He is the author of Sacred Scripture. But the classic catechesis, which is "all we need to know of the Scriptures,"[17] has its classic statement in this one incomparable work called the Roman Catechism.

NOTES

1   "Communis regula atque praescriptio": Praef., 8; p. 3.
    "formula et ratio": Praef., 7; p. 3.
    "communia Sacrae Scripturae loca": Praef.,12; p. 6.

2   See above, Introduction, p. 3.

3   "Multi quidem adhuc in hoc scriptionis genere cum magna pietatis et doctrinae laude versati sunt; sed tamen Patribus visum est maxime referre, si liber sanctae Synodi auctoritate ederetur, ex quo parochi, vel omnes alii, quibus docendi munus impositum est, certa praecepta petere atque depromere ad fidelium aedificationem possent; ut, quemadmodum 'unus est Dominus, una fides,' ita etiam una sit tradendae fidei, ad omniaque pietatis officia populum Christianum erudiendi communis regula atque preaescriptio.

    "Ergo, cum multa sint, quae ad Christianae religionis professionem pertinere videantur, nemo existiment, illud sanctae Synodo propositum fuisse, ut omnia Christianae fidei dogmata uno libro comprehensa subtiliter explicarentur (quod ab iis fieri solet, qui se profitentur universae religionis institutionem et doctrinam tradere; id enim et infiniti paene operis fuisset, et instituto minus convenire perspicuum est); sed, quoniam parochos sacerdotesque animarum curatores earum rerum cognitione instruendos suscepit, quae pastoralis muneris maxime propriae sunt, et ad fidelium captum accomodatae; ea tantum in medium afferri voluit, quae hac in re pium pastorum studium, si in difficilioribus divinarum rerum disputationibus non ita versati fuerint, adiuvare possent." Praef., 8-9; p. 3.

4   See above, Chapter V, pp. 114-15.

    What pre-empted the primary meaning "catechism," i.e., identifying the term with booklets, was the phenomenal success of just such booklets as Luther's and Calvin's (for the Protestants) and Canisius' and Auger's (for the Catholics) "catechisms."

5   The genre of "catechetical directory" thus pioneered by the Roman Catechism has reached fruition in our time with the General Catechetical Directory, issued by the Holy See in 1971 (AAS 64:97-176), and, for the United States, the National Catechetical Directory, issued by the National Conference of Catholic Bishops in 1979.

6   Here are some examples of this blending: a) the "exhortatio" following the "explanatio": I, 8, 11; pp. 52-53; b) the

"exhortatio" in the <u>middle</u> of the "explanatio": II, 2, 22; pp. 104-05; c) the "exhortatio" as a one-sentence "aside": III, 6, 19; pp. 262-63; d) the "exhortatio" addressed to the reader himself: IV, 9, 18; p. 312.

7   The true doctrine of the faith "<u>feeds</u>" (<u>pascit</u>) minds with what they must have if they are truly to love; while the authentic pastoral ministry <u>teaches</u> (<u>docet</u>) hearts that which they must have if they are truly to know, and thus to love. The reciprocity of both functions is based on an organic unity: the unity of the speculative and the practical -- because God Who is the First Truth is also our Last End.

This reciprocity is also well attested etymologically by the one Latin noun, "<u>disciplina</u>." By no coincidence our English derivative, "discipline," means both an ordering of <u>instruction</u> and an ordering of <u>conduct</u>.

8   Although the term "Roman" was not in its official title (see above, Chapter V, note 30, p.   ), the Catechism was seen by the Council of Trent as forming a close-knit triad with the <u>Roman Breviary</u> and the <u>Roman Missal</u>. Note the title of the decree in Session 25 (December 4, 1563): "De Indice Librorum, Catechismo, Breviario et Missali"(<u>CT</u>, IX, p. 1106).

Yet, unlike the Breviary's <u>Quod a Nobis</u> (1568) and the Missal's <u>Quo Primum</u> (1570), both formal Bulls, the Catechism had no formal Papal statement accompanying it except a brief "Moto propio" wherein St. Pius V grants the printer certain publishing rights. See above, Chapter VI, note 5, p. 156.

9   Toth's conclusions on the authority of the Roman Catechism (the title of his monograph) can be summarized as follows: The Roman Catechism is 1) a "public document of the Church," 2) the doctrine in which is "Catholica ac tuta," 3) and the directives from which, as sanctioned by the Ordinary and Universal Magisterium of the Church, 4) are to be received by all the faithful with "religious assent." <u>Op. cit.</u>, p. 46.

There has been no lack of subsequent Papal approbations and recommendations of the Roman Catechism. Following St. Pius V were Gregory XIII, Urban VIII, Clement XI, Clement XII, Benedict XIV, Clement XIII (his encyclical, <u>In Dominico Agro</u>, June 14, 1761, is particularly important), Leo XIII, St. Pius X and Pius XI. <u>ibid.</u>, pp. 37-52. To them can be added John XXIII (see his allocution, <u>Cum heri Romanae Synodi</u>, January 25,1960; <u>AAS</u> 52:203), and John Paul II (<u>Catechesi Tradendae</u>).

10 There has never been, to date, a "universal catechism" except the Roman Catechism. Vatican I approved the publication of one, but its approval was never promulgated. (For the schema, <u>Omnium quie Ecclesiae</u>, voted on and approved by the Council on May 4, 1870, see Mansi, <u>Sacrorum conciliorum nova et amplissima collectio</u>, Vol. 50, cols. 699-702.) The special Synod of

Bishops commemorating the twentieth anniversary of Vatican II (November-December 1985) voted a similar approval, and the preliminary work toward such a publication is now underway.

11 The term "Magisterium" did not have the technical precision it would later receive in the First Vatican Council (Session 3, <u>Dei Filius</u>, April 24, 1870, cap. 3; DS 3011 and 3014); and it is but seldom used in the Roman Catechism (see above, Chapter VI, note 42, p. 163). Yet the verification in the Roman Catechism of its functions and sanctions is self-evident (see below, note 13).

For a brief critique of the term "magisterium" as historically used, see Yves Congar, O.P., <u>op. cit</u>. See also his appended essay, "Bref historique des formes du 'Magistère' et de ses relations avec les docteurs," <u>Revue des Sciences Philosophiques et Théologiques</u>, 60 (1976), 99-112. These two studies, for all their undoubted utility and even brilliance, clearly exemplify -- at a distance of some ten years -- the same historical conditioning they purport to find in "Magisterium."

12 See above, note 3, p. 199.

13 "Ac ne quis verbum auditus Dei ab Ecclesiae ministris, tanquam verbum hominum, sed, sicut vere est, verbum Christi acciperet; ille ipse Salvator noster tantam auctoritatem eorum magisterio tribuendam esse statuit, ut diceret: 'Qui vos audit, me audit; et qui vos spernit, me spernit'; quod quidem non de iis tantum, quibuscum sermo habebatur, intelligi voluit; verum de omnibus etiam, qui legitima successione docendi munus obirent, quibus se omnibus diebus usque ad consummationem saeculi affuturum esse pollicitus est." Praef., 4; p. 2.

14 "La cohésion interne entre la parole et l'organisme qui la porte trace le chemin à la catechèse. Sa structure apparait à travers les evenements principaux de la vie de l'Eglise, qui correspondent aux dimensions essentielles de l'existence chrétienne. Ainsi est née, dès les premiers temps, une structure catéchètique, dont le noyau remonte aux origines de l'Eglise. Luther a utilisé cette structure pour son catéchisme aussi naturellement que les auteurs du Catéchisme du concile de Trente l'ont fait. Cela fut possible parce qu'il ne s'agissait pas d'un synthèse du matériel mnémonique indispensable à la foi, qui reflète en même temps les éléments vitalement indispensable à l'Eglise: le Symbole de Apôtres, les Sacrements, le Décalogue, la Prière du Seigneur. Ces quatre composantes classiques et maitresses de la catéchèse ont servi pendant des siècles comme dispositif et résumé de l'enseignement catéchètique; ils ont aussi ouvert l'acces à la Bible comme à la vie de l'Eglise. Nous venons de dire qu'elles correspondent aux dimensions de l'existence chrétienne. C'est ce qu'affirme le Catéchisme Romain, en disant qu'on y trouve ce que le chrétien doit croire (Symbole), espérer (Notre Père), faire (Décalogue), et dans quel espace vital il doit l'accomplir (Sacraments et Eglise). Ainsi devient perceptible en même temps

l'accord avec les quatre degrés de l'exégèse, dont il est question au Moyen Age, et qui sont aussi considereés comme une réponse aux questions qui se posent au quatre étapes de l'existence humaine." <u>Transmission de la Foi et sources de la Foi</u> (Paris: Tequi, 1983), pp. 33-35.

15   Toth, <u>op. cit.</u>, p. 31, note 105.

16   "Haec vero cognitio nihil aliud est, nisi fides: cuius virtus efficit, ut id ratum habeamus, quod a Dec traditum esse sanctissimae matris Ecclesiae auctoritas comprobarit. Nulla enim fidelibus potest accidere dubitatio in iis, quorum Deus auctor est, qui est ipsa veritas." I, 1, 1; p. 7.

17   "The Catechism is the Bible of the laity, wherein is comprehended the whole sense of Christian teaching, which every Christian needs to know for eternal bliss." Martin Luther, <u>Tishreden</u> (<u>Werke</u>, Weimar ed., Vol. 5, p. 581), as cited by Westerhoff, <u>op.cit.</u>, p. 123.

APPENDIX: A TOPICAL SYNOPSIS OF THE ROMAN CATECHISM

The <u>Parts</u> and <u>Chapters</u> of the Roman Catechism, outlined by divisions (in Roman numerals) and subdivisions (in Roman capitals). Also indicated are the Sections of the "<u>textus receptus</u>" (viz., the "Rovellian numbers," in arabic numerals).

PREFACE: Pastoral Teaching and this Catechism (13 Sections)

I. the general background of this Catechism: the transmission of divine revelation (1-4)
   A. the necessity of divine revelation for salvation (1)
   B. the actuality of divine revelation, mediated by Christ and the Church (2-4)
II. the specific background of this Catechism (5-8)
   A. the current crisis in the Church: mainly catechetical (5-6)
   B. the Church's response to this crisis: a "form and prescription" of catechesis (7-8)
III. the purpose and nature of this Catechism (9-11)
   A. its basic purpose: comprehensive catechetical instruction (9)
   B. its basic content: knowledge of Christ and His love (10)
   C. its basic use: to be adapted to the needs of all the faithful (11)
IV. the sources and components of this Catechism (12-13)
   A. the sources: the Sacred Scripture and Tradition (12a)
   B. the components: the Creed, the sacraments, the Decalogue and the Our Father (12b-13)

PART I: THE CREED

Chapter 1:   the Faith and the Creed (4 Sections)

I. Faith (1)
   A. distinction according to kind: natural and supernatural (1a)
   B. distinction within supernatural faith: according to degree (1b)
II. the Creed (2-4)
   A. the origin and purpose of the Creed: from the Apostles, as a statement and a standard of the faith (2-3)
   B. the division of the Creed into Articles, according to the Trinitarian appropriations (4)

Chapter 2:   the First Article of the Creed (23 Sections)

I. Introduction: both a conviction ("corde") and a profession ("ore") directed to God as Beginning and End (1)
II. "I believe" (2-4)
   A. faith: a unique kind of knowledge (2)
   B. the faithful: a unique relationship to this faith, by conviction and profession (3-4)
III. "in God" (5-8)
   A. the transcendent excellence of the object of faith: God in Himself (5-6)
   B. the unicity of God (7-8)
IV. "the Father" (9-10)
   A. God as Father by virtue of His creation and adoption of us (9)
   B. God as Father as a distinct Person in the Trinity (10)
V. "Almighty" (11-14)
   A. its meaning (11)

    B. its priority and inclusiveness regarding God's attributes (12)
    C. its unity: only one Omnipotence in the Trinity (13)
VI. "Creator of heaven and earth" (15-23)
    A. the nature and cause of Creation as an action: absolute and free (15)
    B. the extent of Creation as a result of God's productive action: "heaven and earth" (16-20)
    C. the continuity of Creation as a result of God's providence (21-22)
    D. the appropriation of Creation to the whole Trinity (23)

Chapter 3:   the Second Article of the Creed (12 Sections)

I. the basic context of this Article: the Redemption (1-4)
    A. its necessity: the Fall of Man (2)
    B. its source: Christ alone (3)
    C. its realization: result of a Promise (the Old Testament) (4)
II. "Jesus Christ" (5-7)
    A. "Jesus": His proper name, from heaven and yet earthly (5-6)
    B. "Christ": His proper title as Prophet, Priest and King (7)
III. "His only Son" (8-10)
    A. His first and unique Sonship, from eternity as God (8-9a)
    B. His secondary Sonship, in time as Man (9b-10)
IV. "Our Lord" (11-12)
    A. the basis of this title in Christ: as both God and Man (11)
    B. the consequences of this title regarding us: being a "Christian" (12)

Chapter 4:   The Third Article of the Creed (11 Sections)

I. the economy of our redemption, yet not affecting the eternity of the Word (1-2)
II. "Conceived by the Holy Spirit" (3-6)
    A. appropriated to the Holy Spirit (3)
    B. Christ's conception: both transcendent and humanly normal (4-5)
    C. application of this truth to us: contemplation, yet not curiosity (6)
III. "Born of the Virgin Mary" (7-10)
    A. the human cooperation with the divine operation (7-8)
    B. the consequent significance of Our Lady in relation to Christ and to us (9-10)
IV. our response to this teaching (11)

Chapter 5:   the Fourth Article of the Creed (16 Sections)

I. "Suffered under Pontius Pilate, was crucified" (1-5)
    A. the singular importance of this Article: knowing nothing but Christ crucified (1)
    B. the reality of Christ's suffering: in His humanity, in history (2-3)
    C. the significance of Christ's Crucifixion: as symbol, as reality (4-5)
II. "Died and was buried" (6-9)
    A. the reality and significance of Christ's death (6-7)
    B. the reality and significance of Christ's burial (8-9)
III. the subject and cause of the Passion (10-13)
    A. Who it was who suffered (10)
    B. why He suffered (11-12)
    C. how He suffered (13)
IV. the effect of the Passion (14-16)

    A. what it effected: forgiveness of sins, opening of heaven (14)
    B. why it effected these: as sacrifice, satisfaction and redemption (15)
    C. the Passion as exemplar of all virtues (16)

Chapter 6:   the Fifth Article of the Creed (15 Sections)

I. "He descended into hell" (1-6)
    A. the fundamental and traditional unity of this Article (1)
    B. the meaning of "hell" in this Article (2-3)
    C. the reality and purpose of Christ's descent into hell (4-6)
II. "He rose again from the dead" (7-9)
    A. the fact itself of the Resurrection (7)
    B. the transcendence of this fact (8)
    C. the ramifications of this fact: "First-born from the dead" (9)
III. two further precisions of this Article (10-11)
    A. "On the third day" (10)
    B. "According to the Scriptures" (11)
IV. the meaning of the Resurrection (12-15)
    A. Why Christ "had to rise again" (12)
    B. What Christ by His Resurrection offers us (13)
    C. conclusions from this as affecting our Christian living (14-15)

Chapter 7:   The Sixth Article of the Creed (9 Sections)

I. "He ascended into heaven" (1-2)
    A. the place of this mystery in the life of the faithful (1)
    B. the place of this mystery in the overall Mystery of Christ (2)
II. "And is seated at the right hand of God" (3)
    A. the obvious metaphor and its obvious signification (3a)
    B. the underlying reality of what is here signified (3b)
III. the significance of the Ascension (4-5)
    A. the term and culmination of all Christ's mysteries (4)
    B. the full import of this final Mystery (5)
IV. the effects of the Ascension (6-9)
    A. the source of these effects: Christ's activity in the Ascension (6)
    B. the effects themselves: our activity now made possible to grow (7)
    C. the full dimension of these effects (8-9)

Chapter 8:   the Seventh Article of the Creed (11 Sections)

I. "He shall come to judge the living and the dead" (1-3)
    A. the three-fold role of Christ: here completed (1)
    B. the two Comings of Christ (2)
    C. the two Judgments by Christ: particular and general (3)
II. the General Judgment: integral to God's plan (4)
    A. the reasons for a second Judgment (4a)
    B. the motives which this Judgment should presently instill in us (4b)
III. the Judge and the signs of His Coming (5-7)
    A. the Person: Jesus Christ (5-6)
    B. the signs: clear yet obscure (7)
IV. the Judgment itself, and its consequences (8-10)
    A. the testimony of Scripture on this (8a)
    B. the sentence on the just: "Come...blessed" (8b)
    C. the sentence on the wicked: "Depart ...cursed" (9-10)

V. the pastoral importance of this Article (11)

Chapter 9:   the Eighth Article of the Creed (8 Sections)

I. the place and importance of this Article (= "Article III") (1)
II. "the Holy Spirit" (2-3)
   A. a common name, yet here specific (2)
   B. the reason for this name for the Third Person of the Trinity (3)
III. the Nature and Personality of the Holy Spirit (4-6)
   A. the absolute divinity of the Holy Spirit (4)
   B. the relationship of the Holy Spirit with the Father and the Son (5-6)
IV. the activity of the Holy Spirit regarding us (7-8)
   A. the basis of the appropriation of the work of sanctification to the Holy Spirit: "Gift" and "Love" (7)
   B. the Gifts of the Holy Spirit (8)

Chapter 10: the Ninth Article of the Creed (27 Sections)

I. the special importance of this Article, and its continuity with the preceding Article (1)
II. "the Church" (2-10)
   A. the term "ecclesia" (2-4)
   B. the component parts of the Church: triumphant and militant (5-8)
   C. those who are not component parts of the Church (9)
III. "holy and Catholic": the marks of the Church (11-17)
   A. the unity of the Church (11-14)
   B. the holiness of the Church (15)
   C. the catholicity of the Church (16)
   D. the apostolicity of the Church (17)
IV. the Church and the faith (18-22)
   A. the Church as subject of faith: infallible in her believing and teaching (18-19)
   B. the Church as object of faith: her mysterious reality, yet still a creature (20-22)
V. "the Communion of Saints" (23-27)
   A. the significance of this phrase: "communion" = the true finality of the Church (23)
   B. the essential nature of this communion: of the sacraments and of charity (24-25)
   C. the derivative blessings of this communion: to sinners, and the charisms (26-27)

Chapter 11: the Tenth Article of the Creed (12 Sections)

I. the importance of this Article: Christ's first formal injunction to His Apostles (1)
II. the power of the Church to remit sins (2-6)
   A. the fact of this power (2)
   B. the extent of this power: unlimited (3-5)
   C. the exercise of this power: limited -- to certain members and signs (6)
III. the basis of the Church's power: the divine power (7-10)
   A. the radical necessity for infinite power (7)
   B. this power: exclusive to God and His Church (8-10)
IV. our response to this power (11-12)

   A. our appreciation of its necessity for us (11)
   B. our use of its efficacy for us (12)

Chapter 12: the Eleventh Article of the Creed (14 Sections)

I. the importance of this Article (1)
II. the fact of the Resurrection of the Body (2-5)
   A. as revealed (2-3)
   B. as reasoned to (4-5)
III. the extent of the resurrection of the body (6-8)
   A. its universality: all mankind without exception (6)
   B. its individuality: each risen body numerically identical with each mortal body (7-8)
IV. the state of the risen body (9-13)
   A. its integrity: all parts integral to human nature, restored to all (9-11)
   B. its qualities: for all, immortality; for the blessed, certain special gifts (12-13)
V. some pastoral considerations consequent to this Article (14)

Chapter 13: the Twelfth Article of the Creed (13 Sections)

I. the place and significance of this Article (1)
II. "Life everlasting": (2-4)
   A. the term itself (2)
   B. the reason for the term (3)
   C. the transcendence of the term (4)
III. the nature of "Everlasting life" (5-12)
   A. Its summary, from revelation (5-6)
   B. the essential beatitude (7-10)
   C. the "accessory" beatitude (11-12)
IV. a pastoral conclusion to this Article, in principle and in practice (13)

PART II: THE SACRAMENTS

Chapter 1: the Sacraments in General (32 Sections)

Introduction: importance of instruction in the sacraments (1)
I. the definition of a sacrament (2-13)
   A. as a word and as a thing (2-4)
   B. as a sign (5-9)
   C. as a sacred thing (10-13)
II. the reasons for the sacraments: integral to the Economy (14)
III. the parts of a sacrament (15-17)
   A. the dual composition of a sign: element and word (15)
   B. the pre-eminence of the form (word) in the composition (16-17)
IV. Ceremonies of the sacraments (18)
   A. not essential (18a)
   B. yet not unimportant (18b)
V. the order of the sacraments (19-22)
   A. the number of the sacraments: seven, no more nor less (19-21)
   B. the rank of the sacraments: according to necessity, to dignity (22)
VI. the minister of the sacraments (23-26)
   A. the principal minister: God alone, in Christ (23)
   B. the instrumental minister: its necessity, its conditions (24-26)

VII. the effects of the sacraments (27-31)
   A. the first effect: sanctifying grace (27-29)
   B. the second effect: the character (30-31)
Conclusion: need for reverence and use of the sacraments (32)

Chapter 2:   the Sacrament of Baptism (77 Sections)

Introduction: the importance of this instruction (1-2)
I. the definition of Baptism (3-6)
   A. the various words used: "Baptism," "Illumination," "Purification," etc. (3-4)
   B. the reality itself (5-6)
II. the parts of Baptism (7-19)
   A. the matter of Baptism: water (7-11)
   B. the form of Baptism: the formula (12-16)
   C. the action itself: the ablution (17-19)
III. the institution of Baptism (20-22)
   A. Christ's own Baptism, and His promulgation of Baptism (20a, 21a)
   B. the relation of both these events to Christ's Passion (20b, 21b)
   C. our reflection on this: our union with Christ in Baptism (22)
IV. the ministers and sponsors of Baptism (23-30)
   A. the ministers: ordinary and extraordinary (23-25)
   B. the sponsors: their responsibilities and their selection (26-30)
V. the necessity of Baptism (31-37)
   A. the basic principle: its absolute necessity for salvation (31)
   B. the application of this principle: to infants, to adults (32-37)
VI. the disposition for Baptism (38-41)
   A. the essential disposition for validity: intention to receive it (38-39)
   B. the non-essential disposition for validity, but essential for liceity: faith and contrition (40)
   C. a reflection: need to renew our dispositions (41)
VII. the effects of Baptism (42-58)
   A. the first effect (negative): the remission of sin (42-49)
   B. the second effect (positive): the infusion of grace (50-53)
   C. the third effect: the character (54-57)
   D. the final effect: heaven itself now opened (58)
VIII. the ceremonies of Baptism (59-76)
   A. the nature and importance of these ceremonies (59-60)
   B. the sequence of the ceremonies themselves: before, accompanying and following the actual conferral of the sacrament (61-76)
Conclusion: a summary and reminder of its pastoral character (77)

Chapter 3:   The Sacrament of Confirmation (26 Sections)

Introduction: need for instruction in this sacrament (1)
I. the identity of Confirmation as a sacrament (2-5)
   A. Confirmation in itself (2-4)
   B. Confirmation as related to Baptism (5)
II. the institution of Confirmation: argued from tradition, from reason (6)
III. the parts of Confirmation (7-12)
   A. the matter of Confirmation: olive oil and balm (7-10)
   B. the form of Confirmation (11-12)
IV. the minister and sponsors of Confirmation (13-15)

    A. the minister: the Apostolic connection (13-14)
    B. the sponsors (15)
V. the necessity of Confirmation: its importance and applicability (16-18)
VI. the dispositions for Confirmation : for validity, for liceity (19)
VII. the effects of Confirmation (20-23)
    A. the first effect: sanctifying grace (20-22)
    B. the second effect: the character (23)
VIII. the ceremonies of Confirmation (24-26)

Chapter 4:   the Sacrament of the Holy Eucharist (81 Sections)

Introduction: the supreme greatness of the Eucharist (1-2)
I. the names given to the Eucharist: no one name really adequate (3-6)
    A. the meaning of "Eucharist" (3)
    B. other names: "Mass," "Communion," "Viaticum," "Supper" (4-6)
II. the sacramentality of the Eucharist (7-11)
    A. the fact of its being a sacrament (7)
    B. its uniqueness among the sacraments (8-9)
    C. its own unity and its variety: one sign and three "signed" (10-11)
III. the matter of the Eucharist (12-18)
    A. the bread: conditions for validity, for liceity (12-14)
    B. the wine: conditions for validity, for liceity (15-17)
    C. the symbolism of the matter: various analogies (18)
IV. the form of the Eucharist (19-24)
    A. the consecration of the bread (19-20)
    B. the consecration of the wine (21-24)
V. the reality-and-sign of the Eucharist (25-46)
    A. the fact of the Real Presence (25-32)
    B. the mode of the Real Presence: "by virtue of the sacrament" and concomitance (33-36)
    C. the reason for the Real Presence: Transubstantiation (37-45)
    D. the "economy" of the Real Presence: its fittingness (46)
VI. the effects of the Eucharist (47-54)
    A. in general: grace itself (analogy with food) (47-48)
    B. more specifically: grace as life, as prevention of death, as anticipation of glory (49-54)
VII. the recipient of the Eucharist (55-66)
    A. the various ways of receiving it: sacramentally, spiritually, both (55)
    B. preparation for Holy Communion (56-58)
    C. frequency of Holy Communion: the minimum, the maximum (59-61)
    D. the various kinds of recipients: children, the retarded, etc. (62-64)
    E. the species to be received: why only one species sufficient (65-66)
VIII. the minister of the Eucharist (67-68)
    A. the priest alone: his power, his responsibility (67)
    B. the relationship of personal worthiness to the ministry (68)
IX. the Sacrifice of the Mass (69-81)
    A. the fact of the Sacrifice: its importance, its institution, its distinction from the sacrament as such (69-72)
    B. the nature of the Sacrifice: its object, its identification with the Sacrifice of the Cross (73-77)
    C. the purpose of the Sacrifice: propitiation as well as praise, for the dead as for the living (78-79)
    D. the liturgy of the Sacrifice: its essentially public character, its attendant ceremonies (80-81)

Chapter 5:   the Sacrament of Penance (79 Sections)

Introduction: importance of instruction in this sacrament (1)
I. Penance in general (2-10)
   A. the word "penance" (2-3)
   B. Penance as a virtue: "interior penance" (4-9)
   C. "exterior penance" and its relation to the sacrament (10)
II. the sacramentality of penance (11-12)
   A. Penance: a true sacrament (11)
   B. its special feature: its indefinite repeatability (12)
III. the parts of Penance as a sacrament (13-17)
   A. the matter of Penance (or "quasi-matter") (13)
   B. the form of Penance (14-17)
IV. the effects of the sacrament (18-19)
   A. reconciliation with God (18a)
   B. the range of this forgiveness: unlimited (18b-19)
V. the necessity of the sacrament (20-22)
   A. what requires the sacrament: the forgiveness of any sin after Baptism (20)
   B. what the sacrament requires: the "integral parts of the sacrament" (21-22)
VI. the first integral part of Penance: Contrition (23-35)
   A. the nature of contrition (23-26)
   B. the necessity of contrition (27-30)
   C. the requisites for contrition (31-33)
   D. the efficacy and practice of contrition (34-35)
VII. the second integral part of Penance: Confession (36-53)
   A. the utility and necessity of confession (36-37)
   B. the nature and efficacy of confession (38-45)
   C. the qualities of confession (46-52)
   D. the frequency of confession (53)
VIII. the minister of confession (54-61)
   A. the power of the keys: conferred on priests alone (54-55)
   B. the qualities of the priest as minister of this sacrament (56-61)
IX. the third integral part of Penance: Satisfaction (62-79)
   A. the nature and kinds of satisfaction (62-64)
   B. the object of "canonical" satisfaction: temporal punishment due to sin (65-70)
   C. the subject of satisfaction: Christ's role and ours (71-73)
   D. the works of satisfaction: in general and for others (74-77)
   E. the "penance" imposed by the confessor in the sacrament (78-79)

Chapter 6:   the Sacrament of Extreme Unction (16 Sections)

Introduction: the special moment of this sacrament (1)
I. the name and nature of this sacrament (2-4)
   A. its names: "Extreme Unction," "Anointing of the Sick" (2)
   B. its nature as a sacrament (3-4)
II. the matter and form of Extreme Unction (5-7)
   A. the matter: oil (5)
   B. the form: a prayer compared with that of the other sacraments (6-7)
III. the institution of this sacrament by Christ (8)
IV. the recipient of this sacrament (9-12)
   A. for all in danger of death from illness, with use of reason (9)
   B. the where and the when of the anointing (10-11)

    C. the dispositions proper to this sacrament (12)
V. the minister of this sacrament (13)
    A. the priest alone (13a)
    B. yet not necessarily any priest, i.e., jurisdiction required (13b)
VI. the effects of this sacrament (14-16)
    A. its spiritual effects (14-15)
    B. its corporal effects (16)

Chapter 7:   the Sacrament of Orders (34 Sections)

Introduction: the importance of this sacrament for everyone in the Church (1)
I. the unique position of this sacrament (2-5)
    A. its special dignity (2)
    B. the corresponding specialness of the vocation to it (3-5)
II. Orders as a power (6-8a)
    A. the two-fold power of the Church, with respect to the Body of Christ: orders and jurisdiction (6)
    B. the power of order: in itself, in relation to previous priesthoods (7-8a)
III. Order as a sacrament (8b-10)
    A. the name of this sacrament (8b-9)
    B. the true sacramentality of Orders (10)
IV. the different degrees -- "orders" -- of the sacrament (11-22)
    A. the basic division and distribution of this power (11-12)
    B. the Minor Orders (13-18)
    C. the Major Orders (19-22)
V. the Priesthood in more detail (23-28)
    A. its premise: the two-fold priesthood, interior and exterior (23-25)
    B. its exercise: the degrees of jurisdiction (26-28)
VI. the minister of this sacrament: the bishop alone (29)
VII. the recipient of this sacrament (30-33)
    A. the premise of the requisites: this sacrament, for others (30)
    B. the requisites themselves, positive and negative (31-33)
VIII. the effects of this sacrament (34)
    A. the main effect: the Church herself (34a)
    B. in the recipient: grace and the character (34b)

Chapter 8:   the Sacrament of Matrimony (34 Sections)

Introduction: the greatness of this sacrament and its importance (1a)
I. the nature of matrimony as such (1b-8)
    A. its definition (2-3)
    B. the essence of this union: the bond and the consent necessary for it (4-8)
II. natural marriage (9-14)
    A. the relation here between nature and grace (9)
    B. its origin: in the beginning, by God Himself (10)
    C. its properties (11-12)
    D. its purposes: two-fold, coordinate (13-14)
III. supernatural marriage: the sacrament (15-27)
    A. its sacramentality (15-19)
    B. its indissolubility (20-22)
    C. its blessings (bona): children, fidelity, sacramentality (23-27)
IV. the ceremonies of Matrimony (28-29)
    A. the "form" of this sacrament (28)
    B. the importance of this "form" (29)

V. the requisites for Matrimony (30-32)
   A. the impediments to Matrimony (30)
   B. the dispositions for Matrimony (31-32)
VI. the consummation of Matrimony (33-34)
   A. its use (33)
   B. its occasional non-use (34)

PART III: THE COMMANDMENTS

Chapter 1:   the Commandments in General (14 Sections)

I. the importance of the Commandments (1-2)
   A. the summary of the entire Law of God (1)
   B. the importance of instruction in them (2)
II. the motives for observing the Commandments (3-10)
   A. the divine authority of the Commandments (3-7)
   B. the Commandments necessary for salvation (8)
   C. the benefits deriving from their observance (9-10)
III. the universality of the Commandments (11-14)
   A. already written in men's hearts, from the beginning and everywhere (11a)
   B. yet reserved for full revelation and mediation via the Jewish nation (11b-14)

Chapter 2:   the First Commandment (34 Sections)

I. "I am the Lord your God Who brought you out of the land of Egypt"(1-2)
   A. its applicability to all, i.e., not just to the Jews (1)
   B. our response to this preamble (2)
II. "You shall have no strange gods before Me": the scope of this Commandment (3-6)
   A. its unity and its parts (3-5)
   B. its position among all the Commandments: the greatest (6)
III. the specific content of this Commandment (7-24)
   A. faith, hope and love "with all our heart" in God our Creator and Father (7)
   B. the veneration of creatures: angels and saints (8-15)
   C. the veneration of images: "You shall not make graven images " (16-24)
IV. "I am a jealous God..." the appendix to this Commandment (25-34)
   A. applicability of this appendix to all the Commandments (25)
   B. its special applicability here (26-29)
   C. the warning included here (30-32)
   D. the final phrase: a summation of all morality (33-34)

Chapter 3:   the Second Commandment (30 Sections)

I. the position and importance of this Commandment (1-2)
   A. its relation to the First Commandment (1)
   B. the importance of instruction in it (2)
II. the scope of this Commandment: both positive and negative (3-4)
   A. the positive and negative aspects, and the priority of the former (3)
   B. the object of each aspect: the Name of God (4)
III. the positive aspect of this Commandment (5-19)
   A. honoring God's Name unambiguously and always: prayer, etc. (5-6a)
   B. honoring God's Name ambiguously and rarely: oath-taking (6b-19)
IV. the negative aspect of this Commandment (20-30)

A. the generic sin against this Commandment: making God a liar (20)
  B. specific sins against it: involving oaths, and other sins (21-29)
  C. a final warning: the sanction of severe punishment (30)

Chapter 4:   the Third Commandment (28 Sections)

Introduction: the relation of this Commandment with the two preceding ones, and its importance (1-3a)
I. this Commandment, compared with the other Commandments (3b-7)
   A. its difference: not based directly on natural law and changed in New Testament (4-5)
   B. its similarity: based indirectly on natural law (6-7a)
   C. division of this instruction into four parts (7b)
II. the 1st part: this Commandment taken as a whole (8-11)
   A. "Remember": reasons for this preliminary statement (8)
   B. "the Sabbath" (9)
   C. "keep holy" (10)
   D. a summary: rest and prayer (11)
III. the 2nd part: the object of Sabbath observance (12-20)
   A. its basic premise: a sign of God's own rest (12)
   B. its elaboration in Scripture and tradition (13-19)
   C. the meaning of "work" here (20)
IV. the 3rd part: the manner of Sabbath observance (21-25)
   A. work that is forbidden (21,24)
   B. work that is permitted (22-23)
   C. work that is enjoined (25)
V. the 4th part: motives for observing this Commandment (26-28)
   A. its reasonableness (26)
   B. its blessings (27)
   C. its punishments (28a)
   D. both blessings and punishments to be "remembered" (28b)

Chapter 5:   the Fourth Commandment (22 Sections)

I. the two "great commandments" and this Commandment (1-6)
   A. this Commandment: where the two "great commandments" merge (1-2)
   B. the distinction between the two "great commandments" (3-6)
II. the wording of this Commandment (7-8)
   A. "honor": the best single comprehensive term (7)
   B. "father": likewise the best single comprehensive term (8)
III. the object of this Commandment (9-16)
   A. our natural parents (9-12)
   B. other superiors (13-16)
IV. the promise attached to this Commandment (17-20)
   A. the reward explicitly promised: "long life" (17-19)
   B. the punishment implicitly attached (20)
V. the corresponding duties of parents toward their children (21-22)
   A. their duty to be real parents (21a)
   B. specifically: the avoiding of certain failings (21b-22)

Chapter 6:   the Fifth Commandment (25 Sections)

I. the importance and content of this Commandment (1-2)
   A. its importance: the importance of peace itself (1)

B. its content: both negative and positive (2)
II. the negative or prohibitory part of this Commandment (3-15)
  A. killing that is not prohibited by this Commandment (3-8)
  B. killing that is absolutely prohibited by this Commandment (9-11)
  C. anger: when it is sinful and when not (12-13)
  D. reasons for the prohibition of murder (14-15)
III. the positive or hortatory part of this Commandment (16-25)
  A. the virtue of love, and its extension (16-19a)
  B. rooting out revenge (19b-25)

Chapter 7:   the Sixth Commandment (13 Sections)

I. Introduction (1-2)
  A. the special position of this Commandment (1)
  B. the two parts of this Commandment: negative and positive (2)
II. the negative part of this Commandment: "adultery" (3-5)
  A. adultery itself (3a)
  B. all other sins of impurity (3b-4)
  C. the reason why "adultery" is explicitly mentioned (5)
  D. the need for private instruction here (6)
III. the positive part of this Commandment: chastity (6-13)
  A. this virtue: proper to every vocation (6)
  B. the motives for this virtue (7-9)
  C. the practice of this virtue (10-13)

Chapter 8:   the Seventh Commandment (25 Sections)

I. Introduction (1-2)
  A. the importance of this Commandment (1)
  B. the object of this Commandment (2)
II. the negative part of this Commandment (3-14a)
  A. stealing, in general (3-8a)
  B. more specifically: theft and robbery, and their various kinds (8b-14a)
III. the positive part of this Commandment (14b-19)
  A. restitution (14b-15)
  B. almsgiving (16-19)
IV. some concluding considerations regarding this Commandment (20-25)
  A. its rewards and punishments (20)
  B. various excuses for not observing this Commandment: an a compounding of one's guilt (21-25)

Chapter 9:   The Eighth Commandment (23 Sections)

I. Introduction (1-2)
  A. the importance of this Commandment (1)
  B. the parts of this Commandment (2)
II. the negative part of this Commandment (3-13)
  A. the terms: "false witness" and "neighbor" (3-4)
  B. lying: its extent and gravity (5-7)
  C. detraction (8-10)
  D. flattery (11-12)
  E. other sins: jokes, actions, etc. (13)
III. the positive part of this Commandment (14-18)
  A. in the judicial process, i.e., "true witness" in court (14-18a)

    B. outside the judicial process, i.e., in everyday life (18b)
IV. some concluding considerations regarding this Commandment (19-23)
    A. motives for observing this Commandment (19-20)
    B. various excuses for not observing this Commandment (21-23)

Chapter 10: the Ninth and Tenth Commandments (23 Sections)

I. Introduction (1-5)
    A. an appropriate conclusion to the Decalogue (1)
    B. the basic sense of these two Commandments (2-3)
    C. the benefits of these two Commandments (4-5)
II. the meaning of "covetousness" (concupiscence) (6-12)
    A. concupiscence as such (6-9)
    B. concupiscence as in these two Commandments (10-12)
III. the negative part of these Commandments (13-20)
    A. "covetousness" in general (13)
    B. its object in particular: under the 10th Commandment (14-18)
    C. its object in particular: under the 9th Commandment (19-20)
IV. the positive part of these Commandments (21)
    A. immediately: detachment (21a)
    B. fundamentally: seeking the will of God, i.e., the truth (21b)
V. motives for observing these Commandments (22-23)
    A. the consequences of the sins against these Commandments (22)
    B. some particular dangers from certain occupations (23)

PART IV: PRAYER

Chapter 1: the Necessity of Prayer (4 Sections)

I. Introduction: the importance of instruction in prayer (1)
II. the necessity of prayer (2-4)
    A. its necessity for salvation itself (2)
    B. its necessity in view of our own needs (3-4)

Chapter 2: the Benefits of Prayer (11 Sections)

I. the primary benefits: honor to God and salvation for us (1-2)
    A. honor to God (1)
    B. salvation for us (2)
II. the efficacy of prayer (3-5)
    A. every prayer answered by God (3-4)
    B. often our prayer, anticipated by God (5)
III. further benefits of prayer (6-11)
    A. increase in our union with God, by faith and charity (6-9)
    B. increase in our purification from evil (10-11)

Chapter 3: the Kinds and Degrees of Prayer (7 Sections)

I. the kinds of prayer (1-3a)
    A. given the need and benefits of prayer: need for instruction here (1)
    B. the two main kinds: petition and thanksgiving (2-3a)
II. the degrees of prayer (3b-7)
    A. the value of knowing these degrees (3b)

B. the four degrees of prayer: the prayer of the just, of the believing sinner, of the unbelieving sinner, of the insincere sinner (4-7)

Chapter 4:   the Objects of Prayer (5 Sections)

I. in general: the basic rule of prayer (1)
II. in particular: the good things to be prayed for (2-5)
   A. the supreme Good: to be sought in itself (2)
   B. the various created goods: to be sought as means to God (3-5)

Chapter 5:   For Whom to Pray (8 Sections)

I. in our prayer of petition (1-6)
   A. generically: all men (1)
   B. specifically: certain persons, viz., our superiors, our enemies, the faithful departed, sinners (2-6)
II. in our prayer of thanksgiving (7-8)
   A. generically: for all God's gifts to all men (7)
   B. specifically: for the saints, and most specifically of all, for Our Lady (the Hail Mary) (8)

Chapter 6:   To Whom to Pray (4 Sections)

I. prayer to God (1)
   A. the basis of this prayer: by all law, natural and positive (1a)
   B. the recipient of this prayer: the Three Persons (1b)
II. prayer to the saints (2-4)
   A. a constant and certain tenet of Catholic faith (2)
   B. difference between our prayer to them and our prayer to God (3-4)

Chapter 7:   Preparation for Prayer (6 Sections)

I. negatively: the obstacles to be removed (1-2)
   A. pride: removed by humility (1a)
   B. actual sin: removed by contrition (1b-2)
II. Positively: the dispositions to be cultivated (3-4)
   A. faith: at once the basis and culmination of prayer (3)
   B. hope: grounded on faith in the triune God (4)
III. ultimately: the direct action of the Holy Spirit, Who is Love (5-6)
   A. all true prayer: the Holy Spirit's action in us (5)
   B. our abiding in Christ: the charity that is prayer (6)

Chapter 8:   Method in Prayer (9 Sections)

I. the importance of "method" in prayer (1a)
II. the respective roles of mental and vocal prayer (1b-4)
   A. mental prayer: essential to all genuine prayer (1b, 4a)
   B. vocal prayer: always appropriate and sometimes essential (2-3, 4b)
III. internal helps to praying rightly (5-8)
   A. privately: interiority and perseverence (5-6)
   B. publicly: all prayer "through Christ our Lord," imitating the saints (7-8)
IV. external helps to praying rightly (9)
   A. the classic triad: prayer, fasting, almsgiving (9a)
   B. the more direct application of these three: to God, self, neighbor (9b)

Chapter 9: the Lord's Prayer: Prologue (20 Sections)

I. Introduction: the Prologue (1a)
II. "Father" (1b-13)
    A. Christ's choice of this Name over all others (1b)
    B. the first basis of His Fatherhood: His creation of us (2)
    C. the second basis: His providence over us (3-9)
    D. the third and supreme basis: HIs redemption of us (10-13)
III. "Our (Father)" (14-18)
    A. our relationship to God as common Father of us all (14-15)
    B. our relationship with one another as brothers (16-17)
    C. our prayer therefore: essentially filial (18)
IV. "Who art in heaven" (19-20)
    A. God's omnipresence (19a)
    B. yet His special presence in "heaven" (19b-20)

Chapter 10: the First Petition of the Lord's Prayer (9 Sections)

I. Introduction to all the Petitions: their order (1a)
II. the Supreme Good: God in Himself (1b-3)
    A. the primacy of prayer: the primacy of charity (1b)
    B. God's Glory: intrinsic and extrinsic (2-3)
III. our glorification of HIs Name: its object and agent (4-7)
    A. in general: God to be honored by all (4)
    B. in particular: God to be honored for His gifts of grace and nature (5-7)
IV. our glorification of His Name: its source and culmination (8-9)
    A. God's glorification in and by His holy Church (8)
    B. our responsibility as members of the Church to glorify God (9)

Chapter 11: the Second Petition of the Lord's Prayer (19 Sections)

I. the context of this Petition (1-6)
    A. the comprehensive theme of the Gospel (1-2)
    B. the compendium of the Christian life (3-6)
II. "Thy Kingdom" (7-11)
    A. in the natural order: the cosmos (7)
    B. in the supernatural order: the Church (8-11)
III. "Come!" (12-14)
    A. for the entrance of all mankind into the Church (12)
    B. for the restoration of life to all members of the Church (13)
    C. for the final and definitive establishment of Christ's rule (14)
IV. the pastoral application of this Petition (15-19)
    A. the incomparable value of the Kingdom (15-16)
    B. the price of the Kingdom, in terms of our present life (17-18)
    C. in summary: Christ the King (19)

Chapter 12: the Third Petition of the Lord's Prayer (24 Sections)

I. the situation of this Petition and our approach to it (1-2)
II. the realism of this Petition: our will vs. God's will (3-10)
    A. the plight of our fallen nature as a consequence of our will (3-7)
    B. the remedy: following God's will (8-10)
III. "Thy Will be done" (11-18)

     A. the primary meaning of "God's Will" (11)
     B. the primary meaning of "be done" (12-13)
     C. some secondary meanings in this Petition (14-18)
IV. "on earth as it is in heaven" (19-24)
     A. the perfect fulfillment of this Petition: the angels' obedience to God, in execution and motive (19-21)
     B. some complements to the fulfillment of this Petition: thanksgiving, humility, peace (22-24)

Chapter 13: the Fourth Petition of the Lord's Prayer (25 Sections)

I. Petition for the goods of this temporal life: its meaning (1-7)
     A. the true order between this temporal life and the next (1-7)
     B. this truth illustrated by contrast between man's condition before the Fall and his present fallen condition (4-7)
II. the principal word in this Petition: "bread" (8-10)
     A. its meaning: our sustenance, in comprehensive and Scriptural sense (8)
     B. the propriety of this sustenance being an object of prayer (9-10)
III. the other words in this Petition (11-17)
     A. "our (bread)" (11-12)
     B. "daily (bread)" (13)
     C. "give us" (14-16)
     D. "this day" (17)
IV. the derivative meaning of this Petition: our spiritual sustenance (18-23)
     A. "bread": the Word and the Eucharist (18-21)
     B. our complete trust in God's providence (22-23)

Chapter 14: the Fifth Petition of the Lord's Prayer (23 Sections)

I. the special character of this Petition (1-3)
     A. the cumulative wisdom and goodness of God, and our response to it (1-2)
     B. the distinction of this Petition from the preceding ones (3)
II. the reality of our sinfulness, our response (4-11)
     A. the basic statement of this two-fold truth (4)
     B. the recognition of the fact of our sinfulness (5-8)
     C. our response to this recognition: prayer for forgiveness (9-11)
III. "forgive us our trespasses" (12-16)
     A. "trespasses" (12-14)
     B. "our (trespasses)" (15)
     C. "forgive us" (16)
IV. "as we forgive those who trespass against us" (17-23)
     A. "as": its two-fold meaning (17)
     B. "forgive": a two-fold sanction (18)
     C. the difficulty of obeying this precept, and aids to overcome this difficulty (19-21)
     D. a general rule of life based on this precept (22-23)

Chapter 15: the Sixth Petition of the Lord's Prayer (20 Sections)

I. the position of this Petition in the Christian life (1-3)
     A. the perennial danger of relapse from forgiveness and grace into sin (1)
     B. to meet this danger: this explicit Petition (2-3)
II. the source of temptation (4-8)
     A. in general: both within and without us (4)

    B. in particular: the Tempter par excellence = the devil (5-8)
III. "lead us not into temptation" (9-15)
    A. the meaning of "to tempt" (9-10)
    B. the meaning of "to lead into temptation" to evil (11-13)
    C. hence, the meaning of this Petition (14-15)
IV. the pastoral implications of this Petition (16-20)
    A. the basic disposition of the soul: patience (16-17)
    B. the basic strategy: counter-attack (18-19)
    C. the reward promised: eternal victory with Christ (20)

Chapter 16: the Seventh Petition of the Lord's Prayer (12 Sections)

I. the position of this Petition in relation to the whole Prayer (1-3)
    A. the summary of all the Petitions (1-2)
    B. the order of the Petitions: the reason why this one is the last (3)
II. the essentially Christian orientation of this Petition (4-5)
    A. the pagan's view of deliverance from evil (4a)
    B. the Christian's view of deliverance from evil (4b-5)
III. "deliver us from evil" (6-10)
    A. the "evils" proper to this Petition (6-7)
    B. "deliverance" by God from these evils (8)
    C. "evil," i.e., the singular, not the plural (9-10)
IV. the habitual attitude resulting from this Petition (11-12)
    A. patience in enduring the evils of this life (11)
    B. gladness in embracing the evils of this life (12)

Chapter 17: the Conclusion to the Lord's Prayer (6 Sections)

I. the specific importance of the conclusion in prayer (1-3)
    A. proper conclusion to prayer: even more important than its proper beginning (1)
    B. the changes effected by prayer in the one who prays (2-3)
II. "amen": the conclusion itself (4-6)
    A. a most appropriate conclusion to our prayer (4-5)
    B. the meaning and value of the word itself (6)

BIBLIOGRAPHY

I. **SOURCES**

A. THE ROMAN CATECHISM

Catechismus ex decreto Concilii Tridentini ad parochos Pii Quinti Pont. Max. iussu editus
Romae: in Aedibus Populi Romani apud Paulum Manutium, MDLXVI [1566]
cum privilegio Pii V, Pont. Max.

Catechismus ex decreto Concilii Tridentini ad parochos Pii V. Pont. Max. iussu editus
Romae: in aedibus Populi Romani apud Paulum Manutium, MDLXVII [1567]
cum privilegio Pii V. Pont. Max. et Philippi Hispaniarum Regis per universam Neapolitanam et Mediolanensem ditionem

Catechismus ex decreto Sacrosancti Concilii Tridentini iussu Pii V Pont. Max. nunc primum in capita, sectionesque distinctus, variisque Patrum senten- tiis et auctoribus munitus
Lugduni: apud Guliel. Rovillium, sub scuto Veneto, MDLXXXVIII [1588]

Catechismus ex decreto Sacrosancti Concilii Triden- tini iussu Pii V. Pont. Max. editus: in capita sectionesque distinctus, variisque Patrum senten- tiis et auctoribus munitus
Venetiis: ex typographica Ioannis Alberti ad S. Fuscae, MDCXV [1615]

Catechismus Concilii Tridentini Pii V. Pont. Max. iussu promulgatus, sincerus et integer mendisque repurgatus opera D.P.L.H.P., a quo est additus apparatus ad Catechismum in quo ratio, auctoritas, approbatores et usus declarantur
Lugduni: apud fratres Duplain, Bibliopolis in vico Mercatorio, MDCCXLI [1741]

Catechismus ex decreto Concilii Trindentini ad parochos Pii V. Pont. Max. primum, nunc Sanctis. D. N. Clementis XIII iussu editus
Romae: ex officina Joan. Bapt. Bernabo et Iosephi Lazarini, MDCCLXI [1761]
Typis Camerae Apostolicae

Catechismus ex Decreto SS. Concilii Tridentini ad Parochos Pii V. Pont. Max. iussu editus
Padua: Typis Seminarii Patavini, 1930

Bradley, Robert I., S. J., and Eugene Kevane (eds.)
The Roman Catechism: Translated and Annotated in accord with Vatican II and post-conciliar documents and the new Code of Canon Law
Boston: St. Paul Editions, 1985

B. THE MAGISTERIUM

Acta Apostolicae Sedis
Romae: Typis Polyglottis Vaticanis, 1909 -

Canones et Decreta Sacrosancti Oecumenici Concilii Tridentini
Turino: Marietti, 1913

Conciliorum Ecumenicorum Decreta
Basel: Herder, 1962

Denzinger, Henricus and Adolfus Schönmetzer (eds.)
Enchiridion Symbolorum: definitionum et declarationum de rebus fidei et morum
Freiburg im Breisgau: Herder, 1963
   (22nd edition)

Kevane, Eugene (ed.)
Teaching the Catholic Faith Today: Twentieth Century Catechetical Documents of the Holy See
Boston: St. Paul Editions, 1982

Mansi,,J.-D.(ed.)
Sacrorum Conciliorum nova et amplissima Collectio
Paris, 1758-98

Missale Romanum
Vatican: Typis Polyglottis Vaticanis, 1971

Rite of Christian Initiation of Adults (RCIA)
Washington, D.C.: United States Catholic Conference, 1974

Societas Goerresiana
Concilium Tridentinum: Diariorum, Actorum, Epistolarum, Tractatuum: Nova Collectio
Tomus IV: Concilii Tridentini Actorum: Prima Pars
Freiburg-im-Breisgau: Herder, 1904

C. FATHERS AND SCHOLASTICS

[St. Augustine]
Christopher, Joseph P. (ed.)
St. Augustine: The First Catechetical Instruction [De Catechizandis Rudibus]
New York: Newman Press, 1946

Migne, J.-P. (ed.)
Patrologia Cursus Completus ... Series Graeca)
Paris, 1857 - ; 161 vols.

Patrologia Cursus Completus ...Series Latina
Paris, 1866 - ; 217 vols.

Mingana, A. (ed.)
Woodbrooke Studies: Christian Documents Edited and Translated
Vols. V and VI
Cambridge, 1932-33

S. Thomas Aquinatis Doctoris Angelici Ordinis Praedicatorum Opera Omnia
Parma: Fiaccadori, 1852 -
(New York: Musurgia, 1948-49; 25 vols.)

[St. Thomas Aquinas]
Collins, Joseph B. (ed.)
The Catechetical Instructions of St. Thomas Aquinas
New York: Wagner, 1939

Wenger, Antoine (ed.)
Huit catéchèses baptismales inédites [of St. John Chrysostom]
Paris: Cerf, 1957
("Sources Chrétiennes," Vol. 50)

D. CATECHISMS (15th & 16th centuries, other than Roman Catechism)

[Auger, Edmond]
Brank, Friedrich Josef
Die Katechismen des Edmundus Augerius, S. J., In Historischer, Dogmatisch-Moralischen und Kate- chetischer Bearbeitung
Freiburg-im-Breisgau: Herder, 1917
(Freiburger Theologischer Studien, Vol. XX, pp. xvi-186)

Calvin, John
Catéchisme, c'est a dire le formulaire d'instruire les enfans en la Chrestienté,faict en manière de dialogue, où le Ministre interrogue, et l'enfant respond
Genève, 1553

---

l'Institution chrétienne
Geneve: Labor et Fides, 1958

[Canisius, St. Peter]
Streicher, Fredericus, S. J. (ed.)
S. Petri Canisii Catechismi Latini et Germanici
Roma: Gregorian, 1933

[Carranza, Bartolomé]
Tellecheria Idigoras, Jose Ignacio (ed.)
Carranza de Miranda, Bartolomé, O.P.: Comentarios sobre el Catechismo Christiano
Madrid: Bibl. de Autores Christianos (BAC), 1972
2 vols.

Erasmus, Desiderius
Dilucida et pia explanatio Symboli quod Apostolorum dicitur, Decalogi praeceptorum et Dominicae Pre- cationis
in: Opera Omnia, Tom. 5 (Leiden, 1704), cols. 1133-96.

Ratio seu Methodus compendio perveniendi ad veram theologiam
Prague, 1786

Gerson, Jean
Oeuvres complètes
(ed., Mgr. Glorieux)
Paris: Desclée, 1960-73; 10 vols.

Summa Theologica et Canonica
Venetiis, 1587

[Heidelberg Catechism]
Good and Harbach (eds.)
The Heidelberg Catechism, or Short Instruction in Christian Doctrine, as it is conducted in the churches and schools of the Palatinate and elsewhere, explained and confirmed with proofs from the Holy Scriptures; the whole adapted to the use of catechetical classes, Sabbath schools and family instruction
Chambersburg, Pennsylvania, 1849

Gropper, Joannes
Enchiridion Christianae Institutionis
Paris, 1545

Janz, Denis (ed.)
Three Reformation Catechisms: Catholic, Anabaptist, Lutheran
New York: Edwin Mullen Press, 1982
("Texts and Studies in Religion," Vol.13)

Luther, Martin
Der Kleine Catechismus fur die gemeine Pfarrherr und Prediger
Werke, Vol. 30 (Weimar, 1910), pp. 239-345

Ein Kurcz form deer zeehn gepott D.M.L., Ein kurcz form des Glaubens, Ein kurcz form dess Vatter unssers
Werke, Vol. 7 (Weimar, 1897), pp. 204-29

[Luther, Martin]
Gausewitz, C. (ed.)
Doctor Martin Luther's Small Catechism
Milwaukee: Northwestern Publishing House, n.d.

Moufang, Christopher
Katholische Katechismen des sehtzehnten Jahrhunderts in deutscher Sprache
Mainz: Kirchheim, 1881

Nausea, Fredericus
Catholicus Catechismus
Cologne, 1543

II. SECONDARY WORKS

A. ON THE ROMAN CATECHISM

Alexandre, Noël, O.P.
Theologia dogmatica et moralis secundum ordinem Catechismi Concilii Tridentini
Venetiis, 1697

Andrianopoli, Luigi
Il Catechismo Romano Commentato: con note di aggiornamento teologico-pastorale
Milano: Edizioni Ares, 1983

Bellarinus, Joannes
Doctrina sacri Concilii Tridentini et Catechismi Romani de sacramentis et de iustificatione et in Symbolum Apostolorum
Venetiis, 1609

Bellinger, Gerhard
Der Catechismus Romanus und die Reformation: die katechetische Antwort des Trienter Konzils auf die Haupt-Katechismen der Reformation
Paderborn: Bonifacius, 1970

Corvin von Skibniewski, Stephan Leo Ritter
Geschichte des Romischen Katechismus
Roma: Pustet, 1903

Eder, Georgius
Oeconomia Bibliorum sive Partitionum Theologicarum
Venetiis, 1572

Paschini, Pio
Il Catechismo Romano del Concilio di Trento: sue origini e sua prima diffusione
Roma: Pont. Sem. Rom. Maggiore "Lateranum", 1923

Reginaldus [Regnault, Antoine, O.P.]
De Catechismi Romani auctoritate dissertatio
Naples, 1765

Rodriguez, Pedro and Raul Lanzetti
El Catecismo Romano: Fuentes e Historia del Texto y de la Redaccion: Bases Criticas para el Estudio Teologico del Catecismo del Concilio de Trento
Pamplona: Ediciones Universidad de Navarra, 1982

El Manuscrito Original del Catecismo Romano: Description del Material y los Trabajos al Servicio de la Edicion Critica del Catecismo del Concilio de Trento
Pamplona: Ediciones Universidad de Navarra, 1985

Toth, John Baptist de
De Auctoritate Theologica Catechismi Romani
Budapest, 1941

B. OTHER MONOGRAPHS

Adler, Gilbert and Gérard Vorgeleisen
Un siècle de catéchèse en France, 1893-1980
Paris: Beauchêne, 1981
("Theologie Historique", Vol. 60)

Benoit, Pierre, O.P.
Exégèse et théologie
Paris: Cerf, 1961
2 vols.

Bourgeault, Guy, S. J.
Decalogue et morale chrétienne: enquête patristique sur l'utilisation et l'interprétation chrétiennes du decalogue de c 60 à c 220
Montréal: Bellarmin, 1971

Coppens, Joseph, S. J.
Les harmonies des deux Testaments: Essai sur les divers sens des Ecritures et sur l'unité de la révélation
Paris: Casterman, 1949

Daniélou, Jean, S. J.
La catéchèse aux premiers siècles
Paris: Fayard-Mame, 1968
("Ecole de la foi": Collection de l'Institut Superieur de Pastorale catéchètique)

Sacramentum Futuri: études sur les origines de la typologie biblique
Patris: Beauchêne, 1950

Dawson, Christopher
The Historic Reality of Christian Culture
New York: Harper & Row, 1960

Dhôtel, Jean, S. J.
Les origines du catéchisme moderne: d'après les premiers manuels imprimés en France
Paris: Aubier, 1967

Dillistone, F. W. (et al)
Scripture and Tradition
London: Lutterworth, 1955

Duroux, Benoit, O. P.
La psychologie de la foi chez St. Thomas d'Aquin
Tournai: Desclée, 1963

Flicoteaux, Dom E., O.S.B.
Le sens du Carême
Paris: Cerf, 1956

Fontaine, J., S. J.
Le prône catéchètique d'après le Concile de Trente: sa méthode et ses sources de développement
Paris: Retaux, 1892

Gatterer, Michael, S. J.
Katechetik
Innsbruck: Rauch, 1924

Germain, Elisabeth
Langages de la foi à travers l'histoire: mentalités et catéchèse
Paris: Institut Catholique, 1972
(Collection de l'Institut Superieur de Pastorale catéchètique)

Gilbey, Thomas, O.P.
Christian Theology
(Vol. I of Summa Theologiae)
New York: McGraw-Hill, 1964

Hebert, Arthur G.
The Throne of David: a Study of the Fulfillment of the Old Testament in Jesus Christ and His Church
London: Faber & Faber, 1956

Hézard, Charles
Histoire du catéchisme depuis la naissance de l'Eglise jusqu'à nos jours
Paris: Retaux, 1908

Holstein, Henri, S. J.
La tradition dans l'Eglise
Paris: Grasset, 1960

Jedin, Hubert
Geschichte des Konzils von Trent
Freiburg-im-Breisgau: Herder, 1949-75
4 vols.

Jedin, Hubert
Papal Legate to the Council of Trent
St. Louis: Herder, 1947

Journet, Charles
Le dogme, chemin de la foi
Paris: Fayard, 1963

Jungmann, Josef, S. J.
Katechetik: Aufgabe und Methode der religiösen Unterweisun
Freiburg: Herder, 1955

Kevane, Eugene
Creed and Catechetics
Westminster, Maryland: Christian Classics, 1977

Ladner, Gerhart B.
The Idea of Reform: its Impact on Christian Thought and Action in the Age of the Fathers
Cambridge: Harvard University Press, 1959

[Lallement,   ]
Pour la formation chrétienne des enfants
n.p., 1976

de Lubac, Henri, S. J.
L'Ecriture dans la Tradition
Paris: Aubier, 1966

Exégèse medievale: les quatre sens de l'Ecriture
Paris: Aubier, 1961

La foi chrétienne: essai sur la structure du Symbole des Apôtres
Paris: Aubier, 1950

Histoire et Esprit: l'intélligence de l'Ecriture d'après Origène
Paris: Aubier, 1969

Orsenigo, Cesare
Life of St. Charles Borromeo
St. Louis: Herder, 1943

Pastor, Ludwig von
The History of the Popes from the Close of the Middle Ages
Vol. XVI [on the close of the Council of Trent]
St. Louis: Herder, 1928

Pontifical Biblical Institute
Institutiones Biblicae
Roma, 1951

Rahner, Karl, S.J. and Josef Ratzinger
The Episcopacy and the Primacy
New York: Herder, 1962

Ratzinger, Josef Cardinal
Transmission de la foi et sources de la foi
Paris: Tequi, 1983

Schaff, Philip
The Creeds of Christendom, with a History and Critical Notes
New York: Harper, 1877
3 vols.

Schauf, Heribert
Die Lehre der Kirche über Schrift und Tradition in den Katechismen
Essen, 1963

Smalley, Beryl
The Study of the Bible in the Middle Ages
Oxford: Blackwell, 1952

Soulages, Gérard
Dossier sur le problème de la catéchèse
Paris: Téqui, 1977

Spicq, Ceslaus, O.P.
Esquisse d'une histoire de l'exégèse latine au moyen-âge
Paris: Vrin, 1944
("Bibliotheque Thomiste," Vol. 26)

Tacchi-Venturi, Pietro, S.J.
Storia della Compagnia di Gesú in Italia
Roma: Civiltà Cattolica, 1938; 2nd ed.

Tellechea Idigores, Jose I.
El Catecismo del Arzobispo Carranza
Madrid: Fundacion Univ. Española, 1972

Van den Eynde, Damian
Les normes de l'enseignement chrétien dans la littérature patristique des trois premiers siècles
Gembloux-Paris, 1933
(Louvain: "Dissertations théologiques", Ser. II, vol. 25)

Vischer, Wilhelm
The Witness of the Old Testament to Christ
London: Lutterworth, 1949

Walz, Angelo, O.P.
I Domenicani al Concilio di Trento
Roma: Herder, 1961

Westerhoff, John H. and O. C. Edwards
A Faithful Church: Issues in the History of Catechesis
Wilton, Connecticut: Morehouse-Barlow, 1981

Wilkinson, John
Elgeria's Travels
London: S.P.C.K., 1971

C. ARTICLES

Batiffol, Pierre
"Theologia, Theologi"
Ephemerides Theologicae Lovanienses, 5 (1928), 205-20

Boyer, Charles, S. J.
"Le Concile de Trente et l'insuffisance de l'Ecriture"
Doctor Communis, 16 (1963), 5-17

Congar, Yves, O.P.
"Pour une histoire semantique du terme 'Magistère'"
Revue des sciences philosophiques et théologiques,
    60 (1976), 85-98

"Bref historique des formes du 'Magistère' et de ses rélations avec les docteurs"
Revue des sciences philosphiques et théologiques 60 (1976), 99-112

Daniélou, Jean, S. J.
"Les divers sens de l'Ecriture dans la tradition chrétienne primitive"
Ephemerides Theologicae Lovanienses, 24 (1948), 119-28

de Ghellinck, Joseph, S. J.
"'Pagina' et 'Sacra Pagina': histoire d'un mot et transformation de l'objet primitivement designé"
Mélanges Auguste Pelzer
Louvain: Inst. Sup. de Phil., 1947
pp. 23-59

Grasso, Domenico, S. J.
"'Pour" ou "Contre' un Catéchisme universel"
Catéchèse, 1:5 (1961), 483-93

Gribomont, Jean, O.S.B.
"Le lieu des deux testaments salon la théologie de St.-Thomas: notes sur le sens spirituel et implicite des Stes-Ecritures"
Ephemerides Theologiae Lovanienses, 22 (1946), 70-89

Guellay, Robert
"L'évolution des méthodes théologiques à Louvain d'Erasme à Jansénius"
Revue d'histoire ecclésiastique, 37 (1941), 31-144

Halkin, Léon-E.,
"La piété d'Erasme"
Revue d'histoire ecclésiastique, 79 (1984), 671-708

Hofinger, J., S.J.
"De apta divisione materiae catechisticae: Tentamen historico-criticum"
Collectanea commissionis synodalis, 13 (1940), 583-99; 729-49; 845-59; 950-65.

Kasper, Walter
"The Church's profession of faith: on drafting a new Catholic catechism for adults"
Communio, 12 (1985), 49-70

de Lubac, Henri, S. J.
"Sens spirituel"
Revue des sciences religieuses, 36 (1949), 542-76.

"Sur un vieux distique: la doctrine du 'quadruple sens'"
Melanges Ferdinand Cavallera
Toulouse: Institut Catholique, 1948
pp. 347-66

Moingt, Joseph
"La transmission de la foi"
Etudes 342 (1975), 107-29

Ortigues, Edmond
"Ecriture et Traditiones apostoliques au Concile de Trente"
Revue des sciences religieuses, 36 (1949), 271-99

Rodriguez, Pedro
"El sentido de los sacramentos segun el Catecismo Romano"
Scripta Theologica, 9 (1977), 951-84

Schauf, Heribert
"De traditione constitutiva ad mentem catechismorum"
Seminarium, 4 (1964), 267-77

D. MISCELLANEOUS

Bacci, Antonius
Lexicon eorum vocabulorum quae difficilius Latine redduntur
Roma: Soc. Lib. "Studium," 1949

Busa, Robert, S.J.
Index Thomisticum: S. Thomae Aquinatis Operum Omnium Indices et Concordantiae
Stuttgart: Frommann, 1974

Lampe, Geoffry W. H.
Patristic Greek Lexicon
Oxford: Clarendon Press, 1961

Liddell, Henry G., and Robert Scott
Greek-English Lexicon
Oxford: Clarendon Press, 1961; 9th ed.

Zorell, Francis, S.J.
Lexicon Graecum Novi Testamenti
Paris: Lethieulleux, 1961; 3rd ed.